Looking Awry

OCTOBER Books
Joan Copjec, Rosalind Krauss, and Annette Michelson, editors

Looking Awry
An Introduction to Jacques Lacan through Popular Culture

SLAVOJ ŽIŽEK

An OCTOBER *Book*

The MIT Press
Cambridge, Massachusetts
London, England

First MIT Press paperback edition, 1992

© 1991 Massachusetts Institute of Technology

This book was set in ITC Garamond by DEKR Corporation and printed and bound in the United States of America.

Library of Congress Cataloging-in-Publication Data

Žižek, Slavoj.
  Looking awry : an introduction to Jacques Lacan through popular
culture / Slavoj Žižek.
    p.   cm.
  "October books."
  Includes bibliographical references (p.
  ISBN 0-262-24031-9 (HB), 0-262-74015-X (PB)
    1. Lacan, Jacques, 1901–   2. Psychoanalysis and culture.
3. Psychoanalysis and literature. 4. Psychoanalysis and motion
pictures. 5. Popular culture—Psychological aspects. 6. Popular
literature—Psychological aspects. 7. Hitchcock, Alfred, 1899–
I. Title.
BF175.4.C84Z59   1991
150.19′5′092—dc20   90-13460
                                                           CIP

20 19 18 17 16 15 14 13 12

Contents

Walter Benjamin commended as a theoretically productive and subversive procedure the reading of the highest spiritual products of a culture alongside its common, prosaic, worldly products. What he had in mind specifically was a reading of
the sublime ideal of the love couple represented in Mozart's *Magic Flute* together
with the definition of marriage found in Immanuel Kant (Mozart's contemporary),
a definition that caused much indignation within moralistic circles. Marriage, Kant
wrote, is "a contract between two adult persons of the opposite sex on the mutual
use of their sexual organs." It is something of the same order that has been put to
work in this book: a reading of the most sublime theoretical motifs of Jacques Lacan
together with and through exemplary cases of contemporary mass culture: not only
Alfred Hitchcock, about whom there is now general agreement that he was, after all,
a "serious artist," but also *film noir*, science fiction, detective novels, sentimental
kitsch, and up—or down—to Stephen King. We thus apply to Lacan himself his own
famous formula "Kant with Sade," i.e., his reading of Kantian ethics through the eyes
of Sadian perversion. What the reader will find in this book is a whole series of "Lacan
with . . .": Alfred Hitchcock, Fritz Lang, Ruth Rendell, Patricia Highsmith, Colleen
McCullough, Stephen King, etc. (If, now and then, the book also mentions "great"
names like Shakespeare and Kafka, the reader need not be uneasy: they are read
strictly as kitsch authors, on the same level as McCullough and King.)

The intention of such an enterprise is twofold. On the one hand, the book is
conceived as a kind of introduction to Lacanian "dogmatics" (in the theological sense
of the term). It mercilessly exploits popular culture, using it as convenient material
to explain not only the vague outlines of the Lacanian theoretical edifice but sometimes also the finer details missed by the predominantly academic reception of
Lacan: the breaks in his teaching, the gap separating him from the field of poststructuralist "deconstructionism," and so on. This way of "looking awry" at Lacan

makes it possible to discern features that usually escape a "straightforward" academic look. On the other hand, it is clear that Lacanian theory serves as an excuse for indulging in the idiotic enjoyment of popular culture. Lacan himself is used to legitimize the delirious race from Hitchcock's *Vertigo* to King's *Pet Sematary*, from McCullough's *An Indecent Obsession* to Romero's *Night of the Living Dead*.

The solidarity of these two movements could be exemplified by a double paraphrase of De Quincey's famous propositions concerning the art of murder, propositions that served as a regular point of reference to both Lacan and Hitchcock:

> If a person renounces Lacan, soon psychoanalysis itself will appear to him dubious, and from here it is just a step to a disdain for Hitchcock's films and to a snobbish refusal of horror fiction. How many people have entered the way of perdition with some fleeting cynical remark on Lacan, which at the time was of no great importance to them, and ended by treating Stephen King as absolute literary trash!

> If a person renounces Stephen King, soon Hitchcock himself will appear to him dubious, and from here it is just a step to a disdain for psychoanalysis and to a snobbish refusal of Lacan. How many people have entered the way of perdition with some fleeting cynical remark on Stephen King, which at the time was of no great importance to them, and ended by treating Lacan as a phallocentric obscurantist!

It is for the reader to decide which of the two versions he or she would choose.

A word or two concerning the general outline of the book's theoretical argument. Lacan's "return to Freud" is usually associated with his motto "the unconscious is structured like a language," i.e., with an effort to unmask imaginary fascination and reveal the symbolic law that governs it. In the last years of Lacan's teaching, however, the accent was shifted from the split between the imaginary and the symbolic to the barrier separating the real from (symbolically structured) reality. So, the first part of the book—"How Real Is Reality?"—attempts to develop the dimension of the Lacanian real, *first* by describing how what we call "reality" implies the surplus of a fantasy space filling out the "black hole" of the real; *then* by articulating the different modalities of the real (the real returns, it answers, it can be rendered via the symbolic form itself, and there is knowledge in the real); and *finally* by confronting the reader with two ways of avoiding the encounter with the real. This last will be exemplified by the two main figurations of the detective in crime novels: the classic "logic and deduction" detective and the hard-boiled detective.

Although it might seem that all has already been said in the endless list of literature on Alfred Hitchcock, the second part of this book—"One Can Never Know Too Much about Hitchcock"—takes the risk of proposing three new approaches: *first* an articulation of the dialectic of deception at work in Hitchcock's films, a dialectic in which those who really err are the non-duped; *then* a conception of the famous Hitchcockian tracking shot as a formal procedure whose aim is to produce a "blot," a point from which the image itself looks at the spectator, the point of the "gaze of the Other"; and, *finally*, a proposal that would enable us to grasp the succession of the main stages in Hitchcock's development, from the Oedipal journey of the 1930s to the "pathological narcissism," dominated by a maternal superego, of the 1960s.

The third part—"Fantasy, Bureaucracy, Democracy"—draws some conclusions from Lacan's late theory, concerning the field of ideology and politics. *First*, it delineates the contours of the ideological *sinthome* (a superegoic voice, for example) as a core of enjoyment at work in the midst of every ideological edifice and thus sustaining our "sense of reality." *Then* it proposes a new way of conceptualizing the break between modernism and postmodernism, centered on the obscenity of the bureaucratic apparatus as rendered in Kafka's work. The book *concludes* with an analysis of the inherent paradoxes that pertain to the very notion of democracy: the source of these paradoxes is the ultimate incommensurability between the symbolic domain of equality, duties, rights, etc., and the "absolute particularity" of the fantasy space, i.e., of the specific ways individuals and communities organize their enjoyment.

Acknowledgments

Preliminary versions of some of the material have appeared in "Hitchcock," *October*, no. 38 (Fall 1986); "Looking Awry," *October*, no. 50 (Fall 1989); "Undergrowth of Enjoyment," *New Formations*, no. 9 (1989); and "The Real and Its Vicissitudes," *Newsletter of the Freudian Field*, no. 5 (1990).

Since it is needless to add that Joan Copjec was present from the very conception of this book, encouraging the author to write it, that her work served as a theoretical point of reference, or that she spent considerable time improving the manuscript, we will not do so!

I   How Real Is Reality?

The Paradoxes of Objet Petit a

LOOKING AWRY AT ZENO'S PARADOXES

What is at stake in the endeavor to "look awry" at theoretical motifs is not just a kind of contrived attempt to "illustrate" high theory, to make it "easily accessible," and thus to spare us the effort of effective thinking. The point is rather that such an exemplification, such a mise-en-scène of theoretical motifs renders visible aspects that would otherwise remain unnoticed. Such a procedure already has a respectable line of philosophical predecessors, from late Wittgenstein to Hegel. Is not the basic strategy of Hegel's *Phenomenology of Spirit* to undermine a given theoretical position by "staging" it as an existential subjective attitude (that of asceticism, that of the "beautiful soul," etc.) and thus to reveal its otherwise hidden inconsistencies, that is, to exhibit the way its very subjective position of enunciation undermines its "enunciated," its positive contents?

To demonstrate the fecundity of such an approach, let us turn to the first proper philosopher, Parmenides, who asserted the sole existence of Being as One. What are of interest are the famous paradoxes by means of which Zeno, his disciple, tried to prove his master's thesis *a contrario,* by disclosing the nonsensical, contradictory consequences that follow from the hypothesis of the existence of multitude and movement. At first sight—which is, of course, that sight which pertains to the traditional historian of philosophy—these paradoxes appear as exemplary cases of pure, hollow, artificial logomachy, contrived logical trifling attempting to prove an obvious absurdity, something that goes against our most elementary experience. But in his brilliant essay "The literary technique of Zeno's paradoxes,"[1] Jean-Claude Milner effectuates a kind of "staging" of them: he gives sufficient reasons to allow us to conclude that all four of the paradoxes by means of which Zeno tried to prove the impossibility of movement originally referred to literary commonplaces. The final form in which these paradoxes became part of our tradition results moreover from a typical carnevalesque-burlesque procedure of confronting a tragic, noble topic with its vulgar, common counterpart, in a manner recalling later Rabelais. Let us take the best known of Zeno's paradoxes, the one about Achilles and the tortoise. Its first point of reference is, of course, the *Iliad,* book XXII, lines 199–200, where Achilles tries in vain to catch up with Hector. This noble reference was then crossed with its popular counterpart, Aesop's fable about the hare and the tortoise. The version universally known today, the one about "Achilles and the tortoise," is thus a later condensation of two literary models. The interest of Milner's argument lies not solely in the fact that it proves that Zeno's paradoxes, far from being purely a game of logical reasoning, belong to a precisely defined literary genre; that is, that they use the established literary technique of subverting a noble model by confronting it with its banal, comical counterpart. What is of crucial importance from our—Lacanian—perspective is the very *contents* of Zeno's literary points of reference. Let us return to the first, most famous paradox mentioned; as already noted, its original literary reference is the following lines from the *Iliad*: "As in a dream, the pursuer never succeeds in catching up with the fugitive whom he is after, and the fugitive likewise cannot ever clearly escape his pursuer; so Achilles that day did not succeed in attaining Hector, and Hector was not able to escape him definitely." What we have here is thus the relation of the subject to the object experienced by every one of us in a dream: the subject, faster than the object, gets closer and closer to it and yet can never attain it— the dream paradox of a continuous approach to an object that nevertheless preserves a constant distance. The crucial feature of this inaccessibility of the object was nicely indicated by Lacan when he stressed that the point is not that Achilles could not *overtake* Hector (or the tortoise)—since he is faster than Hector, he can easily leave him behind—but rather that he cannot *attain* him: Hector is always too fast or too slow. There is a clear parallel here with the well-known paradox from Brecht's *Threepenny Opera*: do not run after luck too arduously, because it might happen that you will overrun it and that luck will thus stay behind. The libidinal economy of the case of Achilles and the tortoise is here made clear: the paradox stages the relation of the subject to the object-cause of its desire, which can never be attained. The object-cause is always missed; all we can do is encircle it. In short, the topology of this paradox of Zeno is the paradoxical topology of the object of desire that eludes our grasp no matter what we do to attain it.

The same may be said of the other paradoxes. Let us go on to the next: the one about the arrow that cannot move because at any given moment, it occupies a definite point in space. According to Milner, its model is a scene from the *Odyssey,* book

XI, lines 606–607, in which Heracles is continually shooting an arrow from his bow. He completes the act again and again, but in spite of this incessant activity on his part, the arrow remains motionless. Again, it is almost superfluous to recall how this resembles the well-known dream experience of "moving immobility": in spite of all our frenetic activity, we are stuck in the same place. As Milner points out, the crucial characteristic of this scene with Heracles is its location—the infernal world in which Odysseus encounters a series of suffering figures—among them Tantalus and Sisyphus—condemned to repeat the same act indefinitely. The libidinal economy of Tantalus's torments is notable: they clearly exemplify the Lacanian distinction between need, demand, and desire, i.e., the way an everyday object destined to satisfy some of our needs undergoes a kind of transubstantiation as soon as it is caught in the dialectic of demand and ends up producing desire. When we demand an object from somebody, its "use value" (the fact that it serves to satisfy some of our needs) *eo ipso* becomes a form of expression of its "exchange value"; the object in question functions as an index of a network of intersubjective relations. If the other complies with our wish, he thereby bears witness to a certain attitude toward us. The final purpose of our demand for an object is thus not the satisfaction of a need attached to it but confirmation of the other's attitude toward us. When, for example, a mother gives milk to her child, milk becomes a token of her love. The poor Tantalus thus pays for his greed (his striving after "exchange value") when every object he obtains loses its "use value" and changes into a pure, useless embodiment of "exchange value": the moment he bites into food, it changes to gold.

It is Sisyphus, however, who bears on our interest here. His continuous pushing of the stone up the hill only to have it roll down again served, according to Milner, as the literary model for the third of Zeno's paradoxes: we never can cover a given distance X, because, to do so, we must first cover half this distance, and to cover half, we must first cover a quarter of it, and so on, ad infinitum. A goal, once reached, always retreats anew. Can we not recognize in this paradox the very nature of the psychoanalytical notion of *drive,* or more properly the Lacanian distinction between its *aim* and its *goal*? The goal is the final destination, while the aim is what we intend to do, i.e., the way itself. Lacan's point is that the real purpose of the drive is not its goal (full satisfaction) but its aim: the drive's ultimate aim is simply to reproduce itself as drive, to return to its circular path, to continue its path to and from the goal. The real source of enjoyment is the repetitive movement of this closed circuit.[2] Therein consists the paradox of Sisyphus: once he reaches his goal, he experiences the fact that the real aim of his activity is the way itself, the alternation of ascent and descent. Where do we detect the libidinal economy of the last of Zeno's paradoxes according to which it follows, from the movement of two equal masses in opposite directions, that *half* of a certain amount of time equals its *double* amount? Where do we encounter the same paradoxical experience of an *increase* in the libidinal impact of an object whenever attempts are made to diminish and destroy it? Consider the way the figure of the Jews functioned in Nazi discourse: the more they were exterminated, eliminated, the fewer their numbers, the more dangerous their remainder became, as if their threat grew in proportion to their diminution in reality. This is again an exemplary case of the subject's relation to the horrifying object that embodies its surplus enjoyment: the more we fight against it, the more its power over us grows.

The general conclusion to be drawn from all this is that there is a certain domain in which Zeno's paradoxes are fully valid: the domain of the subject's impossible relation to the object-cause of its desire, the domain of the drive that circulates endlessly around it. This is, however, the very domain Zeno is obliged to exclude as "impossible" in order that the reign of the philosophical One can establish itself. That is, the exclusion of the real of the drive and the object around which it circulates is constitutive of philosophy as such, which is why Zeno's paradoxes, by means of which he tries to prove the impossibility and consequently the nonexistence of movement and multitude, are the reverse of the assertion of One, the immovable Being, in Parmenides, the first proper philosopher.[3] Perhaps we can now understand what Lacan meant when he said that the object small *a* "is what philosophical reflection lacks in order to be able to locate itself, i.e., to ascertain its nullity."[4]

GOAL AND AIM IN FANTASY

In other words, what Zeno excludes is the very dimension of *fantasy,* insofar as, in Lacanian theory, fantasy designates the subject's "impossible" relation to *a,* to the object-cause of its desire. Fantasy is usually conceived as a scenario that realizes the subject's desire. This elementary definition is quite adequate, on condition that we take it *literally*: what the fantasy stages is not a scene in which our desire is fulfilled, fully satisfied, but on the contrary, a scene that realizes, stages, the desire as such. The fundamental point of psychoanalysis is that desire is not something given in advance, but something that has to be constructed—and it is precisely the role of fantasy to give the coordinates of the subject's desire, to specify its object, to locate the position the subject assumes in it. It is only through fantasy that the subject is constituted as desiring: *through fantasy, we learn how to desire.*[5] To exemplify this crucial theoretical point, let us take a famous science fiction short story, Robert Scheckley's "Store of the Worlds."

Mr. Wayne, the story's hero, visits the old and mysterious Tompkins, who lives alone in a shack, ruined and filled with decaying waste, in an abandoned part of town. Rumor has it that, by means of a special kind of drug, Tompkins is capable of transposing people into a parallel dimension where all their desires are fulfilled. To pay for this service, one was required to hand over to Tompkins one's most valuable material goods. After finding Tompkins, Wayne engages him in conversation; the former maintains that most of his clients return from their experience well satisfied; they do not, afterward, feel deceived. Wayne, however, hesitates, and Tompkins advises him to take his time and think things over before making up his mind. All the way home, Wayne thinks about it; but at home, his wife and son are waiting for him, and soon he is caught up in the joys and small troubles of family life. Almost daily, he promises himself that he will visit old Tompkins again and afford himself the experience of the fulfillment of his desires, but there is always something to be done, some family matter that distracts him and causes him to put off his visit. First, he has to accompany his wife to an anniversary party; then his son has problems in school; in summer, there are vacations and he has promised to go sailing with his son; fall brings its own new preoccupations. The whole year goes by in this way, with Wayne having no time to take the decision, although in the back of his mind, he is constantly aware that sooner or later he will definitely visit Tompkins. Time passes thus until . . . he awakens suddenly in the shack beside Tompkins, who asks him kindly: "So, how do you feel now? Are you satisfied?" Embarrassed and perplexed, Wayne mumbles "Yes, yes, of course," gives him all his worldly possessions (a rusty knife, an old can, and a few other small articles), and leaves quickly, hurrying between the decaying ruins so that he will not be too late for his evening ration of potatoes. He arrives at his underground shelter before darkness, when flocks of rats come out from their holes and reign over the devastation of nuclear war.

This story belongs, of course, to postcatastrophe science fiction, which describes everyday life after nuclear war—or some similar event—has caused the disintegration of our civilization. The aspect that interests us here, however, is the trap into which the reader of the story necessarily falls, the trap upon which the whole effectiveness of the story is based and in which the very paradox of desire consists: we mistake for postponement of the "thing itself" what is already the "thing itself," we mistake for the searching and indecision proper to desire what is, in fact, the realization of desire. That is to say, the realization of desire does not consist in its being "fulfilled," "fully satisfied," it coincides rather with the reproduction of desire as such, with its circular movement. Wayne "realized his desire" precisely by transposing himself, in a hallucination, into a state that enabled him to postpone indefinitely his desire's full satisfaction, i.e., into a state that reproduced the lack constitutive of desire. We can in this way also grasp the specificity of the Lacanian notion of anxiety: anxiety occurs not when the object-cause of desire is lacking; it is not the lack of the object that gives rise to anxiety but, on the contrary, the danger of our getting too close to the object and thus losing the lack itself. Anxiety is brought on by the disappearance of desire.

Where exactly, in this futile circular movement, is the *objet a*? The hero of Dashiell Hammett's *Maltese Falcon,* Sam Spade, narrates the story of his being hired to find a man who had suddenly left his settled job and family and vanished. Spade is unable to track him down, but a few years later the man is spotted in another city, where he lives under an assumed name and leads a life remarkably similar to the one he had fled when a beam from a construction site fell and narrowly missed hitting him on the head. In Lacanian terms this beam became for him the mark of the world's inconsistency: $s(\cancel{A})$. In spite of the fact that his "new" life so closely resembles the old, he is firmly convinced that his beginning again was not in vain, i.e., that it was well worth the trouble to cut his ties and begin a new life. Here we see the function of the *objet petit a* at its purest. From the point of view of "wisdom," the break is not worth the trouble; ultimately, we always find ourselves in the same position from which we have tried to escape, which is why, instead of running after the impossible, we must learn to consent to our common lot and to find pleasure in the trivia of our everyday life. Where do we find the *objet petit a*? The *objet a* is precisely that surplus, that elusive make-believe that drove the man to change his existence. In "reality," it is nothing at all, just an empty surface (his life after the break is the same as before), but because of it the break is nonetheless well worth the trouble.

A Black Hole in Reality

How Nothing Can Beget Something

Patricia Highsmith's story "Black House" perfectly exemplifies the way fantasy space functions as an empty surface, as a kind of screen for the projection of desires: the fascinating presence of its positive contents does nothing but fill out a certain emptiness. The action takes place in a small American town where men gather in the evenings in the local saloon and revive nostalgic memories, local myths—usually their youthful adventures—that are always somehow associated with a desolate old building on a hill near the town. A certain malediction hangs over this mysterious "black house"; there is a tacit agreement among the men that one is not allowed to approach it. Entering it is supposed to involve mortal danger (it is rumored that the house is haunted, that it is inhabited by a lonely lunatic who kills all intruders, etc.) but, at the same time, the "black house" is a place that links all their adolescent memories, the place of their first "transgressions," above all those related to sexual experience (the men endlessly retell stories of how, years ago, they had their first sexual encounter in the house with the prettiest girl in the town, how they had their first cigarette in it). The hero of the story is a young engineer who has just moved into town. After listening to all the myths about the "black house," he announces to the company his intention of exploring this mysterious house the next evening. The men present react to this announcement with silent but nonetheless intense disapproval. The next evening, the young engineer visits the house, expecting something terrible or at least something unexpected to happen to him. With tense anticipation, he approaches the dark, old ruin, climbs the creaking staircase, examines all the rooms, but finds nothing except a few decaying mats on the floor. He immediately returns to the saloon and triumphantly declares to the gathered men that their "black house" is just an old, filthy ruin, that there is nothing mysterious or fascinating about it. The men are horrified and when the engineer begins to leave, one of them wildly attacks him. The engineer unfortunately falls to the ground and soon afterward dies. Why were the men so horrified by the action of the newcomer? We can grasp their resentment by remarking the difference between reality and the "other scene" of the fantasy space: the "black house" was forbidden to the men because it functioned as an empty space wherein they could project their nostalgic desires, their distorted memories; by publicly stating that the "black house" was nothing but an old ruin, the young intruder reduced their fantasy space to everyday, common reality. He annulled the difference between reality and fantasy space, depriving the men of the place in which they were able to articulate their desires.[6]

The gaze of the men in the saloon, capable of discerning the fascinating contours of the object of desire where a normal view sees nothing but a trivial everyday object, is literally a gaze capable of seeing nothingness, i.e., of seeing an object "begot by nothing," as Shakespeare formulated it in a short scene in *Richard II,* one of his most interesting plays. *Richard II* proves beyond any doubt that Shakespeare had read Lacan, for the basic problem of the drama is that of the *hystericization of a king,* a process whereby the king loses the second, sublime body that makes him a king, is confronted with the void of his subjectivity outside the symbolic mandate-title "king," and is thus forced into a series of theatrical, hysterical outbursts, from self-pity to sarcastic and clownish madness.[7] Our interest is limited, however, to a short dialogue between the Queen and Bushy, the King's servant, at the beginning of act II, scene II. The King has left on an expedition of war, and the Queen is filled with presentiments of evil, with a sorrow whose cause she cannot discern. Bushy attempts to console her by pointing out the illusory, phantomlike nature of her grief:

Bushy: Each substance of a grief hath twenty shadows,
Which show like grief itself, but are not so.
For sorrow's eye, glazed with blinding tears,
Divides one thing entire to many objects;
Like perspectives, which rightly gaz'd upon
Show nothing but confusion; ey'd awry
Distinguish form: so your sweet majesty,
Looking awry upon your lord's departure,
Finds shapes of grief more than himself to wail;
Which, look'd on as it is, is nought but shadows
Of what is not. Then, thrice-gracious queen,
More than your lord's departure weep not: more's not seen;
Or if it be, 'tis with false sorrow's eye,
Which for things true weeps things imaginary.

Queen: It may be so; but yet my inward soul
Persuades me it is otherwise: howe'er it be,
I cannot but be sad, so heavy sad,
As, though in thinking on no thought I think,
Makes me with heavy nothing faint and shrink.

Bushy: 'Tis nothing but conceit, my gracious lady.

Queen: 'Tis nothing less: conceit is still deriv'd
From some forefather grief; mine is not so,
For nothing hath begot my something grief;
Or something hath the nothing that I grieve:
'Tis in reversion that I do possess;
But what it is, that is not yet known; what
I cannot name; 'tis nameless woe, I wot.

By means of the metaphor of anamorphosis, Bushy tries to convince the Queen that her sorrow has no foundation, that its reasons are null. But the crucial point is the way his metaphor splits, redoubles itself, that is, the way Bushy entangles himself in contradiction. First ("sorrow's eye, glazed with blinding tears, / Divides one thing entire to many objects"), he refers to the simple, commonsense opposition between a thing as it is "in itself," in reality, and its "shadows," reflections in our eyes, subjective impressions multiplied by our anxieties and sorrows. When we are worried, a small difficulty assumes giant proportions, the thing appears to us far worse than it really is. The metaphor at work here is that of a glass surface sharpened, cut in a way that causes it to reflect a multitude of images. Instead of the tiny substance, we see its "twenty shadows." In the following lines, however, things get complicated. At first sight, it seems that Shakespeare only illustrates the fact that "sorrow's eye . . . divides one thing entire to many objects" with a metaphor from the domain of painting ("like perspectives which rightly gaz'd upon show nothing but confusion; ey'd awry distinguish form"), but what he really accomplishes is a radical change of terrain—from the metaphor of a sharpened glass surface, he passes to the metaphor of anamorphosis, the logic of which is quite different: a detail of a picture that "gaz'd rightly," i.e., straightforwardly, appears as a blurred spot, assumes clear, distinguished shapes once we look at it "awry," at an angle. The lines that apply this metaphor back to the Queen's anxiety and sorrow are thus profoundly ambivalent: "so your sweet majesty, *looking awry* upon your lord's departure, finds shapes of grief more than himself to wail; which, look'd on as it is, is nought but shadows of what is not." That is to say, if we take the comparison of the Queen's gaze with the anamorphotic gaze literally, we are obliged to state that *precisely by "looking awry," i.e., at an angle, she sees the thing in its clear and distinct form,* in opposition to the "straightforward" view that sees only an indistinct confusion (and, incidentally, the further development of the drama fully justifies the Queen's most sinister presentiments). But, of course, Bushy does not "want to say" this, his intention was to say quite the opposite: by means of an imperceptible subreption, he returns to the *first* metaphor (that of a sharpened glass) and "intends to say" that, because her gaze is distorted by sorrow and anxiety, the Queen sees cause for alarm, whereas a closer, matter-of-fact view attests to the fact that there is nothing to her fear.

What we have here are thus two realities, two "substances." On the level of the first metaphor, we have commonsense reality seen as "substance with twenty shadows," as a thing split into twenty reflections by our subjective view, in short, as a substantial "reality" distorted by our subjective perspective. If we look at a thing straight on, matter-of-factly, we see it "as it really is," while the gaze puzzled by our desires and anxieties ("looking awry") gives us a distorted, blurred image. On the level of the second metaphor, however, the relation is exactly the opposite: if we look at a thing straight on, i.e., matter-of-factly, disinterestedly, objectively, we see nothing but a formless spot; the object assumes clear and distinctive features only if we look at it "at an angle," i.e., with an "interested" view, supported, permeated, and "distorted" by *desire.* This describes perfectly the *objet petit a,* the object-cause of desire: an object that is, in a way, posited by desire itself. The paradox of desire is that it posits retroactively its own cause, i.e., the object *a* is an object that can be perceived only by a gaze "distorted" by desire, an object that *does not exist* for an "objective" gaze. In other words, the object *a* is always, *by definition,* perceived in a distorted way, because outside this distortion, "in itself," *it does not exist,* since it is *nothing but* the embodiment, the materialization of this very distortion, of this surplus of confusion and perturbation introduced by desire into so-called "objective reality." The object *a* is "objectively" nothing, though, viewed from a certain perspective, it assumes the shape of "something." It is, as is formulated in an extremely precise manner by the Queen in her response to Bushy, her "something grief" begot by "nothing." Desire "takes off" when "something" (its object-cause) embodies, gives positive existence to its "nothing," to its void. This "something" is the anamorphotic object, a pure semblance that we can perceive clearly only by "looking awry." It is precisely (and only) the logic of desire that belies the notorious wisdom that "nothing comes from nothing": in the movement of desire, "something comes from nothing." Although it is true that the object-cause of desire is a pure semblance, this does not prevent it from triggering a whole chain of consequences that regulate our "material," "effective" life and deeds.

The "Thirteenth Floor" of the Fantasy Space

It was no accident that Shakespeare was so attentive to these paradoxes of "something begot by nothing" (the same problem lies at the very heart of *King Lear*), for he lived in a period of the rapid dissolution of precapitalist social relations and of the lively emergence of the elements of capitalism, i.e., in a period when he was able daily to observe the way a reference to "nothing," to some pure semblance (speculating with "worthless" paper money that is only a "promise" of itself as "real" money, for example), triggers the enormous machinery of a production process that changes the very surface of the earth.[8] Hence Shakespeare's sensitivity to the paradoxical power of money which converts everything into its opposite, procures legs for a cripple, makes a handsome man out of a freak, etc.—all those memorable lines from *Timon of Athens* quoted again and again by Marx. Lacan was well justified in modeling his notion of surplus enjoyment (*plus-de-jouir*) on the Marxian notion of surplus value: surplus enjoyment has the same paradoxical power to convert things (pleasure objects) into their opposite, to render disgusting what is usually considered a most pleasant "normal" sexual experience, to render inexplicably attractive what is usually considered a loathsome act (of torturing a beloved person, of enduring painful humiliation, etc.).

Such a reversal engenders, of course, a nostalgic yearning for the "natural" state in which things were only what they were, in which we perceived them straightforwardly, in which our gaze had not yet been distorted by the anamorphotic spot. Far from announcing a kind of "pathological fissure," however, the frontier separating the two "substances," separating the thing that appears clearly in an objective view from the "substance of enjoyment" that can be perceived clearly only by "looking awry," is precisely what *prevents us from sliding into psychosis*. Such is the effect of the symbolic order on the gaze. The emergence of language opens up a hole in reality, and this hole shifts the axis of our gaze. Language redoubles "reality" into itself and the void of the Thing that can be filled out only by an anamorphotic gaze from aside.

To exemplify this, let us refer again to a product of popular culture, a science fiction novel by Robert Heinlein, *The Unpleasant Profession of Jonathan Hoag*. The action takes place in contemporary New York where a certain Jonathan Hoag hires the private investigator Randall to find out what happens to him after he enters his working premises on the (nonexistent) thirteenth floor of the Acme building—Hoag is totally unaware of his activity during this time. Next day, Randall follows Hoag on his way to work, but between the twelfth and fourteenth floors Hoag suddenly disappears and Randall is unable to locate the thirteenth floor. The same evening, a double of Randall appears to him in his bedroom mirror and tells Randall to follow him through the mirror where he is called by the committee. On the other side of the mirror, the double leads Randall to a great meeting hall where the president of the committee of twelve informs him that he is now on the thirteenth floor, to which he will be called from time to time for interrogation. During these subsequent interrogations, Randall learns that the members of this mysterious committee believe in a Great Bird supposed to breed small birds, her offspring, and to rule the universe together with them. The denouement of the story: Hoag finally becomes aware of his real identity and he invites Randall and his wife Cynthia to a picnic in the countryside where he relates to them the whole plot. He is, he tells them, an art critic—but of a peculiar kind. Our human universe is just one of the existing universes; the real masters of all worlds are mysterious beings, unknown to us, who create different worlds, different universes as works of art. Our universe was created by one of these universal artists. To control the artistic perfection of their productions, these artists from time to time send into their creations one of their own kind, disguised as an inhabitant of the created universe (in Hoag's case disguised as a man), who acts as a sort of universal art critic. (With Hoag, there was a short circuit; he forgot who he really was and has to ask for the services of Randall.) The members of the mysterious committee interrogating Randall were only representatives of some evil lower divinity striving to interrupt the performance of the real "gods," the universal artists. Hoag then informs Randall and Cynthia that he has discovered in our universe some minor defects that will be quickly repaired in the next few hours. They will never even notice, if they simply make sure that when they drive back to New York, they do not— under any circumstances and despite what they might see—open the window of their car. Thereafter Hoag leaves; still excited, Randall and Cynthia start to drive home. Things proceed without mishap as they follow the prohibition. But then they witness an accident, a child is run over by a car. At first the couple remain calm and continue to drive, but after seeing a patrolman, their sense of duty prevails and they stop the car to inform him of the accident. Randall asks Cynthia to lower the side window a little:

> She complied, then gave a sharp intake of breath and swallowed a scream. He did not scream, but he wanted to.
>
> Outside the open window was no sunlight, no cops, no kids—nothing. Nothing but a grey and formless mist, pulsing slowly as if with inchoate life. They could see nothing of the city through it, not because it was too dense but because it was—empty. No sound came out of it; no movement showed in it.
>
> It merged with the frame of the window and began to drift inside. Randall shouted, "Roll up the window!" She tried to obey, but her hands were nerveless; he reached across her and cranked it up himself, jamming it hard into its seat.
>
> The sunny scene was restored; through the glass they saw the patrolman, the boisterous game, the sidewalk, and the city beyond. Cynthia put a hand on his arm. "Drive on, Teddy!"
>
> "Wait a minute," he said tensely, and turned to the window beside him. Very cautiously he rolled it down—just a crack, less than an inch.
>
> It was enough. The formless grey flux was out there, too; through the glass, city traffic and sunny street were plain, through the opening— nothing.

This "grey and formless mist, pulsing slowly as if with inchoate life," what is it if not the Lacanian real, the pulsing of the presymbolic substance in its abhorrent vitality? But what is crucial for us here is the place from which this real erupts: the very borderline separating the outside from the inside, materialized in this case by the windowpane. Here, we should refer to the basic phenomenological experience of discord, the disproportion between inside and outside, present to anyone who has been inside a car. From the outside, the car looks small; as we crawl into it, we are sometimes seized by claustrophobia, but once we are inside, the car suddenly appears far larger and we feel quite comfortable. The price paid for this comfort is the loss of any continuity between "inside" and "outside." To those sitting inside a car, outside reality appears slightly distant, the other side of a barrier or screen materialized by the glass. We perceive external reality, the world outside the car, as "another reality," another mode of reality, not immediately continuous with the reality inside the car. The proof of this discontinuity is the uneasy feeling that overwhelms us when we suddenly roll down the windowpane and allow external reality to strike us with the proximity of its material presence. Our uneasiness consists in the sudden experience of how close really is what the windowpane, serving as a kind of protective screen, kept at a safe distance. But when we are safely inside the car, behind the closed windows, the external objects are, so to speak, transposed into another mode. They appear to be fundamentally "unreal," as if their reality has been suspended, put in parenthesis—in short, they appear as a kind of cinematic reality projected onto the screen of the windowpane. It is precisely this phenomenological experience of the barrier separating inside from outside, this feeling that the outside is ultimately "fictional," that produces the horrifying effect of the final scene in Heinlein's novel. It is as if, for a moment, the "projection" of the outside reality had stopped working, as if, for a moment, we had been confronted with the formless grey, with the emptiness of the screen, with the "place where nothing takes place but the place," if we may be permitted this—sacrilegious in this context perhaps—quotation from Mallarmé.

This discord, thus disproportion between inside and outside is also a fundamental feature of Kafka's architecture. A series of his buildings (the block of flats in which the court has its seat in *The Trial,* the uncle's palace in *America,* etc.) are characterized by the fact that what appears from the outside a modest house changes miraculously into a endless maze of staircases and halls once we enter it. (We are reminded of Piranesi's famous drawings of the subterranean labyrinth of prison staircases and cells.) As soon as we wall or fence in a certain space, we experience more of it "inside" than appears possible to the outside view. Continuity, proportion is not possible because the disproportion (the surplus of the "inside" in relation to the "outside") is a necessary structural effect of the very barrier separating inside from outside. The disproportion can be abolished only by demolishing the barrier, by letting the outside swallow the inside.

Why, then, does the inside surpass the outside in scale? In what does this surplus of the inside consist? It consists, of course, of fantasy space: in our case, the thirteenth floor of the building where the mysterious committee has its seat. This "surplus space" is a constant motif of science fiction and mystery stories, and is visible in many of classic cinema's attempts to evade an unhappy ending. When the action reaches its catastrophic peak, a radical change of perspective is introduced that refigures the entire catastrophic course of events as merely a bad dream of the hero. The first example that comes to mind is *Woman in the Window* by Fritz Lang: a lonely professor of psychology is fascinated by the portrait of a *female fatale* that hangs in the window of a store next to the entrance to his club. After his family has gone away on vacation, he dozes off in his club. One of the attendants awakens him at eleven, whereupon he leaves the club, casting a glance at the portrait, as usual. This time, however, the portrait comes alive as the picture in the window overlaps with the mirror reflection of a beautiful brunette on the street, who asks the professor for a match. The professor, then, has an affair with her; kills her lover in a fight; is informed by a police inspector friend of the progress of the investigation of this murder; sits in a chair, drinks poison, and dozes off when he learns his arrest is imminent. He is then awakened by an attendant at eleven and discovers that he has been dreaming. Reassured, the professor returns home, conscious that he must avoid ensnarement by fatal brunettes. We must not, however, view the final turnaround as a compromise, an accommodation to the codes of Hollywood. The message of the film is not consoling, not: "it was only a dream, in reality I am a normal man like others and not a murderer!" but rather: *in our unconscious, in the real of our desire, we are all murderers.* Paraphrasing the Lacanian interpretation of the Freudian dream about the father to whom a dead son appears, reproaching him with the words "Father, can't you see that I'm burning?," we could say that the professor awakes *in order to continue his dream* (about being a normal person like his fellow men), that is, to escape the real (the "psychic reality") of his desire. Awakened into everyday reality, he can say to himself with relief "It was only a dream!," thus overlooking the crucial fact that, awake, he is "nothing but the consciousness of his dream."[9] In other words, paraphrasing the parable of Zhuang-Zhi and the butterfly, which is also one of Lacan's points of reference: we do not have a quiet, kind, decent, bourgeois professor dreaming for a moment that he is a murderer; what we have is, on the contrary, a murderer dreaming, in his everyday life, that he is just a decent bourgeois professor.[10]

This kind of retroactive displacement of "real" events into fiction (dreaming) appears as a "compromise," an act of ideological conformism, only if we hold to the naive ideological opposition between "hard reality" and the "world of dreaming." As soon as we take into accunt that it is precisely and only in dreams that we encounter the real of our desire, the whole accent radically shifts: our common everyday reality, the reality of the social universe in which we assume our usual roles of kind-hearted, decent people, turns out to be an illusion that rests on a certain "repression," on overlooking the real of our desire. This social reality is then nothing but a fragile, symbolic cobweb that can at any moment be torn aside by an intrusion of the real. At any moment, the most common everyday conversation, the most ordinary event can take a dangerous turn, damage can be caused that cannot be undone. *Woman in the Window* demonstrates this by means of its looplike progress: events progress in a linear way until, all of a sudden, precisely at the point of catastrophic breakdown, we find ourselves again at an earlier point of departure. The path to catastrophe turns out to be only a fictional detour bringing us back to our starting point. To bring about such an effect of retroactive fictionalization, *Woman in the Window* makes use of the repetition of the same scene (the professor dozes off in a chair, the attendant awakens him at eleven). The repetition retroactively changes what happened in between into a fiction, i.e., the "real" awakening is only one, the distance between the two is the place of the fiction.

In a play by John B. Priestley, *The Dangerous Corner,* it is a gunshot that plays the role of the professor's awakening. The play is about a rich family gathered round the hearth of their country house while its members are returning from the hunt. Suddenly, a shot is heard in the background and this shot gives the conversation a dangerous turn. Long-repressed family secrets erupt, and finally the father, the head of the family who had insisted on clarifying things, on bringing all secrets to the light of day, retires, broken, to the first floor of the house and shoots himself. But this shot turns out to be the same as the one heard at the beginning of the play and the same conversation continues, only this time instead of taking the dangerous turn, it remains on the level of the usual superficial family chatter. The traumas remain buried and the family is happily reunited for the idyllic dinner. This is the image of everyday reality offered by psychoanalysis: a fragile equilibrium that can be destroyed at any moment if, in a quite contingent and unpredictable way, trauma erupts. The space that, retroactively, turns out to be fictional, the space between two awakenings or between two shots, is, according to its formal structure, exactly the same as the nonexistent thirteenth floor of the Acme building in Heinlein's novel, a fictional space, "another scene," where alone the truth of our desire can be articulated—which is why, according to Lacan, truth "is structured like fiction."

THE PSYCHOTIC SOLUTION: THE OTHER OF THE OTHER

Our mention of Kafka apropos of the disproportion between outside and inside was by no means accidental: the Kafkaesque Court, that absurd, obscene, culpabilizing agency, has to be located precisely as this surplus of the inside in relation to the outside, as this fantasy space of the nonexistent thirteenth floor. In the mysterious "committee" that interrogates Randall, it is not difficult to recognize a new verson of the Kafkaesque Court, of the obscene figure of an evil superegoic law; the fact that members of this committee worship the divine Bird only confirms that in the imagery of our culture—up to and including Hitchcock's *The Birds*—birds function as the embodiment of a cruel and obscene superegoic agency. Heinlein eludes this Kafkaesque vision of a world ruled by the obscene agency of a "mad God," but the price he pays for it is the paranoid construction according to which our universe is the work of art of unknown creators. The wittiest variation on this theme—witty in the literal sense, because it concerns wit itself, jokes—is to be found in Isaac Asimov's short story "Jokester." A scientist doing research on jokes comes to the conclusion that human intelligence began precisely with the capacity to produce jokes; so, after a thorough analysis of thousands of jokes, he succeeds in isolating the "primal joke," the original point enabling passage from the animal to the human kingdom, i.e., the point at which superhuman intelligence (God) intervened in the course of life on earth by communicating to man the first joke. The common feature of this kind of ingenious "paranoid" story is the implication of the existence of an "Other of the Other": a hidden subject who pulls the strings of the great Other (the symbolic order) precisely at the points at which this Other starts to speak its "autonomy," i.e., where it produces an effect of meaning by means of a senseless contingency, beyond the conscious intention of the speaking subject, as in jokes or dreams. This "Other of the Other" is exactly the Other of paranoia: the one who speaks through us without our knowing it, who controls our thoughts, who manipulates us through the apparent "spontaneity" of jokes, or, as in Heinlein's novel, the artist whose fantasy creation is our world. The paranoid construction enables us to escape the fact that "the Other does not exist" (Lacan)—that it does not exist as a consistent, closed order—to escape the blind, contingent automatism, the constitutive stupidity of the symbolic order.

When faced with such a paranoid construction, we must not forget Freud's warning and mistake it for the "illness" itself: the paranoid construction is, on the contrary, an attempt to heal ourselves, to pull overselves out of the real "illness," the "end of the world," the breakdown of the symbolic universe, by means of this substitute formation. If we want to witness the process of this breakdown—the breakdown of the the barrier real/reality—in its pure form, we have only to follow the path of the paintings produced in the 1960s, the last decade of his life, by Mark Rothko, the most tragic figure of American abstract expressionism. The "theme" of these paintings is constant: all of them present nothing but a set of color variations of the relationship between the real and reality, rendered as a geometrical abstraction by the famous painting of Kasimir Malevich, *The Naked Unframed Icon of My Time*: a simple black square on a white background. The "reality" (white background surface, the "liberated nothingness," the open space in which objects can appear) obtains its consistency only by means of the "black hole" in its center (the Lacanian *das Ding*, the Thing that gives body to the substance of enjoyment), i.e., by the exclusion of the real, by the change of the status of the real into that of a central lack. All late Rothko paintings are manifestations of a struggle to save the barrier separating the real from reality, that is, to prevent the real (the central black square) from overflowing the entire field, to preserve the distance between the square and what must at any cost whatsoever remain its background. If the square occupies the whole field, if the difference between the figure and its background is lost, a psychotic autism is produced. Rothko pictures this struggle as a tension between a gray background and the central black spot that spreads menacingly from one painting to another (in the late 1960s, the vivacity of red and yellow in Rothko's canvases is increasingly replaced by the minimal opposition between black and gray). If we look at these paintings in a "cinematic" way, i.e., if we put the reproductions one above the other and then turn them quickly to get the impression of continuous movement, we can almost draw a line to the inevitable end—as if Rothko were driven by some unavoidable fatal necessity. In the canvases immediately preceding his death, the minimal tension between black and gray changes for the last time into the burning conflict between voracious red and yellow, witnessing the last desperate attempt at redemption and at the same time confirming unmistakably that the end is imminent. Rothko was one day found dead in his New York loft, in a pool of blood, with his wrists cut. He preferred death to being swallowed by the Thing, i.e., precisely by that "grey and formless mist, pulsing slowly as if with inchoate life" that the two heroes of the Heinlein novel perceive through their open window.

Far from being a sign of "madness," the barrier separating the real from reality is therefore the very condition of a minimum of "normalcy": "madness" (psychosis) sets in when this barrier is torn down, when the real overflows reality (as in autistic breakdown) or when it is itself included in reality (assuming the form of the "Other of the Other," of the paranoiac's prosecutor, for example).

How the Real Returns and Answers

RETURN OF THE LIVING DEAD

Why is the Lacanian matheme for the drive $\$\lozenge D$? The first answer is that the drives are by definition "partial," they are always tied to specific parts of the body's surface—the so-called "erogenous zones"—which, contrary to the superficial view, are not biologically determined but result instead from the signifying parceling of the body. Certain parts of the body's surface are erotically privileged not because of their anatomical position but because of the way the body is caught up in the symbolic network. This symbolic dimension is designated in the matheme as D, i.e., symbolic demand. The final proof of this fact consists in a phenomenon often encountered in hysterical symptoms where a part of the body that usually has no erogenous value starts to function as an erogenous zone (neck, nose, etc.). This classic explanation is, however, insufficient: what escapes it is the intimate relationship between drive and demand. A drive is precisely a demand that is not caught up in the dialectic of desire, that resists dialecticization. Demand almost always implies a certain dialectical mediation: we demand something, but what we are really aiming at through this demand is something else—sometimes even the very refusal of the demand in its literality. Along with every demand, a question necessarily rises: "I demand this, but what do I really want by it?" Drive, on the contrary, persists in a certain demand, it is a "mechanical" insistence that cannot be caught up in dialectical trickery: I demand something and I persist in it to the end.

Our interest in this distinction concerns its relation to the "second death": the apparitions that emerge in the domain "between two deaths" address to us some unconditional demand, and it is for this reason that they incarnate pure drive without desire. Let us begin with Antigone who, according to Lacan, irradiates a sublime beauty from the very moment she enters the domain between two deaths, between her symbolic and her actual death. What characterizes her innermost posture is precisely her insistence on a certain unconditional demand on which she is not prepared to give way: a proper burial for her brother. It is the same with the ghost of Hamlet's father, who returns from his grave with the demand that Hamlet revenge his infamous death. This connection between drive as an unconditional demand and the domain between the two deaths is also visible in popular culture. In the film *The Terminator,* Arnold Schwarzenegger plays a cyborg who returns to contemporary Los Angeles from the future, with the intention of killing the mother of a future leader. The horror of this figure consists precisely in the fact that it functions as a programmed automaton who, even when all that remains of him is a metallic, legless skeleton, persists in his demand and pursues his victim with no trace of compromise or hesitation. The terminator is the embodiment of the drive, devoid of desire.[1]

In two other films, we encounter two versions of the same motive, one comical, the other pathetic-tragic. In George Romero's omnibus *Creepshow* (screenplay by Stephen King), a family is gathered around the dinner table to celebrate the anniversary of their father's death. Years earlier, his sister had killed him at his birthday party by hitting him on the head in response to his endlessly repeated demand, "Daddy wants his cake!" Suddenly, a strange noise is heard from the family cemetery behind the house; the dead father climbs from his grave, kills his murderous sister, cuts off the head of his wife, puts it on the tray, smears it with cream, decorates it with candles and mumbles contentedly: "Daddy got his cake!"—a demand that has persisted beyond the grave until satisfied.[2] The cult film *Robocop,* a futuristic story about a policeman shot to death and then revived after all parts of his body have been replaced by artificial substitutes, introduces a more tragic note: the hero who finds himself literally "between two deaths"—clinically dead and at the same time provided with a new, mechanical body—starts to remember fragments of his previous, "human" life and thus undergoes a process of resubjectivation, changing gradually back from pure incarnated drive to a being of desire.[3]

The ease with which examples from popular culture can be found should come as no surprise: if there is a phenomenon that fully deserves to be called the "fundamental fantasy of contemporary mass culture," it is this fantasy of the return of the living dead: the fantasy of a person who does not want to stay dead but returns again and again to pose a threat to the living. The unattained archetype of a long series—from the psychotic killer in *Halloween* to Jason in *Friday the Thirteenth*—is still George Romero's *The Night of the Living Dead,* where the "undead" are not portrayed as embodiments of pure evil, of a simple drive to kill or revenge, but as sufferers, pursuing their victims with an awkward persistence, colored by a kind of infinite sadness (as in Werner Herzog's *Nosferatu,* in which the vampire is not a simple machinery of evil with a cynical smile on his lips, but a melancholic sufferer longing for salvation). Apropos of this phenomenon, let us then ask a naive and elementary question: why do the dead return? The answer offered by Lacan is the same as that found in popular culture: *because they were not properly buried,* i.e., because something went wrong with their obsequies. The return of the dead is a sign of a disturbance in the symbolic rite, in the process of symbolization; the dead return as collectors of some unpaid symbolic debt. This is the basic lesson drawn by Lacan from *Antigone* and *Hamlet.* The plots of both plays involve improper funeral rites, and the "living dead"—Antigone and the ghost of Hamlet's father—return to settle symbolic accounts. The return of the living dead, then, materializes a certain symbolic debt persisting beyond physical expiration.

It is commonplace to state that symbolization as such equates to symbolic murder: when we speak about a thing, we suspend, place in parentheses, its reality. It is precisely for this reason that the funeral rite exemplifies symbolization at its purest: through it, the dead are inscribed in the text of symbolic tradition, they are assured that, in spite of their death, they will "continue to live" in the memory of the community. The "return of the living dead" is, on the other hand, the reverse of the proper funeral rite. While the latter implies a certain reconciliation, an acceptance of loss, the return of the dead signifies that they cannot find their proper place in the text of tradition. The two great traumatic events of the holocaust and the gulag are, of course, exemplary cases of the return of the dead in the twentieth century. The shadows of their victims will continue to chase us as "living dead" until we give them a decent burial, until we integrate the trauma of their death into our historical memory. The same may be said of the "primordial crime" that founded history itself, the murder of the "primal father" (re)constructed by Freud in *Totem and Taboo*:[4] the murder of the father is integrated into the symbolic universe insofar as the dead father begins to reign as the symbolic agency of the Name-of-the-Father. This transformation, this integration, however, is never brought about without remainder; there is always a certain leftover that returns in the form of the obscene and revengeful figure of the Father-of-Enjoyment, of this figure split between cruel revenge and crazy laughter, as, for example, the famous Freddie from *Nightmare on Elm Street.*

BEYOND PET SEMATARY

The Oedipus myth and the myth of the primal father of *Totem and Taboo* are usually apprehended as two versions of the same myth, that is, the myth of the primal father is conceived as a philogenetic projection into the mythic, prehistorical past of the Oedipus myth as the elementary articulation of the subject's ontogenesis. A close look reveals, however, that the two myths are deeply asymmetrical, even opposed.[5] The Oedipus myth is based on the premise that it is the father, as the agent of prohibition, who denies us access to enjoyment (i.e., incest, the sexual relationship with the mother). The underlying implication is that parricide would remove this obstacle and thus allow us fully to enjoy the forbidden object. The myth of the primal father is almost the exact opposite of this: the result of the parricide is not the removal of an obstacle, enjoyment is not brought finally within our reach. Quite the contrary—the dead father turns out to be stronger than the living one. After the parricide, the former reigns as the Name-of-the-Father, the agent of the symbolic law that irrevocably precludes access to the forbidden fruit of enjoyment.

Why is this redoubling necessary? In the Oedipus myth, the prohibition of enjoyment still functions, ultimately, as an external impediment, leaving the possibility open that without this obstacle, we would be able to enjoy fully. But enjoyment is already, in itself, impossible. One of the commonplaces of Lacanian theory is that access to enjoyment is denied to the speaking being, as such. The figure of the father saves us from this deadlock by bestowing on the immanent *impossibility* the form of a symbolic *interdiction*. The myth of the primal father in *Totem and Taboo* complements—or, more precisely, supplements—the Oedipus myth by embodying this impossible enjoyment in the obscene figure of the Father-of-Enjoyment, i.e., in the very figure who assumes the role of the agent of prohibition. The illusion is that there was at least one subject (the primal father possessing all women) who was able to enjoy fully; as such, the figure of the Father-of-Enjoyment is nothing but a neurotic fantasy that overlooks the fact that the father has been dead from the beginning, i.e., that he never was alive, except insofar as he did not know that he was already dead.

The lesson to be drawn from this is that reducing the pressure of the superego is definitely not to be accomplished by replacing its supposedly "irrational," "counterproductive," "rigid" pressure with rationally accepted renunciations, laws, and rules. The point is rather to acknowledge that part of enjoyment is lost from the very beginning, that it is immanently impossible, and not concentrated "somewhere else," in the place from which the agent of prohibition speaks. At the same time, this allows us to locate the weak point of the Deleuzian polemic against Lacan's "oedipalism."[6] What Deleuze and Guattari fail to take into account is that the most powerful anti-Oedipus is *Oedipus itself*: the Oedipal father—father reigning as his Name, as the agent of symbolic law—is necessarily redoubled in itself, it can exert its authority only by relying on the superego figure of the Father-of-Enjoyment. It is precisely this dependence of the Oedipal father—the agency of symbolic law guaranteeing order and reconciliation—on the perverse figure of the Father-of-Enjoyment that explains why Lacan prefers to write *perversion* as *père-version*, i.e., the version of the father. Far from acting only as symbolic agent, restraining pre-oedipal, "polymorphous perversity," subjugating it to the genital law, the "version of," or turn toward, the father is the most radical perversion of all.

In this respect, Stephen King's *Pet Sematary,* perhaps the definitive novelization of the "return of the living dead," is of special interest to us insofar as it presents a kind of inversion of the motif of the dead father returning as the obscene ghost figure. The novel is the story of Louis Creed, a young physician, who—together with his wife Rachel, two small children, six-year-old Ellie and two-year-old Gage, and their cat Church—moves to a small town in Maine where he will manage the university infirmary. They rent a big, comfortable house near the highway, along which trucks pass continually. Soon after their arrival, Jud Crandall, their elderly neighbor, takes them to visit the "Pet Sematary" in the woods behind their house, a cemetery for the dogs and cats run over by trucks on the highway. On the very first day, a student dies in Louis's arms. After dying, however, he suddenly rises up to tell Louis, "Don't go beyond, no matter how much you feel you need to. The barrier was not made to be broken." The place designated by this warning is precisely the place "between two deaths," the forbidden domain of the Thing. The barrier not to be crossed is none other than the one beyond which Antigone is drawn, the forbidden boundary-domain where "being insists in suffering" (like the living dead in Romero's film). This barrier is designated in *Antigone* by the Greek term *atē,* perdition, devastation: "Beyond *atē* we could stay only for a brief period of time, and it is there that Antigone strives to go."[7] The sybilic warning of the dead student soon acquires meaning when Creed is irresistibly drawn into this space beyond the barrier. A few days later, Church is killed by a passing truck. Aware of the pain that the cat's death will cause little Ellie, Jud initiates Creed into the secret that lies beyond the Pet Sematary—an ancient Indian burial ground inhabited by a malevolent spirit, Wendigo. The cat is buried, but returns the very next day—stinking, loathsome, a living dead, similar in all respects to its former self except for the fact that it seems to be inhabited by an evil spirit. When Gage is killed by another passing truck, Creed buries him, only to witness his return as a monster child who kills old Jud, then his own mother, and is finally put to death by his father. Yet Creed returns to the burial ground once again with the body of his wife, convinced that this time things will turn out all right. As the novel ends, he sits alone in his kitchen, playing patience and waiting for her return.

Pet Sematary is, then, a kind of perverted *Antigone* in which Creed represents the consequent logic of the modern, Faustian hero. Antigone sacrifices herself so that her brother will get a decent burial, whereas Creed deliberately sabotages normal burial. He intervenes with a perverted burial rite that—instead of leaving the dead to their eternal rest—provokes their return as living dead. His love for his son is so boundless that it extends even beyond the barrier of *atē,* into the domain of perdition—he is willing to risk eternal damnation, to have his son return as a murderous monster, just to have him back. It is as if this figure of Creed, with his monstrous act, were designed to give meaning to these lines from *Antigone*: "There are a lot of dreadful things in the world, but none is more dreadful than man." Lacan noted, apropos of *Antigone,* that Sophocles gave us a kind of critique of humanism *avant la lettre,* that he outlined in advance, before its arrival, humanism's self-destructive dimension.[8]

THE CORPSE THAT WOULD NOT DIE

Happily for us, the dead can also return in a more amusing, not to say benevolent way, as in Hitchcock's *The Trouble with Harry.* Hitchcock called *The Trouble with Harry* an exercise in the art of understatement. This fundamental component of English humor is present in the film's ironic subversion of the basic procedure of Hitchcock's other films. Far from diverting a peaceful, everyday situation into the *unheimlich,* far from functioning as the eruption of some traumatic entity that disturbs the tranquil flow of life, the "blot," Harry's body—which serves in this film as Hitchcock's famous "McGuffin"—functions as a minor, marginal problem, not really all that important, indeed, almost petty. The social life of the village goes on, people continue to exchange pleasantries, arrange to meet at the corpse, to pursue their ordinary interests.

Nevertheless, the film's lesson cannot be summed up in a comforting maxim—"Let's not take life too seriously; death and sexuality are, in the final analysis, frivolous and futile things"—nor does it reflect a tolerant, hedonistic attitude. Just like the obsessive personality described by Freud toward the end of his analysis of the "Rat Man," so the "official ego" of the characters in *The Trouble with Harry,* open, tolerant, conceals a network of rules and inhibitions that block all pleasure.[9] The ironic detachment of the characters vis-à-vis Harry's body reveals an obsessional neutralization of an underlying traumatic complex. Indeed, just as obsessional rules and inhibitions arise out of a symbolic indebtedness contracted by the disjunction between the real and symbolic death of the father (the father of the "Rat Man" died "without having settled his accounts"), so "the trouble with Harry" consists in the fact that his body is present without being dead on the symbolic level. The film's subtitle could be "The Corpse That Wouldn't Die," since the tiny community of villagers, each of whose fate is in various ways linked to Harry, does not know what to do with his corpse. The only denouement the story can have is Harry's symbolic death: it is thus arranged that the boy will happen upon the body a second time, so that the accounts can be settled, the rite of burial can finally take place.

Here, we should remind ourselves that Harry's problem is the same as Hamlet's (need we stress that Hamlet furnishes a case of obsession par excellence?): in the end, *Hamlet* is the drama of a real death unaccompanied by a symbolic "settling of accounts." Polonius and Ophelia are surreptitiously buried, without the prescribed rituals, and Hamlet's father, killed at an inopportune moment, remains in a state of sin, left to face his Maker unshriven. It is for this reason, and not because of his murder as such, that the ghost returns and orders his son to avenge him. Or we can go back a step further and recall that the same problem also arises in *Antigone* (which could almost be called *The Trouble with Polynices*): the action is set in motion by the fact that Creon forbids Antigone to bury her brother and perform the burial rites. In this way we can measure the path traveled by "Western civilization" in its settlement of the symbolic debt: from Antigone's sublime features, radiant with beauty and inner calm, for whom the act is an unquestioned, accepted thing; through the hesitation and obsessive doubt of Hamlet who, of course, finally acts, but only after it is too late, when his action fails in its symbolic aim; to the "trouble with Harry," in which the entire affair is treated as some kind of quibble, a minor inconvenience, a welcome pretext for wider social contacts, but in which understatement nevertheless betrays the existence of an utter inhibition, for which we would look in vain in either *Hamlet* or *Antigone*.

Understatement thus becomes a specific way of taking note of the "blot" created by the real of the paternal body: isolate the "blot," act as though it were not serious, keep cool—Dad's dead, okay, it's cool, no cause for excitement. The economy of such an isolation of the "blot," such a blockage of its symbolic effectiveness, is given perfect expression in the familiar paradox of the "catastrophic but not yet serious situation"—in what in Freud's day was called "Viennese philosophy." The key to understatement would thus seem to reside in the split between (real) knowledge and (symbolic) belief: "I know very well (that the situation is catastrophic), but . . . (I don't believe it and will go on acting as though it were not serious)." The current attitude toward the ecological crisis is a perfect illustration of this split: we are quite aware that it may already be too late, that we are already on the brink of catastrophe (of which the death throes of the European forests are just the harbinger), but nevertheless we do not believe it. We act as though it were only an exaggerated concern over a few trees, a few birds, and not literally a question of our survival. The same code enables us to understand the slogan "Let us be realistic and demand the impossible!"—which was scrawled on the buildings of Paris in 1968—as a call to be equal to the real of the catastrophe that had befallen us by demanding what, in the framework of our symbolic belief, might appear to be "impossible."

Another reading of "understatement" is offered by Winston Churchill's well-known paradox. Responding to those detractors of democracy who saw it as a system that paved the way for corruption, demagogy, and a weakening of authority, Churchill said: "It is true that democracy is the worst of all possible systems; the problem is that no other system would be better." That sentence is based on the logic of "everything possible and then some." Its first premise gives us the overall grouping of "all possible systems" within which the questioned element (democracy) appears to be the worst. The second premise states that the grouping "all possible systems" is not all-inclusive, and that compared to additional elements, the element in question turns out to be quite bearable. The procedure plays on the fact that additional elements are *the same* as those included in the overall "all possible systems," the only difference being that *they no longer function as elements of a closed totality.* In relation to the *totality* of systems of government, democracy is the worst; but, within the *non-totalized series* of political systems, none would be better. Thus, from the fact that "no system would be better," we cannot therefore conclude that democracy is "the best"—its advantage is strictly limited to the comparative. As soon as we attempt to formulate the proposition in the superlative, the qualification of democracy is inverted into "the worst."

In the "Postscript" to *The Question of Lay Analysis,* Freud reproduces the same "not-all" paradox with regard to women when he recalls a bit of dialogue in *Simplicissimus,* the satiric Viennese newspaper: "One man was complaining to another about the weaknesses and troublesome nature of the fair sex. 'All the same,' replied his companion, 'women are the best thing we have of the kind.'"[10] Thus the logic of woman as symptom of man: unbearable—thus, nothing is more agreeable; impossible to live with—thus, to live without her is even more difficult. The "trouble with Harry" is thus catastrophic from the overall point of view, but if we take into account the dimension of the "not-all," it is not even a serious difficulty. The secret of "understatement" resides in investigating just that dimension of "not-all" (the *pas-tout*): it is an appropriate, English-language way of evoking the "not-all."

It is for this reason that Lacan invites us "to bet on the worst" (*parier sur le pire*): there can be nothing better than what (within the overall framework) seems to be "the worst," as soon as it is transposed to the "not-all" and its elements compared one by one. Within the overall framework of the orthodox psychoanalytic tradition, Lacanian psychoanalysis is without question "the worst," a total catastrophe, but as soon as we compare it one by one with other theories, it appears that none is better.

The Answer of the Real

The role of the Lacanian real is, however, radically ambiguous: true, it erupts in the form of a traumatic return, derailing the balance of our daily lives, but it serves at the same time as a support of this very balance. What would our daily life be without some support in an *answer of the real*? To exemplify this other aspect of the real, let us recall Steven Spielberg's *Empire of the Sun*, the story of Jim, an English adolescent caught in the turmoil of World War II in Shanghai. Jim's basic problem is survival—not only in the physical sense, but above all psychically, i.e., he must learn to avoid the "loss of reality" after his world, his symbolic universe, literally falls apart. We only have to remember the scenes from the beginning of the film in which the misery of Chinese daily life confronts the world of Jim and his parents (the isolated world of Englishmen whose dreamlike character is rendered a little bit too obvious when, accoutred for the masked ball, they pierce the chaotic flow of Chinese refugees in their limousine). Jim's (social) reality is the isolated world of his parents, he perceives the Chinese misery from a distance. Again we discover a barrier separating the inside from the outside, a barrier that is, as in *The Unpleasant Profession of Jonathan Hoag,* materialized in the car's windowpane. It is through the window of his parent's Rolls Royce that Jim observes the misery and chaos of Chinese everyday life as a kind of cinematic "projection," a fictional experience totally discontinuous with his own reality. When the barrier falls down, i.e., when he finds himself thrown into the obscene and cruel world toward which he has until then been able to sustain a distance, the problem of survival begins. Jim's first, almost automatic reaction to this loss of reality, to this encounter with the real, is to repeat the elementary "phallic" gesture of symbolization, that is to say, to invert his utter impotence into omnipotence, to conceive himself as *radically responsible* for the intrusion of the real. The moment of this intrusion can be exactly located: it is marked by the shot from the Japanese warship that hits the hotel where Jim and his parents have taken refuge, shaking its foundations. Precisely to retain his "sense of reality," Jim automatically assumes responsibility for this shot, that is, he perceives himself as culpable for it. Before the shot, he had been watching the Japanese warship emit light signals and he had answered them with his battery torch. When the gun shell hits the hotel building and his father rushes into the room, Jim cries desperately: "I didn't mean it! It was only a joke!" Up till the end, he is convinced that the war was started by his inadvertent light signals. The same enthusiastic feeling of omnipotence erupts later, in the prison camp, when an English lady dies. Jim desperately massages her and when the woman, although dead, opens her eyes for a moment because of the stimulation of her blood circulation, Jim is thrown into ecstasy, convinced that he is capable of reviving the dead. We can see, here, how such a "phallic" inversion of impotence into omnipotence is bound up with an *answer of the real.* There must always be some "little piece of the real," totally contingent but nonetheless perceived by the subject as a confirmation, as the support of its belief in its own omnipotence.[11] In *Empire of the Sun,* this is first of all the shot from the Japanese warship, perceived by Jim as an "answer of the real" to his signaling, then there are the opened eyes of the dead Englishwoman, and finally there is, toward the end of the film, the flare of the atom bomb over Hiroshima. Jim feels illuminated by a special light, penetrated with some new energy lending his hands unique healing power, and he tries to bring back to life the body of his Japanese friend.[12] The same function of the "answer of the real" is fulfilled by the "merciless cards" that continually predict death in Bizet's *Carmen,* or by the love potion that materializes the cause of the fatal liaison in Wagner's *Tristan und Isolde.*

Far from being limited to so-called "pathological" cases, this "answer of the real" is necessary for intersubjective communication as such to take place. There is no symbolic communication without some "piece of the real" to serve as a kind of pawn guaranteeing its consistency. One of the most recent novels by Ruth Rendell, *Talking to Strange Men,* can be read as a kind of "thesis novel" on this theme (in the sense in which Sartre spoke of his plays as "thesis plays," exemplifying his philosophical propositions). The novel sets up an intersubjective constellation perfectly illustrating the Lacanian thesis that communication is a "successful misunderstanding." As is often the case with Rendell (see also her *Lake of Darkness, The Killing Doll, The Tree of Hands*), the plot is based on the contingent encounter of two series, two intersubjective networks. The hero of the novel is a young man, desperate because his wife has recently left him for another man. Returning home one evening, the hero quite by chance catches sight of a boy putting a piece of paper in the hand of a statue in a lonely suburban park. After the boy leaves, the hero takes the paper, transcribes the coded message on it, and replaces the paper. Since his hobby is the deciphering of secret codes, he eagerly begins work on this one and after considerable effort succeeds in breaking it. It contains, it seems, a secret message for the agents of a spy network. What the hero does not know, however, is that the people communicating through these messages are not real secret agents, but a group of adolescents playing spy games: they are split into two "spy rings," each trying to place a "mole" in the adversary's "ring," to penetrate some of their "secrets" (to enter secretly the apartment of one of the enemies and steal one of his books, for example). Not knowing this, the hero decides to use his knowledge of the secret code to his advantage. He places in the statue's hand a coded message ordering one of the "agents" to liquidate the man for whom his wife has left him. In this way, he unwittingly initiates a series of events in the adolescent group the final result of which is the accidental death of his wife's lover. This pure accident is read by the hero as a result of his successful intervention.

The charm of the novel derives from the parallel description of the two intersubjective networks—the hero and his desperate endeavor to regain his wife on the one hand, the adolescent spy games on the other. There is an interaction, a kind of communication going on between them, but it is incorrectly perceived on both sides. The hero thinks that he is in contact with a real spy ring capable of executing his order; the adolescents are unaware that some outsider has interfered in the circulation of their messages (they attribute the hero's messsage to one of their own members). "Communication" is achieved, but in such a way that one of the participants knows nothing about it (the members of the adolescent group do not know that a strange body has already entered the circulation of their messages; they think they are talking only to themselves and not "to strange men"), while the other misunderstands totally the "nature of the game." The two poles of the communication are thus asymmetrical. The adolescent "network" embodies the great Other, the signifier's mechanism, the universe of ciphers and codes, in its senseless, idiotic automatism, and when this mechanism produces as a result of its blind functioning a body, the other side (the hero) reads this contingency as an "answer of the real," as confirmation of successful communication: he throws into circulation a demand, and this demand is effectively fulfilled.[13]

Some accidentally produced "little piece of the real" (the dead body) attests to the success of the communication. We encounter the same mechanism in fortune telling and horoscopes: a totally contingent coincidence is sufficient for the effect of transference to take place; we become convinced that "there is something to it." The contingent real triggers the endless work of interpretation that desperately tries to connect the symbolic network of the prediction with the events of our "real life." Suddenly, "all things mean something," and if the meaning is not clear, this is only because some of it remains hidden, waiting to be deciphered. The real functions here not as something that resists symbolization, as a meaningless leftover that cannot be integrated into the symbolic universe, but, on the contrary, as its last support.

For things to have meaning, this meaning must be confirmed by some contingent piece of the real that can be read as a "sign." The very word *sign,* in opposition to the arbitrary mark, pertains to the "answer of the real": the "sign" is given by the thing itself, it indicates that at least at a certain point, the abyss separating the real from the symbolic network has been crossed, i.e., that the real itself has complied with the signifier's appeal. In moments of social crisis (wars, plagues), unusual celestial phenomena (comets, eclipses, etc.) are read as prophetic signs.

The crucial point here is that the real that serves as support of our symbolic reality must appear to be *found* and not *produced.* To clarify this, let us turn to another Ruth Rendell novel, *The Tree of Hands.* The French habit of changing the titles of translated novels produces as a rule disastrous results; in this case, however, the rule has fortunately found its exception. *Un enfant pour l'autre* (One Child for Another) accurately designates the peculiarity of this macabre story of a young mother whose little son dies suddenly of a mortal disease. To compensate for the loss, the crazy grandmother steals another child of the same age and offers him to the distressed mother as a substitute. After a series of interlaced intrigues and coincidences, the novel comes to a rather morbid happy end: the young mother consents to the substitution and accepts "one child for another."

At first sight, Rendell seems to provide here an elementary lesson on the Freudian notion of the drive: its object is ultimately indifferent and arbitrary—even in the case of the "natural" and "authentic" relationship of a mother to her child, the object-child proves interchangeable. But the accent of Rendell's story offers a different lesson: if an object is to take its place in a libidinal space, its arbitrary character must remain concealed. The subject cannot say to herself, "Since the object is arbitrary, I can choose whatever I want as the object of my drive." The object must appear to be *found,* to offer itself as support and point of reference for the drive's circular movement. In Rendell's novel, the mother only accepts the other child when she can say to herself "I really cannot do anything, if I refuse him now, things will get even more complicated, the child is practically imposed on me." We can say, in fact, that *The Tree of Hands* works in a way opposite to that of Brechtian drama: instead of making a familiar situation strange, the novel demonstrates the way we are prepared, step by step, to accept as familiar a bizarre and morbid situation. This procedure is far more subversive than the usual Brechtian one.

Herein consists, also, the fundamental lesson of Lacan: while it is true that any object can occupy the empty place of the Thing, it can do so only by means of the illusion that it was always already there, i.e., that it was not placed there by us but *found there as an "answer of the real."* Although any object can function as the object-cause of desire—insofar as the power of fascination it exerts is not its immediate property but results from the place it occupies in the structure—we must, by structural necessity, fall prey to the illusion that the power of fascination belongs to the object as such.

This structural necessity enables us to approach from a new perspective the classic Pascalian-Marxian description of the logic of "fetishistic inversion" in interpersonal relationships. The subjects think they treat a certain person as a king because he is already in himself a king, while in reality this person is king only insofar as the subjects treat him as one. The basic reversal of Pascal and Marx lies, of course, in their defining the king's charisma not as an immediate property of the person-king but as a "reflexive determination" of the comportment of his subjects, or—to use the terms of speech act theory—a performative effect of their symbolic ritual. But the crucial point is that it is a positive, necessary condition for this performative effect to take place that the king's charisma be experienced precisely as an immediate property of the person-king. The moment the subjects take cognizance of the fact that the king's charisma is a performative effect, the effect itself is aborted. In other words, if we attempt to "subtract" the fetishistic inversion and witness the performative effect directly, the performative power will be dissipated.

But why, we may ask, can the performative effect take place only on condition that it is overlooked? Why does the disclosure of the performative mechanism necessarily ruin its effect? Why, to paraphrase *Hamlet,* is the king (also) a thing? Why must the symbolic mechanism be hooked onto a "thing," some piece of the real? The Lacanian answer is, of course: because the symbolic field is in itself always already barred, crippled, porous, structured around some extimate kernel, some impossibility. The function of the "little piece of the real" is precisely to fill out the place of this void that gapes in the very heart of the symbolic.

The psychotic dimension of this "answer of the real" can be clearly grasped via its opposition to another kind of "answer of the real": the coincidence that takes us by surprise and produces a vertiginous shock. Our first associations are to mythical cases, such as that of politician whose platform collapses after he passionately proclaims: "May God strike me down if I have spoken a single lie!" Behind these cases the fear *persists* that if we lie and deceive too much, the real itself will intervene to stop us—like the statue of the Commendatore, who responds to the insolent dinner invitation from Don Giovanni by nodding its assent.

To analyze the logic of this kind of "answer of the real," let us recall the amusing adventure of Casanova analyzed in detail by Octave Mannoni in his classic article, "Je sais bien, mais quand même . . . ."[14] By means of an elaborate deception, Casanova attempts to seduce a naive country girl. To exploit the poor girl's credulity and make an appropriate impression on her, he pretends to be a master of occult knowledge. In the dead of night, he puts on the magician's clothes, marks out a circle on the ground, proclaiming it to be a magic circle, and starts to mumble magic formulae. Suddenly, something totally unexpected happens: a thunderstorm breaks out, lightning flares all around, and Casanova is alarmed. Although he *knows* very well that this storm is a simple natural phenomenon and that its breaking out precisely during his magical act is pure coincidence, he is seized with panic because he *believes* that the thunderstorm is a punishment for his blasphemous playing with magic. His quasi-automatic reaction is to enter his own magic circle, where he feels quite safe: "In the fear that apprehended me, I was convinced that thunderbolts would not strike me because they could not enter the circle. Without this false belief, I could not stay in this place for even a minute." In short, Casanova became a victim of his own deception. The answer of the real (the thunderstorm) functioned here as a shock that dissolved the mask of trickery. Once we are seized by panic, the only way out appears to be to "take seriously" our own pretense and to cling to it. The "answer of the real," which is the psychotic kernel that serves as a support for (symbolic) reality, functions in the perverse economy of Casanova in an opposite way: as a shock provoking the loss of reality.

"Nature Does Not Exist"

Is not the ultimate form of the "answer of the real" confronting all of us today in the ecological crisis? Is not the disturbed, derailed course of nature an "answer of the real" to human praxis, to the human encroachment upon nature, "mediated" and organized by the symbolic order? The radical character of the ecological crisis is not to be underestimated. The crisis is radical not only because of its effective danger, i.e., it is not just that what is at stake is the very survival of humankind. What is at stake is our most unquestionable presuppositions, the very horizon of our meaning, our everyday understanding of "nature" as a regular, rhythmic process. To use the terms of the late Wittgenstein, the ecological crisis bites into "objective certainty"—into the domain of self-evident certitudes about which, within our established "form of life," it is simply meaningless to have doubts. Hence our unwillingness to take the ecological crisis completely seriously; hence the fact that the typical, predominant reaction to it still consists in a variation on the famous disavowal, "I know very well (that things are deadly serious, that what is at stake is our very survival), but just the same . . . (I don't really believe it, I'm not really prepared to integrate it into my symbolic universe, and that is why I continue to act as if ecology is of no lasting consequence for my everyday life)."

Hence also the fact that the typical reaction of those who *do* take the ecological crisis seriously is—on the level of the libidinal economy—obsessional. Wherein lies the kernel of the obsessional's economy? The obsessional participates in frenzied activity, he works feverishly all the time—why? To avoid some uncommon catastrophe that would take place if his activity were to stop; his frenetic activity is based on the ultimatum, "If I don't do this (the compulsive ritual), some unspeakably horrible X will take place." In Lacanian terms, this X can be specified as the barred Other, i.e., the lack in the Other, the inconsistency of the symbolic order; in this case, it refers to the disturbance of the established rhythm of nature. We must be active all the time so that it does not come to light that "the Other does not exist" (Lacan).[15] The third reaction to the ecological crisis is to take it as an "answer of the real," as a sign bearing a certain message. AIDS operates this way in the eyes of the "moral majority," who read it as a divine punishment for our sinful life. From this perspective, the ecological crisis appears as a "punishment" for our ruthless exploitation of nature, for the fact that we have treated nature as a stack of disposable objects and materials, not as a partner in dialogue or the foundation of our being. The lesson drawn by those who react in this way is that we must cease our derailed, perverted way of life and begin to live as part of nature, accommodating ourselves to its rhythms, taking root in it.

What can a Lacanian approach tell us about the ecological crisis? Simply that we must learn to accept the real of the ecological crisis in its senseless actuality, without charging it with some message or meaning. In this sense, we could read the three above-described reactions to the ecological crisis—"I know very well, but just the same . . . "; obsessive activity; grasping it as a sign bearing some hidden meaning— as three forms of avoiding an encounter with the real: a fetishistic split, an acknowledgment of the fact of the crisis that neutralizes its symbolic efficacy; the neurotic transformation of the crisis into a traumatic kernel; a psychotic projection of meaning into the real itself. The fact that the first reaction presents a fetishistic disavowal of the real of the crisis is self-evident. What is not so obvious is that the other two reactions also hinder an adequate response to the crisis. For, if we grasp the ecological crisis as a traumatic kernel to be kept at a distance by obsessive activity, or as the bearer of a message, a call to find new roots in nature, we blind ourselves in both cases to the irreducible gap separating the real from the modes of its symbolization. The only proper attitude is that which fully assumes this gap as something that defines our very *condition humaine,* without endeavoring to suspend it through fetishistic disavowal, to keep it concealed through obsessive activity, or to reduce the gap between the real and the symbolic by projecting a (symbolic) message into the real. The fact that man is a speaking being means precisely that he is, so to speak, constitutively "derailed," marked by an irreducible fissure that the symbolic edifice attempts in vain to repair. From time to time, this fissure erupts in some spectacular form, reminding us of the frailty of the symbolic edifice—the latest went by the name of Chernobyl.

The radiation from Chernobyl represented the intrusion of a radical contingency. It was as if the "normal" enchainment of cause and effect were for a moment suspended—nobody knew what its exact consequences would be. The experts themselves admitted that any determination of the "threshold of danger" was arbitrary; public opinion oscillated between panicked anticipation of future catastrophes and acceptance that there was no cause for alarm. It is precisely this indifference to its mode of symbolization that locates the radiation in the dimension of the real. No matter what we say about it, it continues to expand, to reduce us to the role of impotent witnesses. The rays are thoroughly *unrepresentable,* no image is adequate to them. In their status as real, as the "hard kernel" around which every symbolization fails, they become pure semblance. We do not see or feel radioactive rays; they are entirely chimerical objects, effects of the incidence of the discourse of science upon our life world. After all, it would be quite possible to persist in our commonsense attitude and maintain that all the panic provoked by Chernobyl resulted from the confusion and exaggeration of a few scientists. All the fuss in the media was much ado about nothing, while our everyday life simply followed its course. But the very fact that such an effect of panic was triggered by a series of public communications supported by the authority of the discourse of science demonstrates the degree to which our everyday life is already penetrated by science.

Chernobyl confronted us with the threat of what Lacan calls "the second death": the result of the reign of the discourse of science is that what was at the time of the Marquis de Sade a literary fantasy (a radical destruction that interrupts the life process) has become today a menace threatening our everyday life. Lacan himself observed that the explosion of the atomic bomb exemplified the "second death": in radioactive death, it is as if matter itself, the foundation, the permanent support of the eternal circuit of generation and corruption, dissolves itself, vanishes. Radioactive disintegration is the "open wound of the world," a cut that derails and disturbs the circulation of what we call "reality." To "live with radiation" means to live with the knowledge that somewhere, in Chernobyl, a Thing erupted that shook the very ground of our being. Our relation to Chernobyl can thus be written as $\$ \lozenge a$: in that unrepresentable point where the very foundation of our world seems to dissolve itself, there the subject has to recognize the kernel of its most intimate being. That is to say, what is this "open wound of the world" if not, in the last resort, *man himself*—man insofar as he is dominated by the death drive, insofar as his fixation on the empty place of the Thing derails him, deprives him of support in the regularity of life processes? The very appearance of man necessarily entails a loss of natural balance, of the homeostasis proper to the processes of life.

The young Hegel proposed as a possible definition of man a formula that today, in the midst of the ecological crisis, acquires a new dimension: "nature sick unto death." All attempts to regain a new balance between man and nature, to eliminate from human activity its excessive character and to include it in the regular circuit of life, are nothing but a series of subsequent endeavors to suture an original and irredeemable gap. It is in this sense that the classic Freudian thesis on the ultimate discord between reality and the drive potential of man is to be conceived. Freud's claim is that this original, constitutive discord cannot be accounted for by biology, that it results from the fact that the "drive potential of man" consists of drives that are already radically denaturalized, derailed by their traumatic attachment to a Thing, to an empty place, that excludes man forever from the circular movement of life and thus opens the immanent possibility of radical catastrophe, the "second death."

It is here that we should perhaps look for the basic premise of a Freudian theory of culture: all culture is ultimately nothing but a compromise formation, a reaction to some terrifying, radically inhuman dimension proper to the human condition itself.

This also explains Freud's obsession with Michelangelo's Moses: in him, Freud recognized (wrongly, of course, but this does not really matter) a man who was on the brink of giving way to the destructive fury of the death drive, but who nonetheless found strength to master his fury and to refrain from smashing the tablets on which God's commandments were inscribed.[16] Confronted with catastrophes rendered possible by the incidence of the discourse of science upon reality, such a Mosaic gesture is perhaps our only hope.

The basic weakness of the usual ecological response is thus its obsessive libidinal economy: we must do all in order that the equilibrium of the natural circuit will be maintained, in order that some horrifying turbulence will not derail the established regularity of nature's ways. To rid ourselves of this predominant obsessive economy, we must take a further step and *renounce the very idea of a "natural balance" supposedly upset by the intervention of man as "nature sick unto death."* Homologous to the Lacanian proposition "Woman does not exist," we should perhaps assert that *Nature does not exist*: it does not exist as a periodic, balanced circuit, thrown off its track by man's inadvertence. The very notion of man as an "excess" with respect to nature's balanced circuit has finally to be abandoned. The image of nature as a balanced circuit is nothing but a retroactive projection of man. Herein lies the lesson of recent theories of chaos: "nature" is already, in itself, turbulent, imbalanced; its "rule" is not a well-balanced oscillation around some constant point of attraction, but a chaotic dispersion within the limits of what the theory of chaos calls the "strange attractor," a regularity directing chaos itself.

One of the achievements of the theory of chaos is the demonstration that chaos does not necessarily imply an intricate, impenetrable web of causes: simple causes can produce "chaotic" behavior. The theory of chaos thus subverts the basic "intuition" of classical physics according to which every process, left to itself, tends toward a kind of natural balance (a resting point or a regular movement). The revolutionary aspect of this theory is condensed in the term "strange attractor." It is possible for a system to behave in a "chaotic," irregular way, i.e., never to return to a previous state, and still be capable of formalization by means of an "attractor" that regulates it—an attractor that is "strange," i.e., that acquires the form not of a point or of a symmetrical figure, but of endlessly intertwined serpentines within the contours of a definite figure, an "anamorphotically" disfigured circle, a "butterfly," etc.

One is even tempted to risk a homology between the opposition between a "normal" attractor (a state of balance or of regular oscillation toward which a perturbed system is supposed to tend) and a "strange" attractor, and the opposition between the balance toward which the pleasure principle strives and the Freudian Thing embodying enjoyment. Is not the Freudian Thing a kind of "fatal attractor," perturbing the regular functioning of the psychic apparatus, preventing it from establishing an equilibrium? Is not the very form of the "strange attractor" a kind of physical metaphor for the Lacanian *objet petit a*? We find here another confirmation of Jacques-Alain Miller's thesis that *objet a* is a pure form: it is the form of an attractor drawing us into chaotic oscillation. The art of the theory of chaos consists in *allowing us to see the very form of chaos,* in allowing us to see a pattern where ordinarily we see nothing but a formless disorder.

The traditional opposition between "order" and "chaos" is thus suspended: what appears to be an uncontrollable chaos—from the oscillations on the stock exchange and the development of epidemics to the formation of whirlpools and the arrangement of branches on a tree—follows a certain rule; chaos is regulated by an "attractor." The point is not to "detect order behind chaos," but rather to detect the form, the pattern, of chaos itself, of its irregular dispersion. In opposition to "traditional" science, which is centered on the notion of a uniform law (regular connection of causes and effects, etc.), these theories offer first drafts of a future "science of the real," i.e., of a science elaborating rules that generate contingency, *tuché*, as opposed to symbolic *automaton*. It is here, rather than in the obscurantist essays of a "synthesis" between particle physics and Eastern mysticism, aiming at the assertion of a new holistic, organic approach alleged to replace the old "mechanistic" world view, that the real "paradigm shift" in contemporary science is to be sought.[17]

How the Real Is Rendered and Knows

RENDERING THE REAL

The ambiguity of the Lacanian real is not merely a nonsymbolized kernel that makes a sudden appearance in the symbolic order, in the form of traumatic "returns" and "answers." The real is at the same time contained in the very symbolic form: the real is *immediately rendered* by this form. To clarify this crucial point, let us recall a feature of Lacan's seminar *Encore* that must appear somewhat strange from the point of view of the "standard" Lacanian theory. That is to say, the entire effort of the "standard" Lacanian theory of the signifier is to make us see the pure contingency on which the process of symbolization depends, i.e., to "denaturalize" the effect of meaning by demonstrating how it results from a series of contingent encounters, how it is always "overdetermined." In *Encore,* however, Lacan surprisingly *rehabilitates the notion of the sign,* of the sign conceived precisely in its opposition to the signifier, i.e., as preserving the continuity with the real.[18] What is meant by this move—if, of course, we dismiss the possibility of a simple theoretical "regression"?

The order of the signifier is defined by a vicious circle of differentiality: it is an order of discourse in which the very identity of each element is overdetermined by its articulation, i.e., in which every element "is" only its difference from the others, without any support in the real. By rehabilitating the notion of the "sign," Lacan tries to indicate the status of a letter that cannot be reduced to the dimension of the signifier, that is to say, which is *prediscursive,* still permeated with the substance of enjoyment. If in 1962 Lacan proposed that "*jouissance* is forbidden to him who speaks, as such,"[19] he now theorizes a paradoxical letter that is nothing but materialized enjoyment.

To explain this, let us refer again to film theory, because it is precisely the status of this letter-enjoyment that is delimited by Michel Chion through his concept of *rendu. Rendu* is opposed to the (imaginary) *simulacrum* and the (symbolic) *code* as a third way of rendering reality in cinema: neither by means of imaginary imitation nor by means of symbolically codified representation but by means of its immediate "rendering."[20] Chion refers above all to the contemporary sound techniques that enable us not only to reproduce exactly the "original," "natural" sound but even to reinforce it and to render audible details that would be missed if we were to find ourselves in the "reality" recorded by the film. This kind of sound penetrates us, seizes us on an immediate-real level, like the obscene, mucous-slimy, disgusting sounds that accompany the transformations of humans into their alien clones in the Philip Kaufman version of *The Invasion of the Body Snatchers,* sounds that have associations with some indefinite entity between the sexual act and the act of birth. According to Chion, this shift in the status of the soundtrack points toward a slow but nonetheless far-reaching "soft revolution" that is going on in contemporary cinema. It is no longer appropriate to say that the sound "accompanies" the flow of images, insofar as it is now the soundtrack that functions as the elementary "frame of reference" enabling us to orient ourselves in the diegetic space. Bombarding us with details from different directions (dolby stereo techniques, etc.), the soundtrack takes over the function of the establishing shot. The soundtrack gives us the basic perspective, the "map" of the situation, and guarantees its continuity, while the images are reduced to isolated fragments that float freely in the universal medium of the sound aquarium. It would be difficult to invent a better metaphor for psychosis: in contrast to the "normal" state of things in which the real is a lack, a hole in the midst of the symbolic order (like the central black spot in Rothko's paintings), we have here the "aquarium" of the real surrounding isolated islands of the symbolic. In other words, it is no longer enjoyment that "drives" the proliferation of the signifiers by functioning as a central "black hole" around which the signifying network is interlaced; it is, on the contrary, the symbolic order itself that is reduced to the status of floating islands of the signifier, white *îles flottantes* in a sea of yolky enjoyment.[21]

The fact that the real thus "rendered" is what Freud called "psychic reality" is demonstrated by the mysteriously beautiful scenes from David Lynch's *Elephant Man* which present from the "inside," so to speak, the elephant man's subjective experience. The matrix of the "external," "real" sounds and noises is suspended or at least appeased, pushed to the background; all we hear is a rhythmic beat the status of which is uncertain, somewhere between a heartbeat and the regular rhythm of a machine. Here we have *rendu* at its purest, a pulse that does not imitate or symbolize anything, but that "seizes" us immediately, "renders" immediately the thing—what thing? The closest we can get to describing it is to say that it is again the beat of that "grey and formless mist, pulsing slowly as if with inchoate life." These sounds that penetrate us like invisible but nonetheless material rays are the real of the "psychic reality." Its massive presence suspends so-called "external reality." These sounds render the way the elephant man "hears himself," the way he is caught in the closure of his autistic circle, excluded as he is from intersubjective, "public communication." The film's poetic beauty consists in the way it includes a series of shots that are, from the standpoint of realistic narration, totally redundant and incomprehensible, i.e., the sole function of which is to visualize the pulse of the real. Think, for example, of the mysterious shot of the operating weaving-mill; it is as if it were this mill that, by means of its rhythmic movement, produced the beat we hear.[22]

This effect of *rendu* is not of course limited to the "soft revolution" presently taking place in cinema. Careful analysis already reveals its presence in classical Hollywood cinema, more precisely in some of its limit products, such as three *films noirs* shot in the late 1940s and early 1950s and united by a common feature—all three are built on the prohibition of a formal element that is a central constituent of the "normal" narrative procedure of a sound film:

• Robert Montgomery's *Lady in the Lake* is built on a prohibition of the "objective" shot. Except for the introduction and the end, where the detective (Philip Marlowe) gazes directly into the camera introducing and commenting on events, the entire story in flashback is told through subjective shots, i.e., we literally see only what the principal character sees (we see his face only when he looks at himself in the mirror, for example).

• Alfred Hitchcock's *Rope* is built on a prohibition of montage. The whole film gives the impression of one long shot; even when a cut is necessary because of technical limitations (in 1948, the longest possible take lasted ten minutes), it is made unobtrusively so as to pass unnoticed (a person passes directly in front of the camera and blackens its whole field for a moment, for example).

• Russell Rouse's *The Thief,* the least known of the three, the story of a communist spy (Ray Milland) who finally breaks down under the moral pressure and gives himself up to the FBI, is built on a prohibition of the voice. This is not a silent film; we continually hear the usual background sounds, the noises people and cars make, etc., but except for a few distant murmurs, we never hear a voice, a spoken word (the film avoids all situations in which it would be obliged to resort to dialogue). The purpose of this silence, of course, is to allow us to feel the desperate solitude and isolation from the community of a communist agent.

Each of these three films is an artificial, overstrained formal experiment, but from where does the undeniable impression of failure derive? The first reason lies probably in the fact that each is a *hapax,* each is the only specimen of its kind. One could not repeat the "trick" involved in each, for it can be effectively used only once. And yet a deeper source of failure can also be observed. It is no accident that all three films incite the same feeling of claustrophobic closure. It is as if we had found ourselves in a psychotic universe without symbolic openness. In each film, there is a certain barrier at work that can in no way be trespassed. The presence of this barrier is felt the whole time and thus creates an almost unbearable tension throughout the film. In *Lady in the Lake,* we continually long for release from the "glass house" of the detective's gaze, so that, finally, we can get a "free," objective view of the action; in *Rope,* we wait desperately for a cut to deliver us from the nightmarish continuity; in *The Thief,* we look forward the whole time to some voice to pull us out of the closed, autistic universe in which the meaningless noises render all the more palpable the basic silence, i.e., the lack of a spoken word.

Each of these three prohibitions produces its own kind of psychosis: using the three films as a point of reference, we could elaborate a classification of the three fundamental types of psychosis. By means of a prohibition of the "objective shot," *Lady in the Lake* produces a *paranoiac* effect (since the view of the camera is never "objective," the field of what is seen is continually menaced by the unseen, and the very proximity of objects to the camera becomes menacing; all objects assume a potentially threatening character, there is danger everywhere—when a woman approaches the camera, for example, we experience this as an aggressive intervention into the sphere of our intimacy). By means of a prohibition of montage, *Rope* enacts a psychotic *passage à l'acte* (the "rope" from the title of the film is, of course, ultimately the "rope" connecting "words" and "acts," i.e., it marks the moment at which the symbolic, so to speak, falls into the real: as is later the case with Bruno in *Strangers on a Train,* the homosexual, murderous couple take words "literally," they pass from them immediately to "deeds," realizing the professor's [James Stewart's] pseudo-Nietzschean theories that concern precisely the absence of prohibition—to "superhumans," everything is permitted). Finally, *The Thief,* by prohibiting the voice, renders a psychotic *autism,* the isolation from the discursive network of intersubjectivity. We can see, now, wherein lies the dimension of *rendu*: not in the psychotic contents of these films, but in the way the content, far from being simply "depicted," is immediately "rendered" by the very form of the film—here, the "message" of the movie is immediately the form itself.[23]

What is ultimately prohibited by the untrespassable barrier at work in these films? The ultimate reason for their failure is that we cannot get rid of the feeling that the nature of the prohibition with which we are concerned is too arbitrary and capricious: it is as if the author decided to renounce one of the key constituents of the "normal" sound film (montage, objective shot, voice) for the sake of a purely formal experiment. The prohibition on which these films are based is a prohibition of something that could also not have been prohibited: it is not a prohibition of something that is already in itself impossible (the fundamental paradox that, according to Lacan, defines "symbolic castration," the "prohibition of incest": the prohibition of the *jouissance* that is already in itself impossible to attain). Herein lies the sentiment of an unbearable, incestuous stuffiness evoked by the films. The fundamental prohibition constitutive of the symbolic order (the "prohibition of incest," the "cutting of the rope" through which we achieve symbolic distance toward "reality") *is lacking,* and the arbitrary prohibition that replaces it only embodies, bears witness to this lack, to this lack of a lack itself.

Knowledge in the Real

Now we are obliged to take the final step: if, in every symbolic formation, there is a psychotic kernel at work by means of which the real is immediately rendered, and if this form is ultimately that of a signifying chain, i.e., of a chain of knowledge (S_2), then there must be, at least at a certain level, a kind of knowledge operating in the real itself.

The Lacanian notion of "knowledge in the real" must appear at first sight a purely speculative, shallow extravaganza, far from our everyday experience. The very idea that nature knows its laws and behaves accordingly, that, for example, Newton's famous apple falls because it knows the law of gravity, seems preposterous. Even if this idea were just a hollow sally of wit, however, we would be forced to wonder why it repeats itself with such regularity in cartoons. The cat wildly pursues the mouse, not noticing that there is a precipice ahead; but even when the ground disappears, the cat does not fall, it continues to chase after the mouse and falls only when it looks down and *sees* that it is floating in midair. It is as if the real had for a moment forgotten which laws it has to obey. When the cat looks down, the real "remembers" its laws and acts accordingly. The very persistence of such scenes indicates that they must be supported by a certain elementary fantasy scenario. A further argument in favor of this conjecture is that we find the same paradox in the famous dream, reported by Freud in *The Interpretation of Dreams,* about the father who does not know he is dead:[24] he continues to live because he does not know that he was dead, like the cat in cartoons who continues to run because it does not know that there is no ground under its feet. Our third example is Napoleon at Elba: historically he was already dead (i.e., his moment was over, his role was finished), but he was kept alive (present on the scene of history) by the fact that he was unaware of his death, which is why he had to "die twice," to lose for the second time at Waterloo. With certain state or ideological apparatuses, we often encounter the same feeling: although they are clearly anachronistic, they persist because *they do not know it.* Someone must assume the impolite duty of reminding them of this unpleasant fact.

We are now in a position to specify more clearly the contours of the fantasy scenario that supports this phenomenon pertaining to knowledge in the real: in "psychic reality," we encounter a series of entities that literally exist only on the basis of a certain misrecognition, that is to say, insofar as the subject does not know something, insofar as something is left unspoken, is not integrated into the symbolic universe. As soon as the subject comes to "know too much," he pays for this excess, surplus knowledge "in the flesh," by the very substance of his being. The ego is above all an entity of this order; it is a series of imaginary identifications upon which the consistency of a subject's being depends, but as soon as the subject "knows too much," gets too close to the unconscious truth, his ego dissolves. The paradigmatic example of such a drama is ultimately Oedipus: when he finally learns the truth, he existentially "loses the ground under his feet" and finds himself in an unbearable void.

This paradox deserves our attention because it enables us to rectify a certain misconception. As a rule, the notion of the unconscious is conceived in an opposite way: it is supposed to be an entity about which, because of the defense mechanism of repression, the subject does not (want to) know anything (his perverse, illicit desires, for example). The unconscious must instead be conceived as a positive entity that retains its consistency only on the basis of a certain nonknowledge—its positive ontological condition is that something must remain nonsymbolized, that something must not be put into words. This is also the most elementary definition of the symptom: a certain formation that exists only insofar as the subject ignores some fundamental truth about himself; as soon as its meaning is integrated into the symbolic universe of the subject, the symptom dissolves itself. This, at least, was the position of the early Freud, who believed in the omnipotence of the interpretive procedure. In his short story "Nine Billion Names of God," Isaac Asimov presents the universe itself in terms of the logic of the symptom, thereby confirming Lacan's thesis that the "world" as such, "reality," is always a symptom, i.e., is based on the foreclosure of a certain key signifier. Reality itself is nothing but an embodiment of a certain blockage in the process of symbolization. For reality to exist, something must be left unspoken. Monks from a monastery in the Himalayas hire a computer and two American computer experts for the following reason. According to the religious beliefs of the monks, God has a limited number of names; they consist in all possible combinations of nine letters, with the exclusion of nonsensical series (more than three consonants in a row, for example). The world was created in order that all these names be pronounced or written down; once this happens, the creation will have served its purpose and the world will annihilate itself. The task of the experts is, of course, to program the computer so that the printer will write down all nine billion possible names of God. After the two experts have done their job, the printer starts to spew out endless sheets of paper, and so the two begin the journey back to the valley, commenting ironically on the eccentric demand of their customers. After awhile one of them looks at his watch and remarks with laughter that at just around this time, the computer should finish its work. He then looks up at the night sky and stiffens with astonishment: the stars have begun to expire, the universe starts to vanish. Once all the names of God have been written down, once their total symbolization has been accomplished, the world as symptom dissolves itself.

The first reproach that offers itself here is, of course, that this motif of the "knowledge in the real" has only metaphorical value, that it is to be taken only as a means of illustrating a certain feature of psychic reality. Here, however, contemporary science lies in wait with an unpleasant surprise: subatomic particle physics, i.e., the scientific discipline supposed to be "exact," free from "psychological" overtones, has in recent decades been beset by the problem of "knowledge in the real." That is to say, it repeatedly encounters phenomena that seem to suspend the principle of local cause, i.e., phenomena that seem to imply a transport of information faster than the maximum admissible according to the theory of relativity. This is the so-called Einstein-Podolsky-Rosen effect, where what we did in area A affects what happens in area B, without this being possible along the normal causal chain permitted by the speed of light. Let us take a two-particle system of zero spin: if one of the particles in such a system has a spin UP, the other particle has a spin DOWN. Now suppose that we separate two particles in some way that does not affect their spin: one particle goes off in one direction and the other in the oppositie direction. After we separate them, we send one of the particles through a magnetic field that gives it a spin UP: what happens is that the other particle acquires a spin DOWN (and vice versa, of course). Yet there is no possibility of communication or of a normal causal link between them, because the other particle had a spin DOWN immediately after we gave the first particle a spin UP, i.e., *before* the spin UP of the first particle could cause the spin DOWN of the other particle in the fastest way possible (by giving the signal with the speed of light). The question then arises: *How did the other particle "know" that we had given the first particle a spin UP?* We must presuppose a kind of "knowledge in the real," as if a spin somehow "knows" what happens in another place and acts accordingly. Contemporary particle physics is beset by the problem of creating experimental conditions to test this hypothesis (the famous Alain-Aspect experiment from the early 1980s confirmed it!) and of articulating an explanation for this paradox.

This case is not the only one. A whole series of notions formulated by Lacan in his "logic of the signifier," notions that may seem mere intellectual trifling, playing with paradoxes without any scientific value, correspond surprisingly with some key notions of subatomic particles physics (the paradoxical notion of a particle that "does not exist," although it has properties and produces a series of effects, etc.). There is nothing strange about this if we consider that subatomic physics is a realm of pure differentiality in which every particle is defined not as a positive entity, but as one of the possible combinations of other particles (as with the signifier whose identity consists in the bundle of its differences from other signifiers). We should not be surprised, then, to find in recent physics even the Lacanian logic of the "not-all" (*pas-tout*), i.e., the conception of sexual difference that defines the "masculine" side as a universal function constituted through the phallic exception and the "feminine" side as a set that is "not-all," nonuniversal, but without exception. We are referring here to the consequences of the limits of the universe drawn by Stephen Hawking though his hypothesis about "imaginary time" ("imaginary" not in the psychological sense of "existing only in our imagination," but in a purely mathematical sense of being calculable only in terms of imaginary numbers).[25] That is to say, Hawking attempts to construct an alternative to the standard big bang theory according to which, to explain the evolution of the universe, we must presuppose as a starting point a moment of "singularity" at which universal laws of physics are suspended. The big bang theory would thus correspond to the "masculine" side of the logic of the signifier: the universal function (the laws of physics) is based on a certain exception (the point of singularity). What Hawking attempts to demonstrate, however, is that if we accept the hypothesis of "imaginary time," we do not need to postulate the necessary existence of this "singularity." By introducing "imaginary time," the difference between time and space disappears totally, time begins to function in the same way as space in the theory of relativity: although it is finite, it has no limit. Even if it is "bent," circular, finite, there need be no external point that would limit it. In other words, time is "not-all," "feminine" in the Lacanian sense. Apropos of this distinction between "real" and "imaginary" time, Hawking points out clearly that we are concerned with two parallel ways of conceptualizing the universe: although in the case of the big bang theory we speak of "real" time, and in the second case of "imaginary" time, it does not follow from this that either of these versions possesses an ontological priority, i.e., that it offers us a "more adequate" picture of reality: their duplicity (in all senses of the word) is irreducible.

What conclusion should we draw, then, from this unexpected accordance between the most recent speculations of physics and the paradoxes of the Lacanian logic of the signifier? One conclusion would be, of course, a kind of Jungian obscurantism: "male" and "female" do not concern anthropology only, they are also cosmic principles, a polarity that determines the very structure of the universe; human sexual difference is just a special form of appearance of this universal cosmic antagonism between "masculine" and "feminine" principles, yin and yang. It is almost superfluous to add that Lacanian theory compels us to an opposite conclusion, to a radical "anthropocentric" or, more precisely, symbolocentric version: our knowledge of the universe, the way we symbolize the real, is ultimately always bound, determined by the paradoxes proper to language as such; the split into "masculine" and "feminine," i.e., the impossibility of a "neutral" language not marked by this difference, imposes itself because symbolization as such is by definition structured around a certain central impossibility, a deadlock that is nothing but a structuring of this impossibility. Not even the purest subatomic physics can escape this fundamental impasse of symbolization.

3   Two Ways to Avoid the Real of Desire

The Sherlock Holmes Way

THE DETECTIVE AND THE ANALYST

The easiest way to detect changes in the so-called *Zeitgeist* is to pay careful attention to the moment when a certain artistic (literary, etc.) form becomes "impossible," as the traditional psychological-realist novel did in the 1920s. The '20s mark the final victory of the "modern" over the traditional "realist" novel. Afterward, it was, of course, actually still possible to write "realist" novels, but the norm was set by the modern novel, the traditional form was—to use the Hegelian term—already "mediated" by it. After this break, the common "literary taste" perceived newly written realist novels as ironic pastiches, as nostalgic attempts to recapture a lost unity, as outward inauthentic "regression," or simply as no longer pertaining to the domain of art. What is of interest here, however, is a fact that usually goes unnoticed: the breakdown of the traditional "realist" novel in the '20s coincides with the shift of accent from the detective *story* (Conan Doyle, Chesterton, etc.) to the detective *novel* (Christie, Sayers, etc.) in the domain of popular culture. The novel form is not yet possible with Conan Doyle, as is clear from his novels themselves: they are really just extended short stories with a long flashback written in the form of an adventure story (*The Valley of Fear*) or they incorporate elements of another genre, the Gothic novel (*The Hound of the Baskervilles*). In the '20s, however, the detective story quickly disappears as a genre and is replaced by the classic form of the "logic and deduction" detective novel. Is this coincidence between the final breakdown of the "realist" novel and the rise of the detective novel purely contingent, or is there significance in it? Do the modern novel and the detective novel have something in common, in spite of the gulf separating them?

The answer usually escapes us because of its very obviousness: both the modern novel and the detective novel are centered around the same formal problem—

the *impossibility of telling a story in a linear, consistent way,* of rendering the "realistic" continuity of events. It is of course a commonplace to affirm that the modern novel replaces realistic narration with a diversity of new literary techniques (stream of consciousness, pseudodocumentary style, etc.) bearing witness to the impossibility of locating the individual's fate in a meaningful, "organic" historical totality; but on another level, the problem of the detective story is the same: the traumatic act (murder) cannot be located in the meaningful totality of a life story. There is a certain self-reflexive strain in the detective novel: it is a story of the detective's effort to tell the story, i.e., to reconstitute what "really happened" around and before the murder, and the novel is finished not when we get the answer to "Whodunit?" but when the detective is finally able to tell "the real story" in the form of a linear narrative.

An obvious reaction to this would be: yes, but the fact remains that the modern novel is a form of art, while the detective novel is sheer entertainment governed by firm conventions, principal among them the fact that we can be absolutely sure that at the end, the detective will succeed in explaining the entire mystery and in reconstructing "what really happened." It is, however, precisely this "infallibility" and "omniscience" of the detective that constitutes the stumbling block of the standard deprecatory theories of the detective novel: their aggressive dismissal of the detective's power betrays a perplexity, a fundamental incapacity to explain how it works and why it appears so "convincing" to the reader in spite of its indisputable "improbability." Attempts to explain it usually follow two opposing directions. On the one hand, the figure of the detective is interpreted as "bourgeois" scientific rationalism personified; on the other, he is conceived as successor to the romantic clairvoyant, the man possessing an irrational, quasisupernatural power to penetrate the mystery of another person's mind. The inadequacy of both these approaches is evident to any admirer of a good logic and deduction story. We are immensely disappointed if the denouement is brought about by a pure scientific procedure (if, for example, the assassin is identified simply by means of a chemical analysis of the stains on the corpse). We feel that "there is something missing here," that "this is not deduction proper." But it is even more disappointing if, at the end, after naming the assassin, the detective claims that "he was guided from the very beginning by some unmistakable instinct"—here we are clearly deceived, the detective must arrive at the solution on the basis of *reasoning,* not by mere "intuition."[1]

Instead of striving for an immediate solution to this riddle, let us turn our attention to another subjective position that arouses the same perplexity, that of the analyst in the psychoanalytic process. Attempts to locate this position parallel those made in relation to the detective: on the one hand, the analyst is conceived as somebody who tries to reduce to their rational foundation phenomena that, at first sight, belong to the most obscure and irrational strata of the human psyche; on the other hand, he again appears as successor to the romantic clairvoyant, as a reader of dark signs, producing "hidden meanings" not susceptible to scientific verification. There is a whole series of circumstantial evidence pointing to the fact that this parallel is not without foundation: psychoanalysis and the logic and deduction story made their appearance in the same epoch (Europe at the turn of the century). The "Wolf Man," Freud's most famous patient, reports in his memoirs that Freud was a regular and careful reader of the Sherlock Holmes stories, not for distraction but precisely on account of the parallel between the respective procedures of the detective and the analyst. One of the Sherlock Holmes pastiches, Nicholas Meyer's *Seven Per-Cent Solution,* has as its theme an encounter between Freud and Sherlock Holmes, and it should be remembered that Lacan's *Ecrits* begins with a detailed analysis of Edgar Allan Poe's "The Purloined Letter," one of the archetypes of the detective story, in which Lacan's accent is on the parallel between the subjective position of Auguste Dupin—Poe's amateur detective—and that of the analyst.

THE CLUE

The analogy between the detective and the analyst has been drawn often enough. There are a wide range of studies that set out to reveal the psychoanalytic undertones of the detective story: the primordial crime to be explained is parricide, the prototype of the detective is Oedipus, striving to attain the terrifying truth about himself. What we would prefer to do here, however, is to tackle the task on a different, "formal" level. Following Freud's casual remarks to the "Wolf Man," we will focus on the respective *formal procedures* of the detective and the psychoanalyst. What distinguishes, then, the psychoanalytic interpretation of the formations of the unconscious—of dreams, for example? The following passage from Freud's *Interpretation of Dreams* provides a preliminary answer:

> The dream-thoughts are immediately comprehensible, as soon as we have learnt them. The dream-content, on the other hand, is expressed as it were in a pictographic script, the characters of which have to be transposed individually into the language of the dream-thoughts. If we attempted to read these characters according to their pictorial value instead of according to their symbolic relation, we should clearly be led into error. Suppose I have a picture-puzzle, a rebus, in front of me. It depicts a house with a boat on its roof, a single letter of the alphabet, the

figure of a running man whose head has been conjured away, and so on. Now I might be misled into raising objections and declaring that the picture as a whole and its component parts are nonsensical. A boat has no business to be on the roof of a house, and a headless man cannot run. Moreover, the man is bigger than the house; and if the whole picture is intended to represent a landscape, letters of the alphabet are out of place in it since such objects do not occur in nature. But obviously we can only form a proper judgement of the rebus if we put aside criticisms such as these of the whole composition and its parts and if, instead, we try to replace each separate element by a syllable or word that can be presented by that element in some way or other. The words which are put together in this way are no longer nonsensical but may form a poetical phrase of the greatest beauty and significance. A dream is a picture-puzzle of this sort and our predecessors in the field of dream-interpretation have made the mistake of treating the rebus as a pictorial composition: and as such it has seemed to them nonsensical and worthless.[2]

Freud is quite clear when faced with a dream, we must absolutely avoid the search for the so-called "symbolic meaning" of its totality or of its constituent parts; we must *not* ask the question "what does the house mean? what is the meaning of the boat on the house? what could the figure of a running man symbolize?" What we must do is translate the objects back into words, replace things by words designating them. In a rebus, things literally *stand for their names,* for their signifiers. We can see, now, why it is absolutely misleading to characterize the passage from word presentations (*Wort-Vorstellungen*) to thing presentations (*Sach-Vorstellungen*)—so-called "considerations of representability" at work in a dream—as a kind of "regression" from language to prelanguage representations. In a dream, "things" themselves are already "structured like a language," their disposition is regulated by the signifying chain for which they stand. The signified of this signifying chain, obtained by means of a retranslation of "things" into "words," is the "dream-thought." On the level of meaning, this "dream-thought" is in no way connected in its content with objects depicted in the dream (as in the case of a rebus, whose solution is in no way connected with the meaning of the objects depicted in it). If we look for the "deeper, hidden meaning" of the figures appearing in a dream, we *blind* ourselves to the latent "dream-thought" articulated in it. The link between immediate "dream-contents" and the latent "dream-thought" exists only on the level of wordplay, i.e., of nonsensical signifying material. Remember Aristander's famous interpretation of the dream of Alexander of Macedon, reported by Artemidorus? Alexander "had surrounded Tyre and was besieging it but was feeling uneasy and disturbed because of the length of time the siege was taking. Alexander dreamt he saw a satyr dancing on his shield. Aristander happened to be in the neighborhood of Tyre. . . . By dividing the word for satyr into *sa* and *tyros* he encouraged the king to press home the siege so that he became master of the city." As we can see, Aristander was quite uninterested in the possible "symbolic meaning" of the figure of a dancing satyr (ardent desire? joviality?): instead, he focused on the *word* and divided it, thus obtaining the message of the dream: *sa Tyros* = Tyre is thine.

There is, however, a certain difference between a rebus and a dream, which makes a rebus much easier to interpret. In a way, a rebus is like a dream that has not undergone "secondary revision," whose purpose is to satisfy the "necessity for unification." For that reason, a rebus is immediately perceived as something "nonsensical," a bric-a-brac of unconnected, heterogeneous elements, while a dream conceals its absurdity through "secondary revision," which lends the dream at least a superficial unity and consistency. The image of a dancing satyr is thus perceived as an organic whole, there is nothing in it that would indicate that the sole reason for its existence is to lend an imaginary figuration to the signifying chain *sa Tyros*. Herein lies the role of the imaginary "totality of meaning," the final result of the "dreamwork": to blind us—by means of the appearance of organic unity—to the effective reason for its existence.

The basic presupposition of psychoanalytic interpretation, its methodologic a priori, is, however, that every final product of the dream work, every manifest dream content, contains *at least one* ingredient that functions as a stopgap, as a filler holding the place of what is necessarily *lacking* in it. This is an element that at first sight fits perfectly into the organic whole of the manifest imaginary scene, but which effectively holds within it the place of what this imaginary scene must "repress," exclude, force out, in order to constitute itself. It is a kind of umbilical cord tying the imaginary structure to the "repressed" process of its structuration. In short, secondary revision never fully succeeds, not for empirical reasons, but on account of an a priori structural necessity. In the final analysis, an element always "sticks out," marking the dream's constitutive lack, i.e., representing within it its exterior. This element is caught in a paradoxical dialectic of simultaneous lack and surplus: but for it, the final result (the manifest dream text) would not hold together, something would be missing. Its presence is absolutely indispensable to create the sense that the dream is an organic whole; once this element is in place, however, it is in a way "in excess," it functions as an embarrassing plethora:

> We are of the opinion that in every structure there is a lure, a place-holder
> of the lack, comprised by what is perceived, but at the same time the
> weakest link in a given series, the point which vacillates and only seems
> to belong to the actual level: in it is *compressed* the whole virtual level
> [of the structuring space]. This element is *irrational* in reality, and by
> being included in it, it indicates the place of lack in it.[3]

And it is almost superfluous to add that the interpretation of dreams must begin precisely by isolating this paradoxical element, the "place-holder of the lack," the point
of the signifier's non-sense. Starting from this point, dream interpretation must proceed to "denature," to dissipate the false appearance of the manifest dream-content's
totality of meaning, i.e., to penetrate through to the "dream-work," to render visible
the montage of heterogeneous ingredients effaced by its own final result. With this
we have arrived at the similarity between the procedure of the analyst and that of the
detective: the scene of the crime with which the detective is confronted is also, as a
rule, a false image put together by the murderer in order to efface the traces of his
act. The scene's organic, natural quality is a lure, and the detective's task is to denature it by first discovering the inconspicuous details that stick out, that do not fit
into the frame of the surface image. The vocabulary of detective narration contains
a precise *terminus technicus* for such a detail: *clue,* indicated by a whole series of
adjectives: "'odd'—'queer'—'wrong'—'strange'—'fishy'—'rummy'—'doesn't make
sense,' not to mention stronger expressions like 'eerie,' 'unreal,' 'unbelievable,' up
to the categorical 'impossible.'"[4] What we have here is a detail that *in itself* is usually
quite insignificant (the broken handle of a cup, the changed position of a chair, some
transitory remark of a witness, or even a nonevent, i.e., the fact that something *did
not* happen), but which nonetheless *with regard to its structural position* denatures
the scene of the crime and produces a quasi-Brechtian effect of estrangement—like
the alteration of a small detail in a well-known picture that all of a sudden renders
the whole picture strange and uncanny. Such clues can of course be detected only
if we put in parentheses the scene's totality of meaning and focus our attention on
details. Holmes's advise to Watson not to mind the basic impressions but to take into
consideration details echoes Freud's assertion that psychoanalysis employs interpretation *en détail* and not *en masse*: "It regards dreams from the very first as being
of a composite character, as being conglomerates of psychical formations."[5]

Starting from clues, the detective thus unmasks the imaginary unity of the scene
of the crime as it was staged by the assassin. The detective grasps the scene as a *bricolage* of heterogeneous elements, in which the connection between the murderer's

mise-en-scène and the "real events" corresponds exactly to that between the manifest dream contents and the latent dream thought, or between the immediate figuration of the rebus and its solution. It consists solely in the "doubly inscribed"
signifying material, like the "satyr" that means first the dancing figure of the satyr and
then "Tyre is thine." The relevance of this "double inscription" for the detective story
was already noticed by Victor Shklovsky: "The writer looks for cases in which two
things which do not correspond, coincide nonetheless in some specific feature."[6]
Shklovsky also pointed out that the privileged case of such a coincidence is a wordplay: he refers to Conan Doyle's "The Adventure of the Speckled Band" where the
key to the solution is hidden in the statement of the dying woman: "It was the speckled band. . . . " The wrong solution is based on the reading of *band* as *gang,* and
is suggested by the fact that a band of gypsies was camped near the site of the murder,
thus evoking the "convincing" image of the exotic gypsy murderer, while the real
solution is arrived at only when Sherlock Holmes reads *band* as *ribbon.* In the majority of cases, this "doubly inscribed" element consists of course of nonlinguistic material, but even here it is already structured like a language (Shklovsky himself
mentions one of Chesterton's stories that concerns the similarity between a gentle-
man's evening wear and a valet's dress).

Why is the "False Solution" Necessary?

The crucial thing about the distance separating the false scene staged by the
murderer and the true course of events is *the structural necessity of the false solution*
toward which we are enticed because of the "convincing" character of the staged
scene, which is—at least in the classic logic and deduction story—usually sustained
by representatives of "official" knowledge (the police). The status of the false solution is epistemologically internal to the detective's final, true solution. The key to the
detective's procedure is that the relation to the first, false solutions is not simply an
external one: the detective does not apprehend them as simple obstacles to be cast
away in order to obtain the truth, rather it is only *through* them that he can arrive at
the truth, for there is no path leading immediately to the truth.[7]

In Conan Doyle's "The Red-Headed League," a redheaded client calls on Sherlock Holmes, telling him his strange adventure. He read an advertisement in a newspaper, offering redheaded men a well-paid temporary job. After presenting himself
at the appointed place, he was chosen from among a great number of men, although
the hair of many of the others was much redder. The job was indeed well paid, but

utterly senseless: every day, from nine to five, he copies parts of the Bible. Holmes quickly solves the enigma: next to the house in which the client lives (and where he usually stayed during the day when he was unemployed), there is a large bank. The criminals put the advertisement in the newspaper so that he would respond to it. Their purpose was to ensure his absence from his home during the day so that they could dig a tunnel from his cellar into the bank. The only significance of their specification of hair color was to lure him. In Agatha Christie's *The ABC Murders,* a series of murders take place in which the names of the victims follow a complicated alphabetical pattern: this inevitably produces the impression that there is a pathological motivation. But the solution reveals quite a different motivation: the assassin really intended to kill just one person, not for "pathological" reasons but for very "intelligible" material gain. In order to lead the police astray, however, he murdered a few extra people, chosen so that their names form an alphabetical pattern and thus guaranteeing that the murders will be perceived as the work of some lunatic. What do these two stories have in common? In both cases, the deceitful first impression offers an image of pathological excess, a "loony" formula covering a multitude of people (red hair, alphabet), while the operation, in fact, is aimed at a single person. The solution is not arrived at by scrutinizing the possible hidden meaning of the surface impression (what could the pathological fixation on red hair mean? what is the meaning of the alphabetical pattern?): it is precisely by indulging in this kind of deliberation that we fall into a trap. The only proper procedure is to put in parentheses the field of meaning imposed upon us by the deceitful first impression and to devote all our attention to the details *abstracted from their inclusion in the imposed field of meaning.* Why was this person hired for a senseless job *regardless of the fact that he is a redhead*? Who derives profit from the death of a certain person *regardless of the first letter of this person's name*? In other words, we must continually bear in mind that the fields of meaning imposing the "loony" frame of interpretation on us "*exist only in order to conceal the reason of their existence*":[8] their meaning consists solely in the fact that "others" (*doxa,* common opinion) will think they have meaning. The sole "meaning" of red hair is that the person chosen for the job should believe his red hair played a role in the choice; the sole "meaning" of the ABC pattern is to lure the police into thinking this pattern has meaning.

This intersubjective dimension of the meaning that pertains to the false image is most clearly articulated in "The Adventure of the Highgate Miracle," a Sherlock Holmes pastiche written by John Dickson Carr and Adrian Conan Doyle, son of Arthur. Mister Cabpleasure, a merchant married to a wealthy heiress, suddenly develops a "pathological" attachment to his walking stick: he never parts from it, carrying it day and night. What does this sudden "fetishistic" attachment mean? Does the stick serve as a hiding place for the diamonds that recently vanished from Mrs. Cabpleasure's drawer? A detailed examination of the stick excludes this possibility: it is just an ordinary stick. Finally, Sherlock Holmes discovers that the whole attachment to the stick was staged in order to confer credibility on the scene of Cabpleasure's "magic" disappearance. During the night prior to his planned escape, he slips out of his home unobserved, goes to the milkman, and bribes him into lending him his outfit and letting him take his place. Dressed as a milkman, he appears next morning in front of his house with the milkman's handcart, takes out a bottle, and enters the house as usual to leave the bottle in the kitchen. Once inside the house, he quickly puts on his own overcoat and hat and steps out *without his stick*; halfway through the garden, he grimaces, as if suddenly remembering that he forgot his beloved stick, turns around, and runs quickly into the house. Behind the entrance door, he again changes into the milkman's outfit, walks calmly to the handcart and moves off. Cabpleasure, it turns out, stole his wife's diamonds; he knew that his wife suspected him and that she had hired detectives to watch the house during the day. He counted on his "loony" attachment to the stick being observed so that when, on his way through the garden, after noticing the lack of his stick, he shrinks and runs back, his actions appear natural to the detectives observing the house. In short, the sole "meaning" of his attachment to the stick was to make others think it has meaning.

It should be clear, now, why it is totally misleading to conceive of the detective's procedure as a version of the procedure proper to "precise" natural sciences: it is true that the "objective" scientist also "penetrates through false appearance into the hidden reality," but this false appearance with which he has to deal *lacks the dimension of deception.* Unless we accept the hypothesis of an evil, deceitful God, we can in no way maintain that the scientist is "deceived" by his object, i.e., that the false appearance confronting him "exists only to conceal the reason of its existence." In contrast to the "objective" scientist, however, the detective does not attain the truth by simply canceling the false appearance: he takes it into consideration. When confronted with the mystery of Cabpleasure's stick, Holmes does not say to himself "Let us leave out its meaning, it is just a lure," he asks himself a quite different question: "The stick has no meaning, the special meaning supposedly attached to it is of course just a lure; but what precisely did the criminal achieve by luring us into believing that the stick has special meaning for him?" The truth lies not "beyond" the domain of deception, it lies in the "intention," in the intersubjective function of the very deception. The detective does not simply disregard the meaning of the false scene: he pushes it to the point of self-reference, i.e., to the point at which it becomes obvious that its sole meaning consists in the fact that (others think) it possesses some meaning. At the point at which the murderer's position of enunciation is that of a certain *I am deceiving you,* the detective is finally capable of sending back to him the true significance of his message:

> The *I am deceiving you* arises from the point at which the detective awaits the murderer and sends back to him, according to the formula, his own message in its true significance, that is to say, in an inverted form. He says to him—*in this* I am deceiving you, *what you are sending as message is what I express to you, and in doing so you are telling the truth.*[9]

The Detective as the "Subject Supposed to Know"

Now we are finally in a position to locate properly the detective's ill-famed "omniscience" and "infallibility." The certainty on the part of the reader that, at the end, the detective will solve the case does not include the supposition that he will arrive at the truth notwithstanding all deceitful appearances. The point is rather that he will literally *catch the murderer in his deception,* i.e., that he will trap him by taking into account his cunning. The very deceit the murderer invents to save himself is the cause of his downfall. Such a paradoxical conjunction in which it is the very attempt at deception that betrays us is of course possible only in the domain of "meaning," of a signifying structure; it is on this account that the detective's "omniscience" is strictly homologous to that of the psychoanalyst, who is taken by the patient as the "subject supposed to know" (*le sujet supposé savoir*)—supposed to know what? The true meaning of our act, the meaning visible in the very falseness of the appearance. The detective's domain, as well as that of the psychoanalyst, is thus thoroughly the domain of *meaning,* not of "facts": as we have already noted, the scene of the crime analyzed by the detective is by definition "structured like a language." The basic feature of the signifier is its differential character: since the identity of a signifier consists in the bundle of differences from other signifiers, the absence of a trait itself can have a positive value. Which is why the detective's artifice lies not simply in his capacity to grasp the possible meaning of "insignificant details," but perhaps even more in his capacity to apprehend absence itself (the nonoccurrence of some detail) as meaningful—it is perhaps not by chance that the most famous of all Sherlock Holmes's dialogues is the following from "Silver Blaze":

"Is there any point to which you wish to draw my attention?"
"To the curious incident of the dog in the night."
"The dog did nothing in the night."
"That was the curious incident," remarked Holmes.

This is how the detective traps the murderer: not simply by perceiving the traces of the deed the murderer failed to efface, but by perceiving the very absence of a trace as itself a trace.[10] We could then specify the function of the detective *qua* "subject supposed to know" in the following way: the scene of the crime contains a diversity of clues, of meaningless, scattered details with no obvious pattern (like "free associations" of the analysand in the psychoanalytic process), and *the detective, solely by means of his presence, guarantees that all these details will retroactively acquire meaning*. In other words, his "omniscience" is an effect of *transference* (the person in a relation of transference toward the detective is above all his Watsonian companion, who provides him with information the meaning of which escapes the companion completely).[11] And it is precisely on the basis of this specific position of the detective as "guarantor of meaning" that we can elucidate the circular structure of the detective story. What we have at the beginning is a void, a blank of the unexplained, more properly, of the *unnarrated* ("How did it happen? What happened on the night of the murder?"). The story encircles this blank, it is set in motion by the detective's attempt to reconstruct the missing narrative by interpreting the clues. In this way, we reach the proper beginning only at the very end, when the detective is finally able to narrate the whole story in its "normal," linear form, to reconstruct "what really happened," by filling in all the blanks. At the beginning, there is thus the murder—a traumatic shock, an event that cannot be integrated into symbolic reality because it appears to interrupt the "normal" causal chain. From the moment of this eruption, even the most ordinary events of life seem loaded with threatening possibilities; everyday reality becomes a nightmarish dream as the "normal" link between cause and effect is suspended. This radical opening, this dissolution of symbolic reality, entails the transformation of the lawlike succession of events into a kind of "lawless sequence" and therefore bears witness to an encounter with the "impossible" real, resisting symbolization. Suddenly, "everything is possible," including the impossible. The detective's role is precisely to demonstrate how "the impossible is possible" (Ellery Queen), that is, to resymbolize the traumatic shock, to integrate it into symbolic reality. The very presence of the detective guarantees in advance the transformation of the lawless sequence into a lawful sequence; in other words, the reestablishment of "normality."

What is of crucial importance here is the *intersubjective* dimension of the murder, more properly, of the *corpse*. The corpse as object works to bind a group of individuals together: the corpse constitutes them as a group (a group of suspects), it brings and keeps them together through their shared feeling of guilt—any one of them *could have been* the murderer, each had motive and opportunity. The role of the detective is, again, precisely to dissolve the impasse of this universalized, free-floating guilt by localizing it in a single subject and thus exculpating all others.[12] Here, however, the homology between the procedure of the analyst and that of the detective reveals its limits. That is to say, it is not enough to draw a parallel and affirm that the psychoanalyst analyzes "inner," psychic reality, while the detective is confined to "external," material reality. The thing to do is to define the space where the two of them overlap, by asking the crucial question: how does this transposition of the analytic procedure onto "external" reality bear on the very domain of the "inner" libidinal economy? We have already indicated the answer: the detective's act consists in annihilating the libidinal possibility, the "inner" truth that each one in the group might have been the murderer (i.e., that we *are* murderers in the unconscious of our desire, insofar as the actual murderer realizes the desire of the group constituted by the corpse) on the level of "reality" (where the culprit singled out *is* the murderer and thus the guarantee of *our* innocence). Herein lies the fundamental untruth, the existential falsity of the detective's "solution": the detective plays upon the difference between the factual truth (the accuracy of facts) and the "inner" truth concerning our desire. On behalf of the accuracy of facts, he compromises the "inner," libidinal truth and discharges us of all guilt for the realization of our desire, insofar as this realization is imputed to the culprit alone. In regard to the libidinal economy, the detective's "solution" is therefore nothing but a kind of realized hallucination. The detective "proves by facts" what would otherwise remain a hallucinatory projection of guilt onto a scapegoat, i.e., he proves that the scapegoat is effectively guilty. The immense pleasure brought about by the detective's solution results from this libidinal gain, from a kind of surplus profit obtained from it: our desire is realized and we do not even have to pay the price for it. The contrast between the psychoanalyst and the detective is thus clear: psychoanalysis confronts us precisely with the price we have to pay for the access to our desire, with an irredeemable loss (the "symbolic castration"). The way in which the detective functions as a "subject supposed to know" also changes accordingly: what does he guarantee by his mere presence? He guarantees precisely that we will be discharged of any guilt, that the guilt for the realization of our desire will be "externalized" in the scapegoat and that, consequently, we will be able to desire without paying the price for it.

The Philip Marlowe Way

THE CLASSICAL VERSUS THE HARD-BOILED DETECTIVE

Perhaps the greatest charm of the classical detective narrative lies in the fascinating, uncanny, dreamlike quality of the story the client tells the detective at the very beginning. A young maid tells Sherlock Holmes how, every morning on her way from the train station to work, a shy man with a masked face follows her at a distance on a bicycle and draws back as soon as she tries to approach him. Another woman tells Holmes of strange things her employer demands of her: she is handsomely paid to sit by the window for a couple of hours every evening, dressed in an old-fashioned gown, and braid. These scenes exert such a powerful libidinal force that one is almost tempted to hypothesize that the main function of the detective's "rational explanation" is to break the spell they have upon us, i.e., to spare us the encounter with the real of our desire that these scenes stage. The hard-boiled detective novel presents in this regard a totally different situation. In it, the detective loses the distance that would enable him to analyze the false scene and to dispel its charm; he becomes an active hero confronted with a chaotic, corrupt world, the more he intervenes in it, the more involved in its wicked ways he becomes.

It is therefore totally misleading to locate the difference between the classical and the hard-boiled detective as one of "intellectual" versus "physical" activity, to say that the classical detective of logic and deduction is engaged in reasoning while the hard-boiled detective is mainly engaged in chase and fight. The real break consists in the fact that, existentially, the classical detective is not "engaged" at all: he maintains an eccentric position throughout; he is excluded from the exchanges that take place among the group of suspects constituted by the corpse. It is precisely on the basis of this exteriority of his position (which is of course not to be confused with the position of the "objective" scientist: the latter's distance toward the object of his research is of quite another nature) that the homology between the detective and the analyst is founded. One of the clues indicating the difference between the two types of detective is their respective attitudes toward financial reward. After solving the case, the classical detective accepts with accentuated pleasure payment for the services he has rendered, whereas the hard-boiled detective as a rule disdains money and solves his cases with the personal commitment of somebody fulfilling an ethical mission, although this commitment is often hidden under a mask of cynicism. What is at stake here is not the classical detective's simple greed or his callousness toward human suffering and injustice—the point is much finer: the payment enables him to avoid getting mixed up in the libidinal circuit of (symbolic) debt and its restitution. The symbolic value of payment is the same in psychoanalysis: the fees of the analyst allow him to stay out of the "sacred" domain of exchange and sacrifice, i.e., to avoid getting involved in the analysand's libidinal circuit. Lacan articulates this dimension of payment precisely apropos of Dupin who, at the end of "The Purloined Letter," makes the prefect of police understand that he already has the letter, but is prepared to deliver it only for an appropriate fee:

> Does this mean that this Dupin, who up until then was an admirable, almost excessively lucid character, has all of a sudden become a small time wheeler and dealer? I don't hesitate to see in this action the re-purchasing of what one could call the bad *mana* attached to the letter. And indeed, from the moment he receives his fee, he has pulled out of the game. It isn't only because he has handed the letter over to another, but because his motives are clear to everyone—he got his money, it's no longer of any concern to him. The sacred value of remuneration, of the fee, is clearly indicated by the context. . . . We, who spend our time being the bearers of all the purloined letters of the patient, also get paid somewhat dearly. Think about this with some care—were we not to be paid, we would get involved in the drama of Atreus and Thyestes, the drama in which all the subjects who come to confide their truth in us are involved. . . . Everyone knows that money doesn't just buy things, but that the prices which, in our culture, are calculated at rock-bottom, have the function of neutralizing something infinitely more dangerous than paying in money, namely owing somebody something.[13]

In short, by demanding a fee, Dupin forestalls the "curse"—the place in the symbolic network—that befalls those who come into possession of the letter. The hard-boiled detective is, on the contrary, "involved" from the very beginning, caught up in the circuit: this involvement defines his very subjective position. What causes him to solve the mystery is first of all the fact that he has a certain debt to honor. We can locate this "settlement of (symbolic) accounts" on a wide scale ranging from Mike Hammer's primitive vendetta ethos in Mickey Spillane's novels to the refined sense of wounded subjectivity that characterizes Chandler's Philip Marlowe. Let us take, as an exemplary case of the latter, "Red Wind," one of Chandler's early short stories. Lola Barsley once had a lover who died unexpectedly. As a memento of her great love, she keeps an expensive pearl necklace, a gift from him, but in order to avoid her husband's suspicion she invents the story that the necklace is an imitation. Her ex-chauffeur steals the necklace and blackmails her, guessing that the necklace is real and what it means to her. He wants money for the necklace and for not telling her husband that it is not a fake. After the blackmailer is murdered, Lola asks John Dalmas (a precursor of Marlowe) to find the missing necklace, but when he obtains it and shows it to a professional jeweller, the necklace turns out to be a fake. Lola's great love was also an impostor, it seems, and her memory an illusion. Dalmas, however, does not want to hurt her, so he hires a cheap forger to manufacture a deliberately raw imitation of the imitation. Lola, of course, immediately sees that the necklace Dalmas gives her is not her own and Dalmas explains that the blackmailer probably intended to return her this imitation and to keep the original for himself so that he might resell it later on. The memory of Lola's great love, which gives meaning to her life, is thus left unspoiled. Such an act of goodness is, of course, not without a kind of moral beauty, but it nonetheless runs contrary to the psychoanalytic ethic: it intends to spare the other the confrontation with a truth that would hurt him/her by demolishing his/her ego-ideal.

Such an involvement entails the loss of the "excentric" position by means of which the classical detective plays a role homologous to the "subject supposed to know." That is to say, the detective is never, as a rule, the narrator of the classical detective novel, which has either an "omniscient" narrator or one who is a sympathetic member of the social milieu, preferably the detective's Watsonian companion—in short, the person *for whom* the detective is a "subject supposed to know." The "subject supposed to know" is an effect of transference and is as such *structurally impossible in the first person*: he is by definition "supposed to know" by another subject. For that reason, it is strictly prohibited to divulge the detective's "inner thoughts." His reasoning must be concealed till the final triumphal denouement, except for occasional mysterious questions and remarks whose function is to emphasize even further the inaccessible character of what goes on in the detective's head. Agatha Christie is a great master of such remarks, although she seems sometimes to push them to a mannerist extreme: in the midst of an intricate investigation, Poirot usually asks a question such as "Do you know by any chance what was the color of the stockings worn by the lady's maid?"; after obtaining the answer, he mumbles into his moustache: "Then the case is completely clear!"

The hard-boiled novels are in contrast generally narrated in the first person, with the detective himself as narrator (a notable exception, which would require exhaustive interpretation, is the majority of Dashiell Hammett's novels). This change in narrative perspective has of course profound consequences for the dialectic of truth and deception. By means of his initial decision to accept a case, the hard-boiled detective gets mixed up in a course of events that he is unable to dominate; all of a sudden it becomes evident that he has been "played for a sucker." What looked at first like an easy job turns into an intricate game of criss-cross, and all his effort is directed toward clarifying the contours of the trap into which he has fallen. The "truth" at which he attempts to arrive is not just a challenge to his reason but concerns him ethically and often painfully. The deceitful game of which he has become a part poses a threat to his very identity as a subject. In short, the dialectic of deception in the hard-boiled novel is the dialectic of an active hero caught in a nightmarish game whose real stakes escape him. His acts acquire an unforeseen dimension, he can hurt somebody unknowingly—the guilt he thus contracts involuntarily propels him to "honor his debt."[14]

In this case, then, it is the detective himself—not the terrified members of the "group of suspects"—who undergoes a kind of "loss of reality," who finds himself in a dreamlike world where it is never quite clear who is playing what game. And the person who embodies this deceitful character of the universe, its fundamental corruption, the person who lures the detective and "plays him for a sucker," is as a rule the femme fatale, which is why the final "settlement of accounts" usually consists in the detective's confrontation with her. This confrontation results in a range of reactions, from desperate resignation or escape into cynicism in Hammett and Chandler to loose slaughter in Mickey Spillane (in the final page of *I, the Jury*, Mike Hammer answers "It was easy" when his dying, treacherous lover asks him how he could kill her in the middle of making love). Why is this ambiguity, this deceitfulness and corruption of the universe embodied in a woman whose promise of surplus enjoyment conceals mortal danger? What is the precise dimension of this danger? Our answer is that, contrary to appearance, the femme fatale embodies a radical *ethical* attitude, that of "not ceding one's desire," of persisting in it to the very end when its true nature as the death drive is revealed. It is the hero who, by rejecting the femme fatale, breaks with his ethical stance.

THE WOMAN WHO "DOES NOT CEDE HER DESIRE"

What precisely is meant here by "ethics" can be elucidated by reference to the famous Peter Brooks version of Bizet's *Carmen*. That is to say, our thesis is that, by means of the changes he introduced into the original plot, Brooks made Carmen not only a tragic figure but, more radically, an *ethical* figure of the lineage of Antigone. Again, at first it seems that there could be no greater contrast than that between Antigone's dignified sacrifice and the debauchery that leads to Carmen's destruction. Yet the two are connected by the same ethical attitude that we could describe (according to the Lacanian reading of *Antigone*) as an unreserved acceptance of the death drive, as a striving for radical self-annihilation, for what Lacan calls the "second death" going beyond mere physical destruction, i.e., entailing the effacement of the very symbolic texture of generation and corruption. Brooks was quite justified in making the aria about the "merciless card" the central musical motif of the entire work: the aria about the card that "always shows death" (in the third act) designates the precise moment at which Carmen assumes an ethical status, accepting without reserve the imminence of her own death. The cards that, in their chance fall, always predict death, are the "little piece of the real" to which Carmen's death drive clings. And it is precisely at the moment when Carmen not only becomes aware that she—as a woman marking the fate of the men she encounters—is herself the victim of fate, a plaything in the hands of forces she cannot dominate, but also fully accepts her fate by not ceding her desire that she becomes a "subject" in the strict Lacanian meaning of this term. For Lacan, a subject is in the last resort the name for this "empty gesture" by means of which we freely assume what is imposed on us, the real of the death drive. In other words, up until the aria about the "merciless card," Carmen was an object for men, her power of fascination depended on the role she played in their fantasy space, she was nothing but their symptom, although she lived under the illusion that she was effectively "pulling the strings." When she finally becomes an object *for herself also,* i.e., when she realizes that she is just a passive element in the interplay of libidinal forces, she "subjectifies" herself, she becomes a "subject." From the Lacanian perspective, "subjectification" is thus strictly correlative to experiencing oneself as an object, a "helpless victim": it is the name for the gaze by means of which we confront the utter nullity of our narcissistic pretentions.

To prove that Brooks was fully aware of this, it suffices to mention his most ingenious intervention: the radical change of the denouement of the opera. Bizet's original version is well known. In front of the arena in which the toreador Escamillo pursues his victorious fight, Carmen is approached by the desperate Jose who begs her to live with him again. His demand is met with rebuff, and while the song in the background announces another triumph for Escamillo, Jose stabs Carmen to death— the usual drama of a rejected lover who cannot bear his loss. With Brooks, however, things turn out quite differently. Jose resignedly *accepts* Carmen's final rebuff, but as Carmen is walking away from him, the servants bring her the dead Escamillo—he lost the fight, the bull has killed him. It is Carmen who is now broken. She leads Jose to a lonely place near the arena, kneels down and offers herself to him to be stabbed. Is there a denouement more desperate than this? Of course there is: Carmen might have left with Jose, this weakling, and continued to live her miserable everyday life. The "happy ending," in other words, would be the most desperate of all.

And it is the same with the figure of the femme fatale in hard-boiled novels and in *film noir*: she who ruins the lives of men and is at the same time victim of her own lust for enjoyment, obsessed by a desire for power, who endlessly manipulates her partners and is at the same time slave to some third, ambiguous person, sometimes even an impotent or sexually ambivalent man. What bestows on her an aura of mystery is precisely the way she cannot be clearly located in the opposition between master and slave. At the moment she seems permeated with intense pleasure, it suddenly becomes apparent that she suffers immensely; when she seems to be the victim of some horrible and unspeakable violence, it suddenly becomes clear that she enjoys it. We can never be quite sure if she enjoys or suffers, if she manipulates or is herself the victim of manipulation. It is this that produces the deeply ambiguous character of those moments in the *film noir* (or in the hard-boiled detective novel) when the femme fatale breaks down, loses her powers of manipulation, and becomes the victim of her own game. Let us just mention the first model of such a breakdown, the final confrontation between Sam Spade and Brigid O'Shaughnessy in *The Maltese Falcon*. As she begins to lose her grasp of the situation, Brigid suffers a hysterical breakdown; she passes immediately from one strategy to another. She first threatens, then she cries and maintains that she did not know what was really happening to her, then suddenly she assumes again an attitude of cold distance and disdain, and so on. In short, she unfolds a whole fan of inconsistent hysterical masks. This moment of the final breakdown of the femme fatale—who now appears as an entity without substance, a series of inconsistent masks without a coherent ethical attitude—this moment when her power of fascination evaporates and leaves us with feelings of nausea and disgust, this moment when we see "nought but shadows of what is not" where previously we saw clear and distinct form exerting tremendous powers of seduction, this moment of reversal is at the same time the moment of triumph for the hard-boiled detective. Now, when the fascinating figure of the femme fatale disintegrates into an inconsistent bric-a-brac of hysterical masks, he is finally capable of gaining a kind of distance toward her and of rejecting her.

The destiny of the femme fatale in *film noir,* her final hysterical breakdown, exemplifies perfectly the Lacanian proposition that "Woman does not exist": she is nothing but "the symptom of man," her power of fascination masks the void of her nonexistence, so that when she is finally rejected, her whole ontological consistency is dissolved. But precisely as nonexisting, i.e., at the moment at which, through hysterical breakdown, she *assumes* her nonexistence, she constitutes herself as "subject": what is waiting for her *beyond* hysterization is the death drive in its purest. In feminist writings on *film noir* we often encounter the thesis that the femme fatale presents a mortal threat to man (the hard-boiled detective), i.e., that her boundless enjoyment menaces his very identity as subject: by rejecting her at the end, he regains his sense of personal integrity and identity. This thesis is true, but in a sense that is the exact opposite of the way it is usually understood. What is so menacing about the femme fatale is not the boundless enjoyment that overwhelms the man and makes him woman's plaything or slave. It is not Woman as object of fascination that causes us to lose our sense of judgment and moral attitude but, on the contrary, that which remains hidden beneath this fascinating mask and which appears once the masks fall off: the dimension of the pure subject fully assuming the death drive. To use Kantian terminology, woman is not a threat to man insofar as she embodies pathological enjoyment, insofar as she enters the frame of a particular fantasy. The real dimension of the threat is revealed when we "traverse" the fantasy, when the coordinates of the fantasy space are lost via hysterical breakdown. In other words, what is really menacing about the femme fatale is not that she is fatal for *men* but that she presents a case of a "pure," nonpathological subject fully assuming *her own* fate. When the woman reaches this point, there are only two attitudes left to the man: either he "cedes his desire," rejects her and regains his imaginary, narcissistic identity (Sam Spade at the end of *The Maltese Falcon*), or he *identifies* with the woman as symptom and meets his fate in a suicidal gesture (the act of Robert Mitchum in what is perhaps the crucial *film noir*, Jacques Tourneur's *Out of the Past*).[15]

II   One Can Never Know Too Much about Hitchcock

"The Unconscious Is Outside"

Forward, Backward

One of the best-known Hollywood legends concerns the final scene of *Casablanca*. It is said that even during the shooting itself, the director and writers oscillated between different versions of the denouement (Ingrid Bergman leaves with her husband; she stays with Bogart; one of the two men dies). Like most such legends, this one is false, one of the ingredients of the myth of *Casablanca* constructed afterward (in reality, there were some discussions about possible endings, but they were resolved well before the shooting), but it nevertheless illustrates perfectly how the "quilting point" (*point de capiton*) functions in a narration. We experience the present ending (Bogart sacrifices his love and Bergman leaves with her husband) as something that "naturally" and "organically" follows from the preceding action, but if we were to imagine another ending—say, for example, that Bergman's heroic husband were to die and that Bogart were to take his place on the plane for Lisbon together with Bergman—it, too, would be experienced by viewers as something that developed "naturally" out of earlier events. How is this possible, given that the earlier events are the same in both cases? The only answer is, of course, that the experience of a linear "organic" flow of events is an illusion (albeit a necessary one) that masks the fact that it is the ending that *retroactively* confers the consistency of an organic whole on the preceding events. What is masked is the radical contingency of the enchainment of narration, the fact that, at every point, things might have turned out otherwise. But if this illusion is a result of the very linearity of the narration, how can the radical contingency of the enchainment of events be made visible? The answer is, paradoxically: by proceeding in a reverse way, by presenting the events backward, from the end to the beginning. Far from being just a hypothetical solution, this procedure has been put into practice several times:

• J. B. Priestley's *Time and the Conways* is a three-act play about the fate of the Conway family. In the first act, we witness a family dinner (that took place twenty years ago) where all the members are busy making enthusiastic plans for the future. The second act takes place in the present, i.e., twenty years later, when the family, now a group of broken people whose plans have failed, are again gathered together. The third act transposes us back twenty years once again and continues the dinner from the first act. The effect of this temporal manipulation is extremely depressing, if not outright horrifying. What is so horrifying, however, is not the passage from the first to the second act (first the enthusiastic plans, then the sad reality), but rather the passage from the second to the third. To see the depressing reality of a group of people whose life projects have been mercilessly thwarted, and *then* to witness those same people twenty years earlier, when they were still full of hope and unaware of what lay in wait for them, is fully to experience the dashing of hope.

• The film *Betrayal,* based on Harold Pinter's scenario, tells a trivial story of a love affair. The "trick" of the film is simply that the episodes are arranged in reverse order: first we see the lovers as they encounter each other in an inn a year after their break, then the break itself, then their first conflict, then the passionate climax of the love affair, then their first secret date, and finally the moment when, at a party, they first meet.

Such reversals in the order of narration might be expected to provoke an effect of total fatalism: everything is decided in advance, while the protagonists, like puppets, unwittingly play out their roles in an already written script. Closer analysis reveals, however, quite another logic behind the horror provoked by such an ordering of events, a version of the fetishistic split *je sais bien, mais quand meme*: "I know very well what will follow (because I know in advance the end of the story), but still, I don't quite believe it, which is why I am filled with anxiety. Will the unavoidable really happen?" In other words, it is precisely the reversal of the temporal order that makes us experience in an almost palpable way the utter contingency of the narrative sequence, i.e., the fact that, at every turning point, things might have taken another direction. Another example of the same paradox is probably also one of the great curiosities of the history of religion: a religion noted for driving its followers toward incessant, frenetic activity is Calvinism, which founds itself on a belief in predestination. It is as if the Calvinist subject were driven by an anxious premonition that, after all, the unavoidable *might not happen.*

This same form of anxiety prevades Ruth Rendell's excellent crime novel *Judgement in Stone,* a story of an illiterate maid who—fearing public disgrace if her illiteracy were to become known—kills her employer's entire family, liberal bene-factors who want to help her in every way. The story unfolds linearly except that at the very beginning Rendell reveals the final outcome and at every turning point draws our attention to the chance occurrence that seals the fate of all concerned. When, for example, the daughter of the employer's family, after some lingering, decides to spend the weekend at home and not with her boyfriend, Rendell com-ments directly that "her fate was sealed by this arbitrary decision: she missed the last chance to escape the death that awaited her." Far from transforming the flow of events into a fated enchainment, the eruption of the point of view of the final catas-trophe renders palpable the radical contingency of the events.

"The Other Must Not Know All"

It would be wrong to conclude from the "nonexistence of the big Other," i.e., from the fact that the big Other is just a retroactive illusion masking the radical con-tingency of the real, that we can simply suspend this "illusion" and "see things as they really are." The crucial point is that this "illusion" structures our (social) reality itself: its disintegration leads to a "loss of reality"—or, as Freud puts it in *The Future of an Illusion,* after conceiving religion as an illusion: "Must not the assumptions that determine our political regulations be called illusions as well?"[1]

One of the key scenes in Hitchcock's *Saboteur,* the charity dance in the palace of the wealthy Nazi spy posing as a society lady, demonstrates perfectly the way the very superficiality of the big Other (the field of etiquette, social rules, and manners) remains the place where truth is determined and thus the place from which "the game is run." The scene sets up a tension between the idyllic surface (the politeness of the charity dance) and the concealed real action (the desperate attempt by the hero to snatch his girlfriend from the hands of the Nazi agents and to escape together with her). The scene takes place in a great hall, in full view of hundreds of guests. Both the hero and his adversaries have to observe the rules of etiquette appropriate to such an occasion; they are expected to engage in banal conversation, to accept an invitation to dance, etc., and the actions each of them undertakes against the adver-sary have to accord with the rules of the social game (when a Nazi agent wants to lead the hero's girlfriend away, he simply asks her for a dance, a request that, accord-ing to rules of politeness, she cannot refuse; when the hero wants to run away, he joins an innocent couple just taking their leave—the Nazi agents cannot stop him by

force because this would expose them in the eyes of the couple; and so on). It is true
that this renders action difficult (to deal a blow against the adversary, our action must
inscribe itself in the texture of the surface social game and pass for a socially accept-
able act), but an even more rigorous limitation is imposed upon our adversary: if we
succeed in inventing such a "doubly inscribed" act, he is confined to the role of the
impotent observer, he cannot strike back because he is also prohibited from vio-
lating the rules. Such a situation enables Hitchcock to develop the intimate connection between the gaze and the couple power/impotence. The gaze denotes at the
same time power (it enables us to exert control over the situation, to occupy the position of the master) and impotence (as bearers of a gaze, we are reduced to the role
of passive witnesses to the adversary's action). The gaze, in short, is a perfect embodiment of the "impotent Master," one of the central figures of the Hitchcockian
universe.

    This dialectic of the gaze in its connection with both power and impotence was
articulated for the first time in Poe's "The Purloined Letter." When the minister steals
the incriminating letter from her, the Queen sees what is going on, though she can
do nothing but impotently observe his actions. Any action on her part would betray
her to the King, who is also present but who does not know and must not know anything about the incriminating letter (which probably reveals some amorous indis-
cretion of the Queen). The crucial point to be noted is that the situation of the
"impotent gaze" is never dual, it is never a simple confrontation between a subject
and an adversary. A third element is always involved (the King in "The Purloined Letter," the ignorant guests in the *Saboteur*) that personifies the innocent ignorance of
the big Other (the rules of the social game) from which we must hide our true
designs. What we have then are three elements: an *innocent third* who sees all but
fails to grasp the real significance of what he sees; the *agent* whose act—under the
guise of simply following the rules of the social game taking place—deals a decisive
blow to the adversary; and, finally, the adversary himself, the *impotent observer* who
apprehends perfectly the real implication of the act, but is nonetheless condemned
to the role of a passive witness, since his counteraction would provoke the suspicion
of the innocent, ignorant big Other. The fundamental pact uniting the actors of the
social game is thus that the *Other must not know all*. This nonknowledge of the
Other opens up a certain distance that, so to speak, gives us breathing space, i.e., that
allows us to confer upon our actions a supplementary meaning beyond the one that
is socially acknowledged. For this very reason, the social game (the rules of etiquette,
etc.), in the very stupidity of its ritual, is never simply superficial. We can indulge in
our secret wars only as long as the Other does not take cognizance of them, for at

the moment the Other can no longer ignore them, the social bond dissolves itself. A catastrophe ensues, similar to the one instigated by the child's observation that the emperor is naked. *The Other must not know all*: this is an appropriate definition of the nontotalitarian social field.[2]

THE "TRANSFERENCE OF GUILT"

The very notion of the big Other (of the symbolic order) is founded on the special kind of double deception that becomes visible in a scene from the Marx brothers' *Duck Soup,* where Groucho defends his client before the court of law with the following argument in favor of his insanity: "This man looks like an idiot and acts like an idiot—but this should in no way deceive you: he *IS* an idiot!" The paradox of this proposition exemplifies perfectly the classical topos of the Lacanian theory concerning the difference between animal and human deception: man alone is capable of deceiving *by means of truth itself.* An animal can feign to be or to intend something other than what it really is or intends, but only man can lie by telling a truth that he expects to be taken for a lie. Only man can *deceive by feigning to deceive.* This is, of course, the logic of Freud's joke about two Polish Jews often cited by Lacan. One of these men asks the other in an offended tone: "Why are you telling me that you are going to Cracow,, so that I'll think you're going to Lemberg, when you are really going to Cracow?" This same logic structures the plot of a whole series of Hitchcock's films: the amorous couple is at first united by a pure accident or an external constraint, i.e., they find themselves in a situation in which they must pretend to be married or in love, until, finally, they fall in love for real. The paradox of such a situation could be adequately described by a paraphrase of Groucho's plea: "This couple looks like a couple in love and acts like a couple in love—but this should in no way deceive you: they *ARE* a couple in love!" We find perhaps the most refined version of this in *Notorious,* when Alicia and Devlin, American agents in the house of Sebastian, a rich Nazi supporter and Alicia's husband, furtively enter the wine cellar to explore the secret contents of the champagne bottles. There, they are surprised by the sudden arrival of Sebastian. To conceal the real purpose of their visit to the cellar, they embrace quickly, feigning a clandestine meeting of two lovers. The point is, of course, that they are effectively in love: they succeed in deceiving the husband (for the time being, at least), but what they offer him as a lure is truth itself.

This kind of movement "from outside inward" is one of the key components of the intersubjective relations in Hitchcock's films: we effectively *become* something by pretending that we *already are* that. To grasp the dialectic of this movement, we have to take into account the crucial fact that this "outside" is never simply a "mask" we wear in public but is rather the symbolic order itself. By "pretending to be something," by "acting as if we were something," we assume a certain place in the intersubjective symbolic network, and it is this external place that defines our true position. If we remain convinced, deep within ourselves, that "we are not really that," if we preserve an intimate distance toward "the social role we play," we doubly deceive ourselves. The final deception is that social appearance is deceitful, for in the social-symbolic reality things ultimately *are* precisely what they *pretend* to be. (More precisely, this holds only for those of Hitchcock's films designated by Lesley Brill as "romances," in opposition to the "ironic" films. The "romances" are ruled by the Pascalian logic whereby social play gradually changes into an authentic intersubjective relationship whereas the "ironic" films [*Psycho,* for example] depict a total blockade of communication, a psychotic split where the "mask" is effectively *nothing but a mask,* i.e., where the subject maintains the kind of distance from the symbolic order characteristic of psychoses.)

It is against this background that we should also conceive the "transference of guilt," which is, according to Rohmer and Chabrol, the central motif of the Hitchcockian universe.[3] In Hitchcock's films, murder is never simply an affair between a murderer and his victim; murder always implies a third party, a reference to a third person—the murderer kills *for* this third person, his act is inscribed in the framework of a symbolic exchange with him. By means of his act, the murderer realizes his repressed desire. For this reason, the third person finds himself charged with guilt, although he does not know anything or, more precisely, refuses to know anything of the way he is implicated in the affair. In *Strangers on a Train,* for example, Bruno, by killing Guy's wife, transfers the guilt for the murder onto Guy, although Guy does not want to know anything about the "murder-for-murder" pact referred to by Bruno. *Strangers on a Train* is the middle term of the great "trilogy of the transference of guilt": *Rope, Strangers on a Train, I Confess.* In all three films, murder functions as a stake in an intersubjective logic of exchange, i.e., the murderer expects from the third party something in return for his act—recognition (in *Rope*), another murder (in *Strangers on a Train*), silence before the court of law (in *I Confess*).

The crucial point is, however, that this "transference of guilt" does not concern some psychic interior, some repressed, disavowed desire hidden deep beneath the mask of politeness, but quite the contrary a radically external network of intersubjective relations. The moment the subject finds himself at a certain place (or loses a certain place) in this network, he becomes guilty, although, in his psychic interior, he is totally innocent. Which is why—as Deleuze has pointed out—*Mr. and Mrs. Smith* is a thoroughly Hitchcockian movie. A married couple unexpectedly learns that their marriage is legally invalid. What was for years rightful indulgence in con-jugal pleasures changes suddenly into sinful adultery, i.e., the same activity retro-actively acquires a totally different symbolic value. This is what the "transference of guilt" is about, this is what confers upon Hitchcock's universe its radical ambiguity and lability. At any moment, the idyllic texture of the everyday course of events can disintegrate, not because some iniquitous violence erupts from under the surface of social rules (according to the common notion that, beneath the civilized mask, we are all savages and murderers), but because all of a sudden—as a result of unex-pected changes in the symbolic texture of intersubjective relations—what was a moment ago permitted by the rules becomes an abhorrent vice, although the act in its immediate, physical reality remains the same. To elucidate further this sudden reversal, it is sufficient to recall three great Charlie Chaplin films distinguished by the same melancholic, painful humor: *The Great Dictator, Monsieur Verdoux, Lime-light.* All of them turn on the same structural problem: that of locating a line of demar-cation, of defining a certain feature, difficult to specify at the level of positive properties, whose presence or absence radically changes the symbolic status of the object.

> Between the small Jewish barber and the dictator, the difference is as negligible as that between their respective moustaches. Yet it results in two situations as infinitely remote, as far opposed as those of victim and executioner. Likewise, in *Monsieur Verdoux,* the difference between the two aspects or demeanors of the same man, the lady-assassin and the lov-ing husband of a paralyzed wife, is so thin that all his wife's intuition is required for the premonition that somehow he has "changed." . . . The burning question of *Limelight*: what is that "nothing," that sign of age, that small difference of triteness, that turns the clown's funny routine into a tedious spectacle?[4]

This differential feature that cannot be pinned to some positive quality is what Lacan calls *le trait unaire,* the unitary feature: a point of symbolic identification to which the real of the subject clings. As long as the subject is attached to this feature, we are faced with a charismatic, fascinating, sublime figure; as soon as this attach-ment is broken, the figure is deflated. As proof of the fact that Chaplin was well aware of this dialectic of identification, it is enough to recall his earlier *City Lights,* where the action is set in motion by a coincidence that constitutes an effective pendant to the inaugural accident in Hitchcock's *North by Northwest*: the casual coincidence of the slam of a car door with the steps of a departing customer leads the blind flower girl wrongly to identify Charlot with the owner of the rich car. Later, after regaining her sight, the girl does not recognize Charlot as the benefactor who provided money for her operation. Such an intrigue, which seems at first a banal, melodramatic plot, bears witness to a far more perspicacious apprehension of intersubjective dialectics than that at work in most "serious" psychological dramas.

If tragedy is ultimately a matter of "character," i.e., if the immanent necessity leading to the final catastrophe is inscribed in the very structure of the tragic personality, there is on the contrary always something *comical* in the way the subject is attached to the signifier that determines his place in the symbolic structure, i.e., that "represents him for the other signifiers." This link is ultimately groundless, "irrational," of a radically contingent nature, absolutely incommensurate with the subject's "character." It is no accident that *Mr. and Mrs. Smith,* the Hitchcock film that exposes this constituent of his universe most clearly, is a comedy. All the numerous accidental encounters, coincidences, etc., that set off the plot of his films are of an essentially *comical* nature (recall, for example, the inaugural false identification of Thornhill as the nonexistent "Kaplan" in *North by Northwest*). The film in which Hitchcock wanted to render manifest the tragic side of such an unforeseen coincidence (*The Wrong Man,* where the musician Balestrero is wrongly identified as a robber) demonstrates this principle *a contrario,* by its very failure.

HOW TO HYSTERICIZE CHRISTIANITY

In making the radical externality of the Other the place where the truth of the subject is articulated, Hitchcock echoes Lacan's thesis that "the unconscious is outside." This externality is usually conceived as the external, nonpsychological character of the formal symbolic structure regulating the subject's intimate self-experience. Such an apprehension is, however, misleading: the (Hitchcockian and at the same time Lacanian) Other is not simply a universal formal structure filled out with contingent, imaginary contents (as in Lévi-Strauss, where the symbolic order is equivalent to universal symbolic laws structuring the material of myths, kinship relations, etc.). The structure of the Other is, on the contrary, already at work where we encounter the eruption of what seems to be the purest subjective contingency. Note the role of love in Hitchcock's films: it is a kind of "miracle" that explodes "out of nothing" and renders possible the salvation of the Hitchcockian couple. In other words, love is an exemplary case of what Jon Elster calls "states that are essentially by-products": an innermost emotion that cannot be planned in advance or assumed by means of a conscious decision (I cannot say to myself "now I shall fall in love with that woman": at a certain moment, I just *find* myself in love).[5] Elster's list of such states comprises above all notions such as "respect" and "dignity." If I consciously try to appear dignified or to arouse respect, the result is ridiculous; the impression I make, instead, is that of a miserable impersonator. The basic paradox of these states is that although they are what matters most, they elude us as soon as we make them the immediate aim of our activity. The only way to bring them about is not to center our activity on them but to pursue other goals and hope that they will come about "by themselves." Although they do pertain to our activity, they are ultimately perceived as something that belongs to us on account of what we *are* and not on account of what we *do*. The Lacanian name for this "by-product" of our activity is *objet petit a,* the hidden treasure, that which is "in us more than ourselves," that elusive, unattainable X that confers upon all our deeds an aura of magic, although it cannot be pinned down to any of our positive qualities. It is through the *objet a* that we can grasp the workings of the ultimate "by-product" state, the matrix of all the others: the *transference.* The subject can never fully dominate and manipulate the way he provokes transference in others; there is always something "magic" about it. All of a sudden, one appears to possess an unspecified X, something that colors all one's actions, submits them to a kind of transubstantiation. The most tragic embodiment of this state is probably the good-hearted femme fatale of hard-boiled detective novels. Basically a decent and honest woman, she witnesses with horror the way her mere presence brings about the moral decay of all men around her. From the Lacanian perspective, it is *here* that the Other enters the scene: "states that are essentially by-products" are *states that are essentially produced by the big Other*—the "big Other" designates precisely the agency that decides instead of us, in our place. When, all of a sudden, we find ourselves occupying a certain transferential position, i.e., when our mere presence provokes "respect," or "love," we can be sure that this "magic" transformation has nothing whatsoever to do with some "irrational" spontaneity: it is the big Other that produces the change.

It is therefore no accident that Elster illustrates these "states that are essentially by-products" by means of the Hegelian notion of the "cunning of reason." The subject engages in a certain activity with the purpose of achieving a well-defined goal; in this he fails since the final result of his actions is a different, totally unintended state of things that, however, would not have been brought about had the subject aimed directly at it. The final result could be brought about only as a by-product of an activity aimed at another goal. Compare the classic Hegelian example of the murder of Julius Caesar. The immediate, conscious goal of the conspirators opposed to Caesar was, of course, to reinstate the Republic; the final result—the "essential by-product"—of their conspiracy was, however, the installation of the Empire, i.e., the exact opposite of what they intended. In Hegelian terms, we could say that the Reason of History used them as involuntary means of realizing its aim. This Reason, which pulls the strings of History, is, of course, a Hegelian figuration of the Lacanian "big Other." Hegel tells us that the way to detect Reason at work is not to look for the great proclaimed aims and ideals that have guided historical agents, but rather to devote our attention to the effective "by-products" of their activity. The same holds true for Adam Smith's "invisible hand of the market," one of the historical sources of Hegel's idea of the "cunning of reason." In the market, every participant contributes unknowingly to the common good by following his egotistic interests. It is as if one's activity were guided by a benevolent, invisible hand. Again, we have another figuration of the "big Other."

It is against this background that the Lacanian thesis "the big Other does not exist" has to be read. The big Other does not exist as subject of history; it is not given in advance and does not regulate our activity in a teleological way. Teleology is always a retroactive illusion and "states that are essentially by-products" are radically contingent. It is also against this background that we should approach the classic Lacanian definition of communication, by which the speaker receives from the other his own message in its true, inverted form. It is in the "essential by-products" of his activity, in its unintended results, that his message's true, effective meaning is returned to the subject. The problem with this is that, as a rule, the subject is not prepared to recognize in the mess that results from his actions their true meaning. This brings us back to Hitchcock: in the first two films of the "transference of guilt" trilogy, the addressee of the murder (Professor Caddell in *Rope,* Guy in *Strangers on a Train*) is not prepared to assume the guilt transferred to him by the murder. In other words, he is not prepared to recognize in the murder accomplished by his partner an act of communication. By realizing the desire of the addressee, the murderer returns to him his own message in its true form (witness the shock felt by Professor Caddell and the end of *Rope* when the two murderers remind him that all they did was to take him at his word and act out his conviction about the Superman's right to kill).

I Confess, the final film of the trilogy, presents, however, a significant exception. Here, Father Logan recognizes himself from the very beginning as the addressee of the murderous act. Why? Because of his position as *confessor.* By directly associating the motif of the "transference of guilt" with Christianity (through a series of parallels between Father Logan's suffering and the Way of the Cross), *I Confess* exhibits the subversive character of Hitchcock's relationship to Christianity. The film makes visible the hysterical, "scandalous" kernel of Christianity, later obscured by its institutionalization of the obsessional ritual. That is to say, the suffering of Father Logan consists in the fact that he accepts the transference of guilt, i.e., that he recognizes the desires of the other (the murderer) as his own. From this perspective, Jesus Christ himself, this innocent who took upon himself the sins of humanity, appears in a new light: insofar as he assumes the guilt of sinners and pays the price for it, he recognizes the sinners' desire as his own. *Christ desires from the place of the other (the sinner),* this is the ground of his compassion for sinners. If the sinner is, in terms of his libidinal economy, a pervert, Christ is clearly a hysteric. For hysterical desire is the desire of the other. In other words, the question to ask apropos of a hysteric is not "*What* does he/she desire? What is the *object* of his/her desire?" The real enigma is expressed in the question "From where does he/she desire?" The task is to locate the subject with whom the hysteric must identify to be able to accede to his/her own desire.

Ladies Who Vanish

"THE WOMAN DOES NOT EXIST"

Given the central status of deception in relation to the symbolic order, one has to draw a radical conclusion: the only way *not* to be deceived is to maintain a distance from the symbolic order, i.e., to assume a *psychotic* position. A psychotic is precisely a subject who is *not duped by the symbolic order.*

Let us approach this psychotic position via Hitchcock's *The Lady Vanishes,* probably the most beautiful and effective variation on the theme of the "disappearance that everybody denies." The story is usually told from the point of view of a hero who, quite by chance, becomes acquainted with a pleasant, somewhat eccentric person; soon afterward, this person disappears and when the hero tries to find him or her, all those who saw them together remember nothing about the other (or even remember positively that the hero was alone), so that the very existence of this missing person passes for a hallucinatory *idée fixe* of the hero. In his conversations with Truffaut, Hitchcock himself mentions the original of this series of variations; it is the story of an old lady who disappeared from her hotel room in Paris in 1889, at the time of the Great Exhibition. After *The Lady Vanishes,* the most famous variation is undoubtedly Cornell Woolrich's *roman noir, Phantom Lady,* in which the hero spends the evening with a beautiful, unknown woman whom he encounters at a bar. This woman, who subsequently disappears and whom no one will admit seeing, turns out to be the only alibi the hero has to counter a charge of murder.

In spite of the utter improbability of these plots, there is something "psychologically convincing" about them—as if they touched some chord in our unconscious. To understand the apparent "rightness" of these plots, we should note first of all that the person who disappears is as a rule a very *ladylike* woman. It is difficult not to recognize in this phantomlike figure the apparition of Woman, of the woman who could fill out the lack in man, the ideal partner with whom the sexual relationship would finally be possible, in short, The Woman who, according to Lacanian theory, precisely does not exist. The nonexistence of this woman is rendered manifest to the hero by the absence of her inscription in the sociosymbolic network: the intersubjective community of the hero acts as if she does not exist, as if she were only his *idée fixe.*

Where should we locate the "falsity" and at the same time the attraction, the irresistible charm, of this theme of the "disappearance which everybody denies"? According to the ordinary ending of this kind of story, the lady who disappeared was not, in spite of all evidence to the contrary, simply the hero's hallucination. In other words, The Woman *does* exist. The structure of this fiction is the same as that of a well-known joke about a psychiatrist to whom a patient complains that there is a crocodile under his bed. The psychiatrist tries to convince the patient that this is just a hallucination, that in reality there is no crocodile under his bed. At the next session, the man persists in his complaint and the psychiatrist continues his efforts of persuasion. When the man does not come for the third session, the psychiatrist is convinced that the patient has been cured. Some time later, upon meeting one of the man's friends, the psychiatrist asks him how his former patient is doing; the friend replies: "Whom do you mean exactly? The one who was eaten by a crocodile?"

At first sight, the point of this kind of story seems to be that the subject was right to oppose the *doxa* of the Other: the truth is on the side of his *idée fixe,* even though his insistence on it threatened to exclude him from the symbolic community. Such a reading nevertheless obscures an essential feature, which can be approached via another, slightly different variation on the theme of the "realized hallucination," Robert Heinlein's science fiction short story "They." Its hero, confined to a lunatic asylum, is convinced that the whole of external, objective reality is a gigantic mise-en-scène staged by "them" in order to dupe him. All the people around him are part of this trickery, including his wife. (Things became "clear" to him a few months previously while setting out on a Sunday drive with his family. He was already in the car, it was raining outside, when he suddenly remembered that he had forgotten some small detail and returned to the house. Casually looking through the rear window on the second floor, he noticed that the sun was shining brightly, and realized that "they" had made a small mistake by forgetting to stage the rain behind the house!) His benevolent psychiatrist, his lovely wife, all his friends try desperately to bring him back to "reality"; when he finds himself alone with his wife and she professes her love for him, he is almost duped for an instant into believing her, but his old conviction stubbornly prevails. The end of the story: after leaving him, the women posing as his wife reports to some unidentified agency: "We failed with subject X, he still has doubts, mainly because of our mistake over the rain-effect: we forgot to arrange it behind his house."

Here, as well as with the joke about the crocodile, the denouement is not interpretive, it does not transpose us into another frame of reference. In the end, we are thrown back to the beginning: the patient is convinced that there is a crocodile under his bed, and there really is a crocodile under his bed: Heinlein's hero thinks that objective reality is a mise-en-scène organized by "them," and objective reality actually turns out to be a mise-en-scène organized by "them." What we have here is a kind of *successful encounter*: the final surprise is produced by the fact that a certain gap (that separating "hallucination" from "reality") is abolished. This collapse of "fiction" (the contents of the hallucination) and "reality" defines the psychotic universe. It is, however, only the second story ("They") that enables us to isolate the crucial feature of the mechanism at work; there the deception of the big Other is located in an agent, another subject ("they") who *is not deceived*. This subject, who holds and manipulates the threads of the deception proper to the symbolic order, is what Lacan calls "the Other of the Other." This other emerges as such, acquires visible existence, in paranoia, in the form of the persecutor supposed to master the game of deception.

Herein lies then the crucial feature: the psychotic subject's distrust of the big Other, his *idée fixe* that the big Other (embodied in the intersubjective community) is trying to deceive him, is always and necessarily supported by an unshakable belief in a consistent Other, an Other without gaps, an "Other of the Other" ("they" in Heinlein's story). When the paranoid subject clings to his distrust of the Other of the symbolic community, of "common opinion," he implies thereby the existence of an "Other of this Other," of a nondeceived agent who holds the reins. The paranoiac's mistake does not consist in his radical disbelief, in his conviction that there is a universal deception—here he is quite right, the symbolic order is ultimately the order of a fundamental deception—but rather, in his belief in a hidden agent who manipulates this deception, who tries to dupe him into accepting that "The Woman does not exist," for example. This would be, then, the paranoid version of the fact that "The Woman does not exist": she certainly does exist; the impression of her nonexistence is nothing but an effect of the deception staged by the conspiratory Other, like the gang of conspirators in *The Lady Vanishes* who try to dupe the heroine into accepting that the lady who vanished never existed.

The lady who vanishes is thus ultimately the woman with whom the sexual relationship would be possible, the elusive shadow of a Woman who would not be just another woman; which is why the disappearance of this woman is a means by which filmic romance takes cognizance of the fact that "The Woman does not exist" and that there is, therefore, no sexual relationship. Joseph Mankiewicz's classic Hollywood melodrama *A Letter to Three Wives,* also a story of a lady who vanishes, presents this impossibility of the sexual relationship in another, more refined way. The lady who vanishes, although never seen on screen, is here constantly present in the form of what Michel Chion called *la voix acousmatique.*[6] The story is introduced by the off-screen voice of Attie Ross, a small town femme fatale: she has arranged for a letter to be delivered to three women taking a Sunday trip down the river. The letter informs them that on this very day while they are absent from town, she will run off with one of their husbands. During the trip, each of the three women recalls in a flashback the difficulties of her marriage; each of them fears that Attie has chosen precisely her husband to run off with, because to each of them Attie represents the ideal woman, a refined lady possessing that "something" that the wife lacks, causing the marriage itself to seem less than perfect. The first wife is a nurse, an uneducated, simple-minded girl married to a rich man she met in the hospital; the second is a rather vulgar, professionally active woman, earning much more than her husband, a professor and writer; the third is a working-class parvenu, married, with no illusion of love, to a rich merchant, simply for the purpose of financial security. Naive common girl, active professional wife, cunning parvenu—three ways of introducing disharmony into marriage, three ways to be inadequate in the role of a wife, and in all three cases Attie Ross appears as "the other woman" who possesses what is lacking in them: experience, feminine delicacy, financial independence.[7] The result is of course a happy ending, but with an interesting undertone. It turns out that Attie planned to run off with the third woman's husband, the rich merchant, who, however, at the last moment changes his mind, returns home, and confesses all to his wife. Although she could divorce him and obtain a substantial alimony, she forgives him, discovering that she loves him after all. The three couples are thus reunited at the end; the menace that seemed to threaten their marriages disappears. The lesson of the film is, however, a bit more ambiguous than it might at first appear. The happy ending is never pure, it always implies a kind of renunciation—an acceptance of the fact that the woman with whom we live is never Woman, that there is a permanent threat of disharmony, that at any moment another woman might appear who will embody what seems to be lacking in the marital relation. What enables the happy ending, i.e., a return to the first woman, is precisely the experience that the Other

Woman "does not exist," that she is ultimately just a fantasy figure filling out the void of our relation with a woman. In other words, the happy ending is possible only with the first woman. If the hero were to decide for the Other Woman (whose exemplary case is of course the femme fatale in *film noir*), he would necessarily pay for his choice by catastrophe, even by death. What we encounter here is the same paradox as that of the incest prohibition, i.e., the prohibition of something that is already in itself impossible. The Other Woman is prohibited insofar as she "does not exist"; she is mortally dangerous because of the ultimate discord between her fantasy figure and the "empirical" woman who, quite by chance, finds herself occupying this fantasy place. It is precisely this impossible relationship between the fantasy figure of the Other Woman and the "empirical" woman who finds herself elevated to this sublime place that is the subject of Hitchcock's *Vertigo*.

SUBLIMATION AND THE FALL OF THE OBJECT

Hitchcock's *Vertigo,* another tale of a woman who vanishes, a film whose hero is captivated by a sublime image, is made as if to illustrate the Lacanian thesis that sublimation, while having nothing to do with "desexualization," has all the more to do with death: the power of fascination exerted by a sublime image always announces a lethal dimension.

Sublimation is usually equated with desexualization, i.e., with the displacement of libidinal cathexis from the "brute" object alleged to satisfy some basic drive to an "elevated," "cultivated" form of satisfaction. Rather than making a direct assault upon a woman, we try to seduce and conquer her by writing amorous letters and poetry; rather than beating our enemy senseless, we write an essay containing annihilating criticism of him—the banal psychoanalytic "interpretation" would suggest that our poetic activity was just a sublime, indirect way of providing for our bodily needs, our elaborate criticism a sublime rechanneling of our physical aggression. Lacan breaks completely with this problematic of a zero degree of satisfaction that undergoes a process of sublimation. His starting point is not the object of the allegedly direct, "brute" satisfaction, but its reverse, the primordial void around which the drive circulates, the lack that assumes positive existence in the shapeless form of the Thing (the Freudian *das Ding,* the impossible-unattainable substance of enjoyment). The sublime object is precisely "an object elevated to the dignity of the Thing,"[8] an ordinary, everyday object that undergoes a kind of transubstantiation and starts to function, in the symbolic economy of the subject, as an embodiment of the impossible Thing, i.e., as materialized Nothingness. This is why the sublime object presents the paradox of an object that is able to subsist only in shadow, in an intermediary, half-born state, as something latent, implicit, evoked: as soon as we try to cast away the shadow to reveal the substance, the object itself dissolves; all that remains is the dross of the common object.

In one of his television broadcasts on the wonders of sea life, Jacques Cousteau showed a kind of octopus that, seen its element in the ocean depths, moves with delicate grace and exerts a terrifying and at the same time magnificent power of fascination, but which, when removed from the water, becomes a disgusting lump of slime. In Hitchcock's *Vertigo,* Judy-Madeleine undergoes a similar transformation: as soon as she is removed from her "element," as soon as she no longer occupies the place of the Thing, her fascinating beauty vanishes and she becomes repulsive. The point of these observations is that the sublime quality of an object is not intrinsic, but rather an effect on its position in the fantasy space.

Hitchcock's genius is attested by the film's double scansion, i.e., by the break, the change of modality, between its first and second part. That is to say, the whole first part, up to the "suicide" of the false Madeleine, constitutes a magnificent lure, the story of the hero's progressive obsession with the fascinating image of Madeleine, ending necessarily in death. Let us afford ourselves a kind of mental experiment: if the film had ended at this point, with the hero deeply broken, incapable of consoling himself, refusing to accept the loss of the beloved Madeleine, we would not only obtain an entirely consistent story; we would by this very abridgment even produce a supplementary meaning. We would have the passionate drama of a man who, while striving desperately to save a beloved woman from the demons of her past, unwittingly pushed her toward her death by the very excessive nature of his love. We could even—why not?—give this story a Lacanian twist by interpreting it as a variation on the theme of the impossibility of the sexual relationship. The elevation of an ordinary, earthly woman to the sublime object always entails mortal danger for the miserable creature charged with embodying the Thing, since "Woman does not exist."

But the continuation of the film collapses this passionate drama by displaying its banal background: behind the fascinating story of a woman possessed by demons from the past, behind the existential drama of a man driving a woman to death because of the excessive character of his love, we find a common, although ingenious, criminal plot of a husband who wants to get rid of his wife for the sake of an inheritance. Unaware of this, the hero is not prepared to renounce his fantasy: he starts looking for the lost woman, and when he encounters a girl resembling her, he sets out desperately to recreate her in the image of the dead Madeleine. The trick is, of course, that this *is* the woman he knew before as "Madeleine" (recall the famous lines from the Marx brothers: "You remind me of Emmanuel Ravelli." "But I am Emmanuel Ravelli!" "No wonder, then, that you resemble him so much!") This comical identity of "resembling" and "being" announces, however, a lethal proximity: if the false Madeleine resembles herself, it is because she is in a way *already dead*. The hero loves her as Madeleine, that is to say, *insofar as she is dead*—the sublimation of her figure is equivalent to her mortification in the real. This would then be the lesson of the film: fantasy rules reality, one can never wear a mask without paying for it in the flesh. Although shot almost exclusively from a masculine perspective, *Vertigo* tells us more about the impasse of the woman's being a symptom of man than most "women's films."

Hitchcock's finesse consists in the way he succeeds in avoiding the simple alternative: either the romantic story of an "impossible" love or the unmasking that reveals the banal intrigue behind the sublime facade. Such a disclosure of the secret *beneath* the mask would leave intact the power of fascination exerted by the *mask itself*. The subject could again embark on a search for another woman to fill out the empty place of Woman, a woman who, this time, will not deceive him. Hitchcock is here incomparably more radical: he undermines the sublime object's power of fascination *from within*. Recall the way Judy, the girl resembling "Madeleine," is presented when the hero runs into her for the first time. She is a common redhead with thick makeup who moves in a coarse, ungracious way—a real contrast to the fragile and refined Madeleine. The hero puts all his effort into transforming Judy into a new "Madeleine," into producing a sublime object, when, all of a sudden, he becomes aware that "Madeleine" herself was Judy, this common girl. The point of such a reversal is not that an earthly woman can never fully conform to the sublime ideal; on the contrary, it is the sublime object herself ("Madeleine") that loses her power of fascination.

To locate this reversal properly, it is essential to be attentive to the difference between the two losses that befall Scottie, *Vertigo*'s hero: between the first loss of "Madeleine" and the second, final loss of Judy. The first is the simple loss of a beloved object—as such, it is a variation on the theme of the death of a fragile, sublime woman, the ideal love-object, that dominates romantic poetry and finds its most popular expression in a whole series of stories and poems by Edgar Allan Poe ("The Raven," among others). Although this death comes as a terrible shock, we could say that there is really nothing unexpected about it: it is rather as if the situation itself calls for it. The ideal love-object lives on the brink of death, her life itself is overshadowed by imminent death—she is marked by some hidden curse or suicidal madness, or she has some disease that befits the frail woman. This feature constitutes an essential part of her fatal beauty—from the very beginning, it is clear that "she is too beautiful to last long." For this reason, her death does not entail a loss of her power of fascination; quite the contrary, it is her very death that "authenticates" her absolute hold over the subject. Her loss throws him into a melancholic depression, and, consistent with romantic ideology, the subject is able to pull himself out of this depression only by dedicating the rest of his life to the poetic celebration of the lost object's incomparable beauty and grace. It is only when the poet loses his lady that he finally and truly acquires her, it is precisely through this loss that she gains her place in the fantasy space that regulates the subject's desire.

The second loss is, however, of quite another nature. When Scottie learns that Madeleine—the sublime ideal he was striving to recreate in Judy—*is* Judy, i.e., when, after all, he gets back the real "Madeleine" herself, *the figure of "Madeleine" disintegrates,* the whole fantasy structure that gave consistency to his being falls apart. This second loss is in a way a reversal of the first: we lose the object as fantasy support at the very moment we get hold of it in reality:

> For if Madeleine was really Judy, if she still exists, then she never existed, was never really anyone. . . . With her second dying he loses himself more finally and desperately because he loses not only Madeleine but his memory of her and probably his belief in her possibility.[9]

To use a Hegelian phrase, Madeleine's "second death" functions as the "loss of loss": by obtaining the object, we lose the fascinating dimension of loss as that which captivates our desire. True, Judy finally gives herself to Scottie, but—to paraphrase Lacan—this gift of her person "is changed inexplicably into a gift of shit": she becomes a common woman, repulsive even. This produces the radical ambiguity of the film's final shot in which Scottie looks down from the brink of the bell tower into the abyss that has just engulfed Judy. This ending is at the same time "happy" (Scottie is cured, he can look down into the precipice) and "unhappy" (he is finally broken, losing the support that gave consistency to his being). This same ambiguity characterizes the final moment of the psychoanalytic process when the fantasy is traversed; it explains why a "negative therapeutic reaction" always lurks as threat at the end of psychoanalysis.[10]

The abyss Scottie is finally able to look into is the very abyss of the hole in the Other (the symbolic order), concealed by the fascinating presence of the fantasy object. We have this same experience every time we look into the eyes of another person and feel the depth of his gaze. This abyss is figured in the shots accompanying the titles of *Vertigo,* the closeups of a woman's eye out of which swirls a nightmarish partial object. We could say that at the end of the film, Scottie is finally able to "look a woman in the eye," i.e., to bear the view shown during the film's titles. This abyss of the "lack in the Other" causes the profound "vertigo" that troubles him. A famous passage from Hegel's manuscripts for the *Realphilosophie* of 1805/1806 can be read proleptically as a theoretical comment on *Vertigo*'s titles. The manuscript thematizes the gaze of the other as the silence preceding the spoken word, as the void of the "night of the world" where nightmarish partial objects appear "out of nowhere," like the strange shapes spiraling their way out of Kim Novak's eye.

> The human being is this night, this empty nothing, that contains every-thing in its simplicity—an unending wealth of presentations, images, none of which occurs to him or is present. This night, the inner one of nature that exists here—this pure self—in phantasmagorical presenta-tions . . . here shoots out a bloody head, there a white shape. . . . One catches sight of this night when one looks human beings in the eye—this night that becomes awful suspends the night of the world in an opposition.[11]

The Phallic Anamorphosis

Oral, Anal, Phallic

In *Foreign Correspondent*, there is a short scene that exemplifies what might be called the elementary cell, the basic matrix of the Hitchcockian procedure. In pursuit of the kidnappers of a diplomat, the hero finds himself in an idyllic Dutch countryside with fields of tulips and windmills. All of a sudden he notices that one of the mills rotates against the direction of the wind. Here we have the effect of what Lacan calls the *point de capiton* (the quilting point) in its purest: a perfectly "natural" and "familiar" situation is denatured, becomes "uncanny," loaded with horror and threatening possibilities, as soon as we add to it a small supplementary feature, a detail that "does not belong," that sticks out, is "out of place," does not make any sense within the frame of the idyllic scene. This "pure" signifier without signified stirs the germination of a supplementary, metaphorical meaning for all other elements: the same situations, the same events that, till then, have been perceived as perfectly ordinary acquire an air of strangeness. Suddenly we enter the realm of double meaning, everything seems to contain some hidden meaning that is to be interpreted by the Hitchcockian hero, "the man who knows too much." The horror is thus internalized, it reposes on the *gaze* of him who "knows too much."[1]

Hitchcock is often reproached for his "phallocentrism"; although meant as a criticism, this designation is quite adequate—on condition that we locate the phallic dimension precisely in this supplementary feature that "sticks out." To explain, let us articulate three successive ways of presenting an event onscreen, three ways that correspond to the succession of "oral," "anal," and "phallic" stages in the subject's libidinal economy.

The "oral" stage is, so to speak, the zero degree of filmmaking: we simply shoot an event and as spectators we "devour it with our eyes"; the montage has no function in organizing narrative tensions. Its prototype is the silent, slapstick film. The effect of "naturalness," of direct "rendering of reality," is, of course, false: even at this stage, a certain "choice" is at work, part of reality is enframed and extracted from the space-time continuum. What we see is the result of a certain "manipulation," the succession of shots partakes of a *metonymical* movement. We see only parts, fragments of a never-shown whole, which is why we are already caught in a dialectic of seen and unseen, of the field (enframed by the camera) and its outside, giving rise to the desire to see what is not shown. For all that, we remain captive of the illusion that we witness a homogeneous continuity of action registered by the "neutral" camera.

In the "anal" stage montage enters. It cuts up, fragments, multiplies the action; the illusion of homogeneous continuity is forever lost. Montage can combine elements of a wholly heterogeneous nature and thus create new *metaphorical* meaning having nothing whatsoever to do with the "literal" value of its component parts (compare Eisenstein's concept of "intellectual montage"). The exemplary display of what montage can achieve at the level of traditional narration is, of course, the case of "parallel montage": we show in alternation two interconnected courses of action, transforming the linear deployment of events into the horizontal coexistence of two lines of action, thus creating an additional tension between the two. Let us take, for example, a scene depicting the isolated home of a rich family encircled by a gang of robbers preparing to attack it; the scene gains enormously in effectiveness if we contrast the idyllic everyday life within the house with the threatening preparations of the criminals outside: if we show in alternation the happy family at dinner, the boisterousness of the children, father's benevolent reprimands, etc., and the "sadistic" smile of a robber, another checking his knife or gun, a third already grasping the house's balustrade . . .

In what would the passage to the "phallic" stage consist? In other words, how would *Hitchcock* shoot the same scene? The first thing to remark is that the content of this scene does not lend itself to Hitchcockian suspense insofar as it rests upon a simple counterpoint of idyllic interior and threatening exterior. We should therefore transpose this "flat," horizontal doubling of the action onto a *vertical* level: the menacing horror should not be placed *outside*, *next to* the idyllic interior, but well *within* it, more precisely: *under* it, as its "repressed" underside. Let us imagine, for example, the same happy family dinner shown from the point of view of a rich uncle, their invited guest. In the midst of dinner, the guest (and together with him ourselves, the public) suddenly "sees too much," observes what he was not supposed to notice, some incongruous detail arousing in him the suspicion that the hosts plan to poison him in order to inherit his fortune. Such a "surplus knowledge" has so to speak an abyssal effect on the perspective of the host (and ours with it): the action is in a way *redoubled in itself*, endlessly reflected in itself as in a double mirror play. The most common, everyday events are suddenly loaded with terrifying undertones, "everything becomes suspicious": the kind mistress of the house asking if we feel well after dinner wants perhaps to learn if the poison has already taken effect; the children who run around in innocent joy are perhaps excited because the parents have hinted that they would soon be able to afford a luxurious voyage . . . things appear in a totally different light, although they stay the same.

Such a "vertical" doubling entails a radical change in the libidinal economy: the "true" action is repressed, internalized, subjectivized, i.e., presented in the form of the subject's desires, hallucinations, suspicions, obsessions, feelings of guilt. What we actually see becomes nothing but a deceptive surface beneath which swarms an undergrowth of perverse and obscene implications, the domain of what is *prohibited*. The more we find ourselves in total ambiguity, not knowing where "reality" ends and "hallucination" (i.e., desire) begins, the more menacing this domain appears. Incomparably more threatening than the savage cries of the enemy is his calm and cold gaze, or—to transpose the same inversion into the field of sexuality— incomparably more exciting than the openly provocative brunette is the cold blonde who, as Hitchcock reminds us, knows how to do many things once we find ourselves alone with her in the back seat of a taxi. What is crucial here is this inversion by means of which silence begins to function as the most horrifying menace, where the appearance of a cold indifference promises the most passionate pleasures—in short, where the prohibition against passing over into action opens up the space of a hallucinatory desire that, once set off, cannot be satisfied by any "reality" whatsoever.

But what has this inversion to do with the "phallic" stage? "Phallic" is precisely the detail that "does not fit," that "sticks out" from the idyllic surface scene and denatures it, renders it uncanny. It is the point of *anamorphosis* in a picture: the element that, when viewed straightforwardly, remains a meaningless stain, but which, as soon as we look at the picture from a precisely determined lateral perspective, all of a sudden acquires well-known contours. Lacan's constant point of reference is Holbein's *Ambassadors*[2]: at the bottom of the picture, under the figures of the two ambassadors, a viewer catches sight of an amorphous, extended, "erected" spot. It is only when, on the very threshold of the room in which the picture is exposed, the visitor casts a final lateral glance at it that this spot acquires the contours of a skull, disclosing thus the true meaning of the picture—the nullity of all terrestrial goods, objects of art and knowledge that fill out the rest of the picture. This is the way Lacan defines the phallic signifier, as a "signifier without signified" which, as such, renders possible the effects of the signified: the "phallic" element of a picture is a meaningless stain that "denatures" it, rendering all its constituents "suspicious," and thus opens up the abyss of the search for a meaning—nothing is what it seems to be, everything is to be interpreted, everything is supposed to possess some supplementary meaning. The ground of the established, familiar signification opens up; we find ourselves in a realm of total ambiguity, but this very lack propels us to produce ever new "hidden meanings": it is a driving force of endless compulsion. The oscillation between lack and surplus meaning constitutes the proper dimension of subjectivity. In other words, it is by means of the "phallic" spot that the observed picture is subjectivized: this paradoxical point undermines our position as "neutral," "objective" observer, pinning us to the observed object itself. This is the point at which the observer is already included, inscribed in the observed scene—in a way, it is the point from which the picture itself looks back at us.[3]

THE BLOT AS THE GAZE OF THE OTHER

The finale of *Rear Window* demonstrates perfectly how the fascinating object that drives the interpretive movement is ultimately the gaze itself: this interpretive movement is suspended when Jeff's (James Stewart's) gaze, inspecting what goes on in the mysterious apartment across the yard, meets the gaze of the other (the murderer). At this point, Jeff loses his position as neutral, distant observer and is caught up in the affair, i.e., he becomes part of what he observed. More precisely, he is forced to confront the question of his own desire: what does he really want from this affair? This *Che vuoi?* is literally pronounced during the final confrontation between him and the perplexed murderer who asks him again and again: "Who are you? What do you want from me?" The whole final scene, in which the murderer approaches as Jeff attempts desperately to stop him by the dazzle of flashbulbs, is shot in a remarkable, totally "unrealistic" way. Where we would expect rapid movement, an intense, swift clash, we get hindered, slowed-down, protracted movement, as if the "normal" rhythm of events had undergone a kind of anamorphotic deformation. This renders perfectly the immobilizing, crippling effect the fantasy object has upon the subject: from the interpretive movement induced by the ambiguous register of symptoms, we have passed over to the register of fantasy, the inert presence of which suspends the movement of interpretation.

Where does this power of fascination come from? Why does the neighbor who killed his wife function for the hero as the object of his desire? There is only one answer possible: *the neighbor realizes Jeff's desire*. The hero's desire is to elude the sexual relation at any price, i.e., to get rid of the unfortunate Grace Kelly. What happens on *this side* of the window, in the hero's apartment—the amorous misadventures of Stewart and Kelly—is by no means a simple subplot, an amusing diversion with no bearing on the central motif on the film, but on the contrary, its very center of gravity. Jeff's (and our) fascination with what goes on in the other apartment functions to make Jeff (and us) overlook the crucial importance of what goes on on this side of the window, in the very place from which he looks. *Rear Window* is ultimately the story of a subject who eludes a sexual relation by transforming his effective impotence into power by means of the gaze, by means of secret observation: he "regresses" to an infantile curiosity in order to shirk his responsibility toward the beautiful woman who offers herself to him (the film is at this point very unequivocal—note the scene where Grace Kelly changes into a transparent nightgown). What we encounter here is, again, one of Hitchcock's fundamental "complexes," the interconnection of the gaze and the couple power/impotence. In this respect, *Rear Window* reads like an ironic reversal of Bentham's "Panopticon" as exploited by Foucault. For Bentham, the horrifying efficacy of the Panopticon is due to the fact that the subjects (prisoners, patients, schoolboys, factory workers) can never know for sure if they are actually observed from the all-seeing central control tower—this very uncertainty intensifies the feeling of menace, of the impossibility of escape from the gaze of the Other. In *Rear Window*, the inhabitants of the apartments across the yard are actually observed all the time by Stewart's watchful eye, but far from being terrorized, they simply ignore it and go on with their daily business. On the contrary, it is Stewart himself, the center of the Panopticon, its all-pervasive eye, who is terrorized, constantly looking out the window, anxious not to miss some crucial detail. Why?

The rear window is essentially a fantasy window (the phantasmatic value of the window in painting has already been pointed out by Lacan): incapable of motivating himself to action, Jeff puts off indefinitely the (sexual) act, and what he sees through the window are precisely *fantasy figurations of what could happen to him and Grace Kelly*. They could become happy newlyweds; he could abandon Grace Kelly, who would then become an eccentric artist or lead a desperate, secluded life like Miss Lonely Hearts; they could spend their time together like the ordinary couple with a small dog, yielding to an everyday routine that barely conceals their underlying despair; or, finally, he could *kill* her. In short, the meaning of what the hero perceives beyond the window depends on his actual situation this side of the window: he has just to "look through the window" to see on display a multitude of imaginary solutions to his actual impasse.

Careful attention to the film's soundtrack, especially if we approach *Rear Window* in retrospect, on the basis of Hitchcock's subsequent films, also reveals unmistakably the agency that hinders the hero's "normal" sexual relation: the *maternal superego* embodied in a *voix acousmatique*, a free-floating voice that is not assigned to any bearer. Michel Chion has already drawn attention to a peculiarity of the film's soundtrack, more precisely, its background sounds: we hear a diversity of voices to which we are always able to assign bearers, i.e., emitters. All *except one*, the voice of an unidentified soprano practicing scales and generally emerging just in time to prevent the fulfillment of sexual union between Stewart and Kelly. This mysterious voice does not originate from a person living on the other side of the courtyard, visible through the window, so the camera never shows the singer: the voice remains *acousmatique* and uncannily close to us, as if its origins were within us.[4] It is on account of this feature that *Rear Window* announces *The Man Who Knew Too Much*, *Psycho*, and *The Birds*: this voice transmutes first into the awkwardly pathetic song by means of which Doris Day reaches her kidnapped son (the famous *Que será será*), then into the voice of the dead mother taking possession of Norman Bates, until it finally dissolves into the chaotic croaking of the birds.

THE TRACKING SHOT

The standard Hitchcockian *formal* procedure for isolating the stain, this remainder of the real that "sticks out," is, of course, his famous tracking shot. Its logic can be grasped only if we take into account the whole range of variations to which this procedure is submitted. Let us begin with a scene from *The Birds* in which the hero's mother, peering into a room that has been ravaged by the birds, sees a pajama-clad body with its eyes torn out. The camera first shows us the entire body; we then expect it to track forward slowly into the fascinating detail, the bloody sockets of the missing eyes. But Hitchcock instead gives us an *inversion* of the process we expect: instead of slowing down, he drastically *speeds up*; with two abrupt cuts, each bringing us closer to the subject, he quickly shows us the corpse's head. The subversive effect of these quickly advancing shots is created by the way in which they frustrate us even as they indulge our desire to view the terrifying object more closely: we approach it too quickly, skipping over the "time for understanding," the pause needed to "digest," to integrate the brute perception of the object.

Unlike the usual tracking shot that endows the object-blot with a particular weight by slowing down the "normal" speed and by *deferring* the approach, here the object is "missed" precisely insofar as we approach it precipitously, too quickly. Thus, if the usual tracking shot is obsessional, forcing us to fix on a detail that is made to function as a blot because of the slow motion of the tracking, the precipitous approach to the object reveals its own hysterical basis: we "miss" the object because of the speed, because this object is already empty in itself, hollow—it cannot be evoked other than "too slowly" or "too swiftly," because in its "proper time" it is nothing. So delay and precipitousness are two modes of capturing the object-cause of desire, object small *a*, the "nothingness" of pure seeming. We thereby touch upon the *objectal* dimension of the Hitchcockian "blot" or "stain": the signifying dimension of the blot, its effect of doubling meaning, of conferring on every element of the image a supplementary meaning that makes the interpretative movement work. None of this should blind us to its other aspect, however, that of an inert, opaque object that must drop out or sink for any symbolic reality to emerge. In other words, the Hitchcockian tracking shot that produces the blot in an idyllic picture is achieved as though to illustrate the Lacanian thesis: "The field of reality rests upon the extraction of the object *a*, which nevertheless frames it."[5] Or, to quote Jacques-Alain Miller's precise commentary:

> We understand that the covert setting aside of the object as real conditions the stabilization of reality, as "a bit of reality." But if the object *a* is absent, how can it still frame reality?

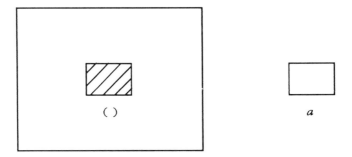

( )   *a*

It is precisely *because* the object *a* is removed from the field of reality that it frames it. If I withdraw from the surface of this picture the piece I represent by a shaded square, I get what we might call a frame: a frame for a hole, but also a frame of the rest of the surface. Such a frame could be created by any window. So object *a* is such a surface fragment, and it is its subtraction from reality that frames it. The subject, as barred subject—as want-of-being—is this hole. As being, it is nothing but the subtracted bit. Whence the equivalency of the subject and object *a*.[6]

We can read Miller's schema as the schema of the Hitchcockian tracking shot: from an overall view of reality, we advance toward the blot that provides it with its frame (the hatched square). The advance of the Hitchcockian tracking shot is reminiscent of the structure of a Moebius strip: by moving away from the side of reality, we find ourselves suddenly alongside the real whose extraction constitutes reality. Here the process inverts the dialectic of montage: there it was a matter of producing, through the discontinuity of the cuts, the continuity of a new signification, of a new diegetic reality, linking the disconnected fragments, whereas here the continual advance itself produces an effect of banking, of radical discontinuity, by showing us the heterogeneous element that must remain an inert, nonsensical "blot" if the rest of the picture is to acquire the consistency of a symbolic reality.

Whence we could return to the succession of "anal" and "phallic" stages in the organization of filmic material: if montage is the "anal" process *par excellence*, the Hitchcockian tracking shot represents the point at which the "anal" economy becomes "phallic." Montage entails the production of a supplementary, metaphorical signification that emerges from the juxtaposition of connected fragments, and, as Lacan emphasized in *The Four Fundamental Concepts of Psycho-Analysis*, metaphor is, in its libidinal economy, an eminently anal process: we give something (shit) to fill out the nothing, that is, to make up for what we do not have.[7] In addition to montage within the framework of traditional narration (as typified by "parallel montage") we have a whole series of "excessive" strategies that are designed to subvert the linear movement of traditional narration (Eisenstein's "intellectual montage," Welles's "inner montage," and the antimontage of Rossellini, who tried to forgo any manipulation of the material and allow for the emergence of the signification from the "miracle" of fortuitous encounters). All such processes are only variations and reversals within the same field of the montage, whereas Hitchcock, with his tracking shots, changes the field itself: in place of montage—the creation of a new metaphoric continuity by the combination of discontinuous fragments—he introduces a radical discontinuity, the shifting from reality to the real, produced by the very continuous movement of the tracking shot. That is, the tracking movement can be described as a moving from an overall view of reality to its point of anamorphosis. To return to

Holbein's *Ambassadors*, the Hitchcockian tracking shot would advance from the total area of the picture toward the erected, "phallic" element in the background that must fall away, remain simply a demented stain—the skull, the inert fantasy-object as the "impossible" equivalent of the subject itself ($8\Diamond a$), and it is no accident that we find this same object in several instances in Hitchcock's own work (*Under Capricorn, Psycho*). In Hitchcock this real object, the blot, the terminal point of the tracking shot, can assume two principal forms: either the gaze of the other insofar as our position as spectator is already inscribed within the film—i.e., the point from which the picture itself gazes at us (the eye sockets in the skull, not to mention the most celebrated of Hitchcock's tracking shots, the shot into the drummer's blinking eyes in *Young and Innocent*)—or the Hitchcockian object *par excellence*, the nonspecularizable object of exchange, the "piece of the real" that circulates from one subject to another, embodying and guaranteeing the structural network of symbolic exchanges between them (the most famous example: the long tracking shot in *Notorious*, from the overall view of the entrance hall down to the key in Ingrid Bergman's hand).

We can categorize Hitchcock's tracking shots, however, without reference to the nature of their terminal object, that is, based on variations in the formal process itself. In addition to the zero degree of tracking (which moves from the overall view of reality to its real point of anamorphosis), we have at least three other variants in Hitchcock:

• The precipitous, "hystericized" tracking shot: see the example from *The Birds* analyzed above, in which the camera draws into the blot too quickly, through jump cuts.

• The reverse tracking shot, which begins at the uncanny detail and pulls back to the overall view of reality: witness the long shot in *Shadow of a Doubt* that starts with the hand of Teresa Wright holding the ring given her by her murdering uncle, and pulls back and up to the overall view of the library reading room in which she appears as nothing but a small dot in the center of the frame; or the famous reverse tracking shot in *Frenzy*.[8]

• Lastly, the paradox of the "immobile tracking shot," in which the camera does not move: the shift from reality to the real is accomplished by the intrusion into the frame of a heterogeneous object. For an example, we can return to *The Birds*, in which such a shift is achieved during one long, fixed shot. A fire caused by a cigarette butt dropped into some gasoline breaks out in the small town threatened by the birds. After a series of short and "dynamic" close-ups and medium shots that draw us immediately into the action, the camera pulls back and up and we are given an overall shot of the entire town taken from high above. In the first instant we read this overall shot as an "objective," "epic" panorama shot, separating us from the immediate drama going on down below and enabling us to disengage ourselves from the action. This distancing at first produces a certain "pacifying" effect; it allows us to view the action from what might be called a "metalinguistic" distance. Then, suddenly, a bird enters the frame from the right, as if coming from behind the camera and thus from behind our own backs, and then three birds, and finally an entire flock. The same shot takes on a totally different aspect, it undergoes a radical *subjectivization*: the camera's elevated eye ceases to be that of a netural, "objective" onlooker gazing down upon a panoramic landscape and suddenly becomes the subjective and threatening gaze of the birds as they zero in on their prey.[9]

The Maternal Superego

WHY DO THE BIRDS ATTACK?
What we must bear in mind is the libidinal content of this Hitchcockian stain: although its logic is phallic, it announces an agency that perturbs and hinders the rule of the Name-of-the-Father—in other words, the stain materializes the *maternal superego*. To prove it, let us return to the last of the above-mentioned cases: that of *The Birds*. Why do they attack? Robin Wood suggests three possible readings of this inexplicable, "irrational" act by which the idyllic, daily life of a small northern California town is derailed: "cosmological," "ecological," "familial."[10]

According to the first, "cosmological" reading, the attack of the birds can be viewed as embodying Hitchcock's vision of the universe, of the (human) cosmos as system—peaceful on the surface, ordinary in its course—that can be upset at any time, that can be thrown into chaos by the intervention of pure chance. Its order is always deceiving; at any moment some ineffable terror can emerge, some traumatic real erupt to disturb the symbolic circuit. Such a reading can be supported by references to many other Hitchcock films, including the most somber of them, *The Wrong Man*, in which the mistaken identification of the hero as a thief, which happens purely by chance, turns his daily life into a hell of humiliation and costs his wife her sanity—the entering into play of the theological dimension in Hitchcock's work, the vision of a cruel, arbitrary, and impenetrable God who can bring down catastrophe at any moment.

For the second, "ecological" reading, the film's title could have been *Birds of the World, Unite!*: in this reading, the birds function as a condensation of exploited nature that finally rises up against man's heedless exploitation. In support of this interpretation, we can cite the fact that Hitchcock selected his attacking birds almost exclusively from species known for their gentle, nonaggressive nature: sparrows, seagulls, a few crows.

The third reading sees the key to the film in the intersubjective relations between the main characters (Melanie, Mitch, and his mother), which are far from being merely an insignificant sideline to the "true" plot, the attack of the birds: the attacking birds only "embody" a fundamental discord, a disturbance, a derailment in those relations. The pertinence of this interpretation emerges if we consider *The Birds* within the context of Hitchcock's earlier (and later) films; in other words, to play on one of Lacan's homophonies, if we are to take the films seriously, we can only do so if we take them serially.[11]

In writing of Poe's "The Purloined Letter," Lacan makes reference to a game of logic: we take a random series of 0s and 1s—100101100, for example—and as soon as the series is articulated into linked triads (100, 001, 010, etc.), rules of succession will emerge (a triad with 0 at the end cannot be followed by a triad that has 1 as its middle term, and so on).[12] The same is true of Hitchcock's films: if we consider them as a whole we have an accidental, random series, but as soon as we separate them into linked triads (and exclude those films that are not part of the "Hitchcockian universe," the "exceptions," the results of various compromises), each triad can then be seen to be linked by some theme, some common structuring principle. For example, take the following five films: *The Wrong Man*, *Vertigo*, *North by Northwest*, *Psycho*, and *The Birds*: no single theme can be found to link all the films in such a series, yet such themes can be found if we consider them in groups of three. The first triad concerns "false identity": in *The Wrong Man*, the hero is wrongly identified as the burglar; in *Vertigo* the hero is mistaken about the identity of the false Madeleine; in *North by Northwest* Soviet spies mistakenly identify the film's hero as the mysterious CIA agent "George Kaplan." As for the great trilogy *Vertigo*, *North by Northwest*, and *Psycho*, it is very tempting to regard these three key Hitchcock films as the articulation of three different versions of filling the gap in the Other. Their formal problem is the same: the relationship between a lack and a factor (a person) that tries to compensate for it. In *Vertigo*, the hero attempts to compensate for the absence of the woman he loves, an apparent suicide, on a level that is literally *imaginary*: he tries, by means of dress, hairstyle, and so forth, to recreate the image of the lost woman. In *North by Northwest*, we are on the *symbolic* level: we are dealing with an empty name, the name of a nonexistent person ("Kaplan"), a signifier without a bearer, which becomes attached to the hero out of sheer chance. In *Psycho*, finally, we reach the level of the *real*: Norman Bates, who dresses in his mother's clothes, speaks with her voice, etc., wants neither to resuscitate her image nor act in her name; he wants to take her place in the real—evidence of a psychotic state.

If the middle triad, therefore, is that of the "empty place," the final one is in its turn united around the motif of the *maternal superego*: the heroes of these three films are fatherless, they have a mother who is "strong," who is "possessive," who disturbs the "normal" sexual relationship. At the very beginning of *North by Northwest* the film's hero, Roger Thornhill (Cary Grant), is shown with his scornful, mocking mother, and it is not difficult to guess why he has been four times divorced; in *Psycho*, Norman Bates (Anthony Perkins) is directly controlled by the voice of his dead mother, which instructs him to kill any woman to whom he is sexually attracted; in the case of the mother of Mitch Brenner (Rod Taylor), hero of *The Birds*, mocking disdain is replaced by a zealous concern for her son's fate, a concern that is perhaps even more effective in blocking any lasting relationship he might have with a woman.

There is another trait common to these three films: from one film to the next, the figure of a threat in the shape of birds assumes greater prominence. In *North by Northwest* we have what is perhaps the most famous Hitchcockian scene, the attack by the plane—a steel bird—that pursues the hero across a flat, sun-baked landscape; in *Psycho*, Norman's room is filled with stuffed mounted birds, and even the body of his mummified mother reminds us of a stuffed bird; in *The Birds*, after the (metaphorical) steel bird and the (metonymic) stuffed birds, we finally have actual live birds attacking the town.

The decisive thing is to perceive the link between the two traits: the terrifying figure of the birds is actually the embodiment in the real of a discord, an unresolved tension in intersubjective relations. In the film, the birds are like the plague in Oedipus's Thebes: they are the incarnation of a fundamental disorder in family relationships—the father is absent, the paternal function (the function of pacifying law, the Name-of-the-Father) is suspended and that vacuum is filled by the "irrational" maternal superego, arbitrary, wicked, blocking "normal" sexual relationship (only possible under the sign of the paternal metaphor). The dead end *The Birds* is really about is, of course, that of the modern American family: the deficient paternal ego-ideal makes the law "regress" toward a ferocious maternal superego, affecting sexual enjoyment—the decisive trait of the libidinal structure of "pathological narcissism": "Their unconscious impressions of the mother are so overblown and so heavily influenced by aggressive impulses, and the quality of her care is so little attuned to the child's needs, that in the child's fantasies the mother appears as a devouring bird."[13]

From the Oedipal Journey to the "Pathological Narcissist"

How should we locate this figuration of the maternal superego in the totality of Hitchcock's work? The three main stages of Hitchcock's career can be conceived precisely as three variations on the theme of the impossibility of the sexual relationship. Let us begin with the first Hitchcockian classic, *The Thirty-Nine Steps*: all the animated action of the film should not deceive us for a minute—its function is ultimately just to put the love couple to the test and thus render possible their final reunion. It is on account of this feature that *The Thirty-Nine Steps* starts the series of Hitchcock's English films of the second half of the 1930s, all of which, with the exception of the last (*Jamaica Inn*), relate the same story of the *initiation of an amorous couple*. They are all stories of a couple tied (sometimes literally: note the role of handcuffs in *The Thirty-Nine Steps*) by accident and then maturing through a series of ordeals. All these films are thus actually variations on the fundamental motif of the bourgeois ideology of marriage, gaining its first and perhaps noblest expression in Mozart's *Magic Flute*. The parallel could be here expanded to details: the mysterious woman who charges the hero with his mission (the stranger killed in Hannay's apartment in *The Thirty-Nine Steps*; the nice old lady who vanishes in the film of the same title), is she not a kind of reincarnation of the "Queen of the Night"? The black Monostatos, is he not reincarnated in the murderous drummer with blackened face in *Young and Innocent*? In *The Lady Vanishes*, the hero attracts the attention of his future love by playing what?—a flute, of course!

The innocence lost on this voyage of initiation is best presented in the remarkable figure of Mr. Memory, whose number in the music hall opens and closes the film. He is a man who "remembers everything," a personification of pure automatism and, at the same time, the absolute ethic of the signifier (in the film's final scene, he answers Hannay's question "What are 'the thirty-nine steps'?", although he knows the answer could cost him his life—he is simply obliged to honor his public engagement, to answer any question whatsoever). There is something of the fairy tale in this figure of a Good Dwarf who must die in order that the liaison of the amorous couple finally be established. Mr. Memory embodies a pure, asexual gapless knowledge, a signifying chain that works absolutely automatically, without any traumatic stumbling block hindering its course. What we must be careful about is the precise moment of his death: he dies after answering the question "What are 'the thirty-nine steps'?", i.e., after revealing the McGuffin, the secret propelling the story. By disclosing it to the public in the music hall (which stands here for the big Other of common opinion), he delivers Hannay from the awkward position of "persecuted persecutor." The two circles (that of the police chasing Hannay and that of Hannay himself in pursuit of the real culprit) rejoin, Hannay is exonerated in the eyes of the big Other, and the real culprits are unmasked. At this point, the story could end since it was sustained solely by this intermediary state, by Hannay's ambiguous position vis-a-vis the big Other: guilty in the eyes of the big Other, he is at the same time on the track of the real culprits.

It is this position of the "persecuted persecutor" that already displays the motif of the "transference of guilt": Hannay is falsely accused, the guilt is transferred onto him—but whose guilt is it? The guilt of the *obscene, "anal" father* personified by the mysterious leader of the spy network. At the film's end, we witness *two* consecutive deaths: first the leader of the spy ring kills Mr. Memory, then the police, this instrument of the big Other, shoot down the leader, who falls from his theater box onto the podium (this is an exemplary place of denouement in Hitchcock's films: *Murder*, *Stage Fright*, *I Confess*). Mr. Memory and the leader of the spy ring represent the two sides of the same pre-Oedipal conjunction: the Good Dwarf with his gapless undivided knowledge, and the mean "anal father," the master who pulls the strings of this knowledge-automaton, a father who exhibits in an obscene way his shortened little finger—an ironic allusion to his castration. (We encounter a homologous split in Robert Rossen's *The Hustler*, in the relationship between the professional billiard player, an incarnation of the pure ethic of the game [Jackie Gleason], and his corrupt boss [George C. Scott].) The story begins with an act of "interpellation" that subjectivizes the hero, i.e., it constitutes him as desiring by evoking the McGuffin, the object-cause of his desire (the message of the "Queen of the Night," the mysterious stranger who is slaughtered in Hannay's apartment). The Oedipal voyage in pursuit of the father, which constitutes the bulk of the film, ends with the "anal" father's death. By means of his death, he can assume his place as metaphor, as the Name-of-the-Father, thus rendering possible the amorous couple's final reunion, their "normal" sexual relation which, according to Lacan, can take place only under the sign of the paternal metaphor.

In addition to Hannay and Pamela in *The Thirty-Nine Steps*, couples tied by chance and reunited through ordeal are Ashenden and Elsa in *The Secret Agent*, Robert and Erica in *Young and Innocent*, Gilbert and Iris in *The Lady Vanishes*—with the notable exception of *Sabotage*, where the triangle of Sylvia, her criminal husband Verloc, and the detective Ted foreshadows the conjuncture characteristic of Hitchcock's next stage (the Selznick period). Here, the story is, as a rule, narrated from the point of view of a woman divided between two men, the elderly figure of a villain (her father or her aged husband, embodying one of the typical Hitchcockian figures, that of a villain who is aware of the evil in himself and who strives after his own

destruction) and the younger, somewhat insipid "good guy" whom she chooses at
the end.[14] In addition to Sylvia, Verloc, and Ted in *Sabotage*, the main cases of such
triangles are Carol Fisher, divided between loyalty to her pro-Nazi father and love
for the young American journalist, in *Foreign Correspondent*; Charlie, divided
between her murderous uncle of the same name and the detective Jack, in *Shadow
of a Doubt*; and, of course, Alicia, divided between her aged husband Sebastian and
Devlin, in *Notorious*. (The notable exception here is *Under Capricorn*, where the
heroine resists the charm of a young seducer and returns to her aged, criminal husband after confessing that the crime her husband was convicted for was her own.)
The third stage again shifts the accent to the male hero to whom the maternal superego blocks access, thus prohibiting a "normal" sexual relation (from Bruno in
Strangers on a Train to the "necktie murderer" in *Frenzy*).

Where should we look for the wider frame of reference enabling us to confer
a kind of theoretical consistency on this succession of the three forms of (the impossibility of) sexual relationship? Here, we are tempted to venture a somewhat quick
"sociological" answer by invoking the three successive forms of the libidinal structure of the subject exhibited in capitalist society during the past century: the "autonomous" individual of the Protestant ethic, the heteronomous "organization man,"
and the type gaining predominance today, the "pathological narcissist." The crucial
thing to emphasize here is that the so-called "decline of the Protestant ethic" and the
appearance of the "organization man," i.e., the replacement of the ethic of individual
responsibility by the ethic of the heteronomous individual, oriented toward others,
leaves intact the underlying frame of the ego-ideal. It is merely its contents that
change: the ego-ideal becomes "externalized" as the expectations of the social group
to which the individual belongs. The source of moral satisfaction is no longer the
feeling that we resisted the pressure of our milieu and remained true to ourselves
(i.e., to our paternal ego-ideal), but rather the feeling of loyalty to the group. The
subject looks at himself through the eyes of the group, he strives to merit its love and
esteem.

The third stage, the arrival of the "pathological narcissist," breaks precisely with
this underlying frame of the ego-ideal common to the first two forms. Instead of the
integration of a symbolic *law*, we have a multitude of *rules* to follow—rules of
accommodation telling us "how to succeed." The narcissistic subject knows only the
"rules of the (social) game" enabling him to manipulate others; social relations constitute for him a playing field in which he assumes "roles," not proper symbolic man-
dates; he stays clear of any kind of binding commitment that would imply a proper
symbolic identification. He is a radical *conformist* who paradoxically experiences

himself as an *outlaw*. All this is, of course, already a commonplace of social psychology; what usually goes unnoticed, however, is that this disintegration of the ego-ideal entails the installation of a "maternal" superego that does not prohibit enjoyment but, on the contrary, imposes it and punishes "social failure" in a far more cruel and severe way, through an unbearable and self-destructive anxiety. All the babble about the "decline of paternal authority" merely conceals the resurgence of this incomparably more oppressive agency. Today's "permissive" society is certainly not less "repressive" than the epoch of the "organization man," that obsessive servant of the bureaucratic institution; the sole difference lies in the fact that in a "society that demands submission to the rules of social intercourse but refuses to ground those rules in a code of moral conduct,"[15] i.e., in the ego-ideal, the social demand assumes the form of a harsh, punitive superego.

We could also approach "pathological narcissism" on the basis of Saul Kripke's criticism of the theory of descriptions, i.e., from his premise that the meaning of a name (proper or of a natural kind) can never be reduced to a set of descriptive features that characterize the object denoted by it. The name always functions as a "rigid designator," referring to the same object even if all properties contained in its meaning prove false.[16] Needless to say, the Kripkian notion of the "rigid designator" overlaps perfectly with the Lacanian notion of the "master signifier," i.e., of a signifier that does not denote some positive property of the object but establishes, by means of its own act of enunciation, a new intersubjective relation between speaker and hearer. If, for example, I tell somebody "You are my master!", I confer upon him a certain symbolic "mandate" that is not contained in the set of his positive properties but results from the very performative force of my utterance, and I create thereby a new symbolic reality, that of a master-disciple relationship between the two of us, within which each of us assumes a certain commitment. The paradox of the "pathological narcissist" is, however, that *for him, language does indeed function according to the theory of descriptions*: the meaning of words is reduced to the positive features of the denoted object, above all those that concern his narcissistic interests. Let us exemplify this apropos of the eternally tedious feminine question: "Why do you love me?" In love proper, this question is, of course, unanswerable (which is why women ask it in the first place), i.e., the only appropriate answer is "Because there is something in you more than yourself, some indefinite X that attracts me, but that cannot be pinned down to any positive quality." In other words, if we answer it with a catalogue of positive properties ("I love you because of the shape of your breasts, because of the way you smile"), this is at best a mocking imitation of love proper. The "pathological narcissist" is, on the other hand, somebody who *is* able to answer such a question by enumerating a definite list of properties: for him, the idea that love is a commitment transcending an attachment to a series of qualities that could gratify his wishes is simply beyond comprehension.[17] And the way to hystericize the "pathological narcissist" is precisely to force upon him some symbolic mandate that cannot be grounded in its properties. Such a confrontation brings about the hysterical question, "Why am I what you are saying that I am?" Think of Roger O. Thornhill in Hitchcock's *North by Northwest*, a pure "pathological narcissist" if ever there was one, who all of a sudden, without any apparent reason, finds himself pinned to the signifier "Kaplan"; the shock of this encounter derails his narcissistic economy and opens up to him the road of gradual access to "normal" sexual relations under the sign of the Name-of-the-Father (which is why *North by Northwest* is a variation of the formula of *The Thirty-Nine Steps*).[18]

We can now see how the three versions of the impossibility of sexual relationship in Hitchcock's films refer to these three types of libidinal economy. The couple's initiating voyage, with its obstacles stirring the desire of reunification, is firmly grounded in the classical ideology of the "autonomous" subject strengthened through ordeal; the resigned paternal figure of Hitchcock's next stage evokes the decline of this "autonomous" subject to whom is opposed the victorious, insipid "heteronomous" hero; and, finally, it is not difficult to recognize in the typical Hitchcockian hero of the 1950s and '60s the features of the "pathological narcissist" dominated by the obscene figure of the maternal superego. Hitchcock is thus staging again and again the vicissitudes of the family in late-capitalist society; the real "secret" of his films is ultimately always the family secret, its tenebrous reverse.

A MENTAL EXPERIMENT: *THE BIRDS* WITHOUT BIRDS

Although Hitchcock's birds do give body to the agency of the maternal superego, the essential thing is nevertheless *not* to seize upon the link between the two traits we have noted—the appearance of the ferocious assailant birds, the blockage of "normal" sexual relations by the intervention of the maternal superego—as a sign relationship, as a correlative between a "symbol" and its "signification": the birds do not "signify" the maternal superego, they do not "symbolize" blocked sexual relations, the "possessive" mother, and so on; they are, rather, the making present in the real, the objectivization, the incarnation of the fact that, on the symbolizing level, something "has not worked out," in short, the objectivization-positivization of a *failed* symbolization. In the terrifying presence of the attacking birds, a certain lack, a certain failure assumes positive existence. At first glance, this distinction may appear factitious, vague; that is why we shall try to explicate it by means of a fairly elementary test question: how might the film have been constructed if the birds were to function *in fact* as the "symbol" of blocked sexual relations?

The answer is simple: first, we must imagine *The Birds* as a film *without birds*. We would then have a typically American drama about a family in which the son goes from one woman to another because he is unable to free himself from the pressure exerted by a possessive mother, a drama similar to dozens of others that have appeared on American stages and screens, particularly in the 1950s: the tragedy of a son playing with the chaos of his sexual life for what was in those days referred to as the mother's inability to "live her own life," to "expend her vital energy," and the mother's emotional breakdown when some woman finally manages to take away her son, all seasoned with a touch of "psychoanalytic" salt à la Eugene O'Neill or Tennessee Williams and acted, if possible, in a psychologistic, Actors' Studio style—the common ground of the American theater at midcentury.

Next, in such a drama we must imagine the appearance from time to time, particularly at crucial moments of emotional intrigue (the son's first encounter with his future wife, the mother's breakdown, etc.), of birds—in the background, as part of the ambience: the opening scene (the meeting of Mitch and Melanie in the pet shop, the purchase of the lovebirds) could perhaps remain as it is; and, after the emotion-charged scene of conflict between mother and son, when the sorrowing mother withdraws to the seacoast, we might hear the cawing of birds. In such a film, the birds, even though or, rather, *because* they do not play a direct role in the development of the story, would be "symbols," they would "symbolize" the tragic necessity of the mother's renunciation, her helplessness, or whatever—and everyone would know what the birds signified, everyone would clearly recognize that the film was depicting an emotional drama of a son facing up to a possessive mother who is trying to transfer onto him the price of her own failure, and the "symbolic" role of the birds would be indicated by the title, which would remain unchanged: *The Birds*.

Now, what did Hitchcock do? In his film, the birds are not "symbols" at all, they play a direct part in the story as something inexplicable, as something outside the rational chain of events, as a *lawless* impossible real. The diegetic action of the film is so influenced by the birds that their massive presence completely overshadows the domestic drama: the drama—literally—*loses its significance*. The "spontaneous" spectator does not perceive *The Birds* as a domestic family drama in which the role of the birds is "symbolic" of intersubjective relationships and tensions; the accent is put totally on the traumatic attacks by the birds, and, within that framework, the emotional intrigue is mere pretext, part of the undifferentiated tissue of everyday incidents of which the first half of the film is made up, so that, against that background, the weird, inexplicable fury of the birds can be made to stand out even more strongly. Thus the birds, far from functioning as a "symbol" whose "signification" can be detected, on the contrary *block, mask,* by their massive presence, the film's "signification," their function being to make us *forget,* during their vertiginous and dazzling attacks, with what, in the end, we are dealing: the triangle of a mother, her son, and the woman he loves. If the "spontaneous" spectator had been supposed to perceive the film's "signification" easily, then the birds should quite simply have been *left out.*

There is a key detail that supports our reading; at the very end of the film, Mitch's mother "accepts" Melanie as her son's wife, gives her consent, and abandons her superego role (as indicated by the fleeting smile she and Melanie exchange in the car)—and that is why, at that moment, they are all able to leave the property that is being threatened by the birds: the birds are no longer needed, their role is finished. The end of the film—the last shot of the car driving away surrounded by hordes of calm birds—is for that reason wholly coherent and not at all the result of some kind of "compromise"; the fact that Hitchcock himself spread the rumor that he would have preferred another ending (the car arriving at a Golden Gate Bridge totally blackened by the birds perched on it) and was forced to accede to studio pressure, is just another of the many myths fomented by the director, who was at pains to dissimulate what was really at stake in his work.

It is clear, therefore, why *The Birds*—according to François Regnault[19]—is the film that closes the Hitchcockian system: the birds, the ultimate incarnation in Hitchcock of the Bad Object, are the counterpart of the reign of maternal law, and it is precisely this conjunction of the Bad Object of fascination and the maternal law that defines the kernel of the Hitchcockian fantasy.

The Perverse Short Circuit

SADIST AS OBJECT

Michael Mann's *Manhunter* is a movie about a police detective famous for his ability to enter intuitively, through his "sixth sense," the mind of perverse, sadistic murderers. His task is to detect a particularly cruel mass murderer who slaughtered a series of quiet, provincial families. The detective reruns again and again super-8 home movies shot by each of the slaughtered families in order to arrive at the *trait unaire,* the feature common to all of them that attracted the murderer and thus directed his choice. But all his efforts are in vain as long as he looks for this common feature on the level of content, i.e., in the families themselves. He finds the key to the identity of the murderer when a certain inconsistency strikes his eye. The investigation at the scene of the last crime shows that to enter the house, to break open the back door, the murderer used a kind of tool that was inappropriate, even unnecessary. The old back door had been replaced a few weeks before the crime with a new type of door. To break open the new door, another kind of tool would have been far more appropriate. So how did the murderer get this piece of wrong or, more precisely, out-of-date information? The old back door could be seen clearly in scenes from a super-8 home movie. The only thing common to all the slaughtered families is then *the home movies themselves,* i.e., the murderer had to have had access to their private movies, there is no other link connecting them. Because these movies are private, the only possible link between them is the laboratory where they were developed. A quick check confirms that all the movies were developed by the same laboratory, and the murderer is soon identified as one of the workers in the lab. Wherein lies the theoretical interest of this denouement? The detective searches for a common feature that will enable him to get at the murderer in the content of the home movies, thus overlooking the form itself, i.e., the crucial fact that he is all the

time viewing a series of home movies. The decisive turn takes place when he
becomes aware that through the very screening of the home movies, *he is already
identified with the murderer,* that his obsessive gaze, surveying every detail of the
scenery, coincides with the gaze of the murderer. The identification is on the level
of the gaze, not on the level of the content. There is something extremely unpleasant
and obscene in this experience of our gaze as already the gaze of the other. Why?
The Lacanian answer is that such a coincidence of gazes defines the position of the
pervert. (Herein consists, according to Lacan, the difference between the "feminine"
and the "masculine" mystic, between, let us say, Saint Theresa and Jacob Boehme.
The "feminine" mystic implies a nonphallic, "not-all" enjoyment, whereas the "masculine" mystic consists precisely in such an overlap of gazes by which he experiences
the fact that his intuition of God is the view by means of which God looks at Himself:
"To confuse his contemplative eye with the eye with which God is looking at him
must surely partake of perverse *jouissance.*")[1]

This coincidence of the subject's view with the gaze of the big Other, which
defines perversion, enables us to conceptualize one of the fundamental features of
the ideological functioning of "totalitarianism": if the perversion of "male" mysticism
consists in the fact that the view by means of which the subject contemplates God is
at the same time the gaze by means of which God contemplates Himself, then the
perversion of Stalinist Communism consists in the fact that the view by means of
which the Party looks at history coincides immediately with history's gaze upon itself.
To use good old Stalinist jargon, today already half-forgotten, Communists act immediately in the name of "objective laws of historical progress"; it is history itself, its
necessity, that speaks through their mouths.

Which is why the elementary formula of Sadean perversion, as formulated by
Lacan in "Kant with Sade," is so convenient to designate the subjective position of
Stalinist Communism. According to Lacan, the Sadean subject tries to elude his constitutive split, his division, by transferring it onto his other (the victim) and by identifying himself with the object, i.e., by occupying the position of the object-
instrument of the will-to-enjoy (*volonté-de-jouir*)—which is not his own will but that
of the big Other, who assumes the form of the "Supreme Evil Being." Herein consists
Lacan's break with the usual notion of "sadism": according to the latter, the "sadist
pervert" assumes the position of an absolute subject usurping the right to enjoy, without restraint, the body of the other, reducing him/her to an object-instrument for the
satisfaction of his own will. Lacan argues, however, that it is the "sadist" himself who
is in the position of the object-instrument, the executor of some radically hetero-

geneous will, while the split subject is precisely his other (the victim). The pervert does not pursue his activity for his own pleasure, but for the enjoyment of the Other—he finds enjoyment precisely in this instrumentalization, in working for the enjoyment of the Other.[2] It should then be clear why in Lacan, the matheme of perversion is written as the inversion of the matheme of fantasy: $a \diamond \mathcal{S}$.[3] And it should also be clear why this matheme designates at the same time the subjective position of Stalinist Communist: he torments his victim (the masses, the "ordinary" people) infinitely, but he does this as an instrument of the big Other ("the objective laws of history," "the necessity of historical progress") behind which it is not difficult to recognize the Sadean figure of the Supreme Evil Being. The case of Stalinism neatly exemplifies why, in perversion, the other (the victim) is split: the Stalinist Communist torments people, but he does so as their own faithful servant, in their own name, as an executor of their own will (their own "true, objective interests").[4]

The final irony of *Manhunter* would, then, be the following: confronted with a perverse-sadistic content, the detective is able to arrive at a solution only by taking into account the fact that his very procedure is, on a formal level, already "perverse." It implies a coincidence between his gaze and the gaze of the other (the murderer). And it is this overlap, this coincidence of our view with the gaze of the other, that helps us to understand pornography.

As it is ordinarily understood, *pornography* is the genre supposed to "reveal all there is to reveal," to hide nothing, to register "all" and offer it to our view. It is nevertheless precisely in pornographic cinema that the "substance of enjoyment" perceived by the view from aside is *radically lost*—why? Let us recall the antinomic relation of gaze and eye as articulated by Lacan in *Seminar XI*: the eye viewing the object is on the side of the subject, while the gaze is on the side of the object. When I look at an object, the object is always already gazing at me, and from a point at which I cannot see it:

> In the scopic field, everything is articulated between two terms that act in an antinomic way—on the side of things, there is the gaze, that is to say, things look at me, and yet I see them. This is how one should understand those words, so strongly stressed, in the Gospel, *They have eyes that they might not see.* That they might not see what? Precisely, that things are looking at them.[5]

This antinomy of gaze and view is lost in pornography—why? Because pornography is inherently *perverse*; its perverse character lies not in the obvious fact that it "goes all the way and shows us all the dirty details"; its perversity is, rather, to be conceived in a strictly formal way. In pornography, the spectator is forced a priori to occupy a perverse position. Instead of being on the side of the viewed object, the gaze falls into ourselves, the spectators, which is why the image we see on the screen contains no spot, no sublime-mysterious point from which it gazes at us. It is only we who gaze stupidly at the image that "reveals all." Contrary to the commonplace according to which, in pornography, the other (the person shown on the screen) is degraded to an object of our voyeuristic pleasure, we must stress that it is the spectator himself who effectively occupies the position of the object. The real subjects are the actors on the screen trying to rouse us sexually, while we, the spectators, are reduced to a paralyzed object-gaze.[6]

Pornography thus misses, reduces the point of the object-gaze in the other. This miss has precisely the form of a missed, failed encounter. That is to say, in a "normal," nonpornographic film, a love scene is always built around a certain insurmountable limit; "all cannot be shown." At a certain point the image is blurred, the camera moves off, the scene is interrupted, we never directly see "that" (the penetration of sexual organs, etc.). In contrast to this limit of representability defining the "normal" love story or melodrama, pornography goes beyond, it "shows everything." The paradox is, however, that by trespassing the limit, it always *goes too far,* i.e., it *misses* what remains concealed in a "normal," nonpornographic love scene. To refer again to the phrase from Brecht's *Threepenny Opera*: if you run too fast after happiness, you may overtake it and happiness may stay behind. If we proceed too hastily "to the point," if we show "the thing itself," we necessarily lose what we were after. The effect is extremely vulgar and depressing (as can be confirmed by anyone who has watched any hard-core movies). Pornography is thus just another variation on the paradox of Achilles and the tortoise that, according to Lacan, defines the relation of the subject to the object of his desire. Naturally, Achilles can easily outdistance the tortoise and leave it behind, but the point is that he cannot come up alongside it, he cannot rejoin it. The subject is always too slow or too quick, it can never keep pace with the object of its desire. The unattainable/forbidden object approached but never reached by the "normal" love story—the sexual act—exists only as concealed, indicated, "faked." As soon as we "show it," its charm is dispelled, we have "gone too far." Instead of the sublime Thing, we are stuck with vulgar, groaning fornication.

The consequence of this is that harmony, congruence between the filmic narrative (the unfolding of the story) and the immediate display of the sexual act, is structurally impossible: if we choose one, we necessarily lose the other. In other words, if we want to have a love story that "takes," that moves us, we must not "go all the way" and "show it all" (the details of the sexual act), because as soon as we "show it all," the story is no longer "taken seriously" and starts to function only as a pretext for introducing acts of copulation. We can detect this gap via a kind of "knowledge in the real," which determines the way actors behave in different film genres. The characters included in the diegetic reality always react as if they knew in which genre of film they were. If, for example, a door creaks in a horror film, the actor will react by turning his head anxiously toward it; if a door creaks in a family comedy, the same actor will shout at his small child not to sneak around the apartment. The same is true to an even greater extent of the "porno" film: before we pass to the sexual activity, we need a short introduction—normally, a stupid plot serving as pretext for the actors to begin copulation (the housewife calls in a plumber, a new secretary reports to the manager, etc.) The point is that even in the manner in which they enact this introductory plot, the actors divulge that this is for them only a stupid although necessary formality that has to be gotten over with as quickly as possible so as to begin tackling the "real thing."[7]

The fantasy ideal of a perfect work of pornography would be precisely to preserve this impossible harmony, the balance between narration and explicit depiction of the sexual act, i.e., to avoid the necessary *vel* that condemns us to lose one of the two poles. Let us take an old-fashioned, nostalgic melodrama like *Out of Africa,* and let us assume that the film is precisely the one shown in cinemas, except for an additional ten minutes. When Robert Redford and Meryl Streep have their first love encounter, the scene—in this slightly longer version of the film—is not interrupted, the camera "shows it all," details of their aroused sexual organs, penetration, orgasm, etc. Then, after the act, the story goes on as usual, we return to the film we all know. The problem is that such a movie is structurally impossible. Even if it were to be shot, it simply "would not function"; the additional ten minutes would derail us, for the rest of the movie we would be unable to regain our balance and follow the narration with the usual disavowed belief in the diegetic reality. The sexual act would function as an intrusion of the real undermining the consistency of this diegetic reality.

NOSTALGIA

In pornography, the gaze *qua* object falls thus onto the subject-spectator, causing an effect of depressing desublimation. Which is why, to extract the gaze-object in its pure, formal status, we have to turn to pornography's opposite pole: nostalgia.

Let us take what is probably today the most notorious case of nostalgic fascination in the domain of cinema: the American *film noir* of the 1940s. What, precisely, is so fascinating about this genre? It is clear that we can no longer identify with it. The most dramatic scenes from *Casablanca, Murder, My Sweet,* or *Out of the Past* provoke laughter today among spectators, but nevertheless, far from posing a threat to the genre's power of fascination, this kind of distance is its very condition. That is to say, what fascinates us is precisely a certain gaze, the gaze of the "other," of the hypothetical, mythic spectator from the '40s who was supposedly still able to identify immediately with the universe of *film noir.* What we really see, when we watch a *film noir,* is this gaze of the other: we are fascinated by the gaze of the mythic "naive" spectator, the one who was "still able to take it seriously," in other words, the one who "believes in it" for us, in place of us. For that reason, our relation to a *film noir* is always divided, split between fascination and ironic distance: ironic distance toward its diegetic reality, fascination with the gaze.

This gaze-object appears in its purest form in a series of films in which the logic of nostalgia is brought to self-reference: *Body Heat, Driver, Shane.* As Fredric Jameson has already observed in his well-known article on postmodernism,[8] *Body Heat* reverses the usual nostalgic procedure in which the fragment of the past that serves as the object of nostalgia is extracted from its historic context, from its continuity, and inserted into a kind of mythic, eternal, timeless present. Here, in this *film noir*—a vague remake of *Double Indemnity,* which takes place in contemporary Florida—present time itself is viewed through the eyes of the *film noir* of the '40s. Instead of transposing a fragment of the past into a timeless, mythic present, we view the present itself as if it were part of the mythic past. If we do not take into consideration this "gaze of the '40s," *Body Heat* remains simply a contemporary film about contemporary times and, as such, totally incomprehensible. Its whole power of fascination is bestowed upon it by the fact that it looks at the present with the eyes of the mythical past. The same dialectic of the gaze is at work in Walter Hill's *Driver*; its starting point is again the *film noir* of the '40s which, as such, *does not exist.* It started to exist only when it was discovered by French critics in the '50s (it is no accident that even in English, the term used to designate this genre is French: *film noir*). What was, in America itself, a series of low-budget B-productions of little critical prestige, was miraculously transformed, through the intervention of the French gaze, into a sublime object of art, a kind of film pendant to philosophical existentialism. Directors who had in America the status of skilled craftsmen, at best, became *auteurs,* each of them staging in his films a unique tragic vision of the universe. But the crucial fact is that this French view of *film noir* exerted a considerable influence on French film production, so that in France itself, a genre homologous to the American *film noir* was established; its most distinguished example is probably Jean-Pierre Melville's *Samurai*. Hill's *Driver* is a kind of remake of *Samurai,* an attempt to transpose the French gaze back onto America itself—a paradox of America looking at itself through French eyes. Again, if we conceive *Driver* simply as an American film about America, it becomes incomprehensible: we must include the "French gaze."

Our last example is *Shane,* the classic western by George Stevens. As is well known, the end of the '40s witnessed the first great crisis of the western as a genre. Pure, simple westerns began to produce an effect of artificiality and mechanical routine, their formula was seemingly exhausted. Authors reacted to this crisis by overlaying westerns with elements of other genres. Thus we have *film noir* westerns (Raoul Welsh's *Pursued,* which achieves the almost impossible task of transposing into a western the dark universe of the *film noir*); musical comedy westerns (*Seven Brides for Seven Brothers*); psychological westerns (*The Gunfighter,* with Gregory Peck); historical epic westerns (the remake of *Cimarron*), etc. In the '50s, André Bazin baptized this new, "reflected" genre the *meta-western.* The way *Shane* functions can be grasped only against the background of the "meta-western." *Shane* is the paradox of a western, the "meta-" dimension of which is the *western itself.* In other words, it is a western that implies a kind of nostalgic distance toward the universe of westerns: a western that functions, so to speak, as its own myth. To explain the effect produced by *Shane,* we must again refer to the function of the gaze. That is to say, if we remain on the commonsense level, if we do not include the dimension of the gaze, a simple and understandable question arises: if the meta-dimension of this western is the western itself, what accounts for the distance between the two levels? Why does the meta-western not simply overlap with the western itself? Why do we not have a western pure and simple? The answer is that, by means of a structural necessity, *Shane* belongs in the context of the meta-western: on the level of its immediate diegetic contents, it is of course a western pure and simple, one of the purest ever made. But the very form of its historical context determines that we perceive it as meta-western, i.e., precisely because, in its diegetic contents, it is a pure western, the dimension "beyond western" opened up by the historical context can be filled out only by the western itself. In other words, *Shane* is a pure western *at a time when pure westerns were no longer possible,* when the western was already perceived from a certain nostalgic distance, as a lost object. Which is why it is highly indicative that the story is told from a child's perspective (the perspective of a little boy, a member of a farming family defended against violent cattle breeders by Shane, a mythic hero appearing suddenly out of nowhere. The innocent, naive gaze of the other that fascinates us in nostalgia is in the last resort always the gaze of a child.

In nostalgic, retrofilms, then, the logic of the gaze *qua* object appears as such. The real object of fascination is not the displayed scene but the gaze of the naive "other" absorbed, enchanted by it. In *Shane,* for example, we can be fascinated by the mysterious apparition of Shane only through the medium of the "innocent" child's gaze, never immediately. Such a logic of fascination by which the subject sees in the object (in the image it views) its own gaze, i.e., by which, in the viewed image, it "sees itself seeing," is defined by Lacan as the very illusion of perfect self-mirroring that characterizes the Cartesian philosophical tradition of the subject of self-reflection.[9] But what happens here with the *antinomy* between eye and gaze? That is to say, the whole point of Lacan's argument is to oppose to the self-mirroring of philosophical subjectivity the irreducible discord between the gaze *qua* object and the subject's eye. Far from being the point of self-sufficient self-mirroring, the gaze *qua* object functions like a blot that blurs the transparency of the viewed image. I can never see properly, can never include in the totality of my field of vision, the point in the other from which it gazes back at me. Like the extended blot in Holbein's *Ambassadors,* this point throws the harmony of my vision off balance.

The answer to our problem is clear: the function of the nostalgic object is precisely to *conceal* the antinomy between eye and gaze—i.e., the traumatic impact of the gaze *qua* object—by means of its power of fascination. In nostalgia, the gaze of the other is in a way domesticated, "gentrified"; instead of the gaze erupting like a traumatic, disharmonious blot, we have the illusion of "seeing ourselves seeing," of seeing the gaze itself. In a way, we could say that the function of fascination is precisely to blind us to the fact that the other is already gazing at us. In Kafka's parable "The Door of the Law," the man from the country waiting at the entrance to the court is fascinated by the secret beyond the door he is forbidden to trespass. In the end, the power of fascination exerted by the court is dispelled. But how, exactly? Its power is lost when the door keeper tells him that this entrance was, from the very start, meant only for him. In other words, he tells the man from the country that the thing that fascinated him was, in a way, gazing back at him all along, addressing him. That is, the man's desire was from the very start "part of the game." The whole spectacle of the Door of the Law and the secret beyond it was staged only to capture his desire. If the power of fascination is to produce its effect, this fact must remain concealed. As soon as the subject becomes aware that the other gazes at him (that the door is meant only for him), the fascination is dispelled.

In his Bayreuth production of *Tristan und Isolde,* Jean-Pierre Ponelle introduced an extremely interesting change in Wagner's original plot, a change that precisely concerns the functioning of the gaze as object of fascination. In Wagner's libretto, the denouement simply resumes the mythic tradition. The wounded Tristan takes refuge in his castle in Cornwall and waits for Isolde to follow him. When, because of a misunderstanding concerning the color of the sail of Isolde's vessel, he becomes convinced that Isolde will not arrive, he dies in agony. Whereupon Isolde arrives together with her lawful husband, King Marke, who is willing to forgive the sinful couple. It is, however, too late; Tristan is already dead. In esctatic agony, Isolde herself dies embracing the dead Tristan. What Ponelle did was simply to stage the last act as if the end of the "real" action were Tristan's death. All that follows—the arrival of Isolde and Marke, Isolde's death—is just Tristan's mortal delirium. In reality, Isolde has simply broken the vow to her lover and returned, repentent, to her husband. The much-celebrated end of *Tristan und Isolde,* Isolde's love-death, appears thus as what it effectively is: the *masculine* fantasy of a finally accomplished sexual relationship by which the couple is forever united in mortal ecstasy, or, more precisely, in which the *woman* follows her man into death in an act of ecstatic self-abandonment.

But the crucial point for us is the way Ponelle staged this delirious apparition of Isolde. Because she appears to *Tristan,* we would expect her to stand *in front of* him and thus fascinate his gaze. In Ponelle's mise-en-scène, however, Tristan looks directly at us, the spectators in the hall, while the dazzlingly illuminated Isolde grows luxuriantly *behind* him, as that which is "in him more than himself." The object at which Tristan stares in fascination is thus literally *the gaze of the other* (embodied in us, the spectators), the gaze that sees Isolde, i.e., the gaze that sees not only Tristan but also his sublime other, that which is in him more than himself, the "treasure," *agalma,* in him. At this point, Ponelle adroitly made use of the words sung by Isolde. Far from plunging into a kind of autistic trance, she continually addresses the gaze of the other: "Friends! Do you see, can't you see, how he [Tristan] glitters more and more?"—that which "glitters more and more" in him being of course *herself* as the illuminated apparition behind him.

If the function of nostalgic fascination is thus to conceal, to appease the disharmonious irruption of the gaze *qua* object, how is this gaze consequently *produced*? Which cinematic procedure opens up, hollows the void of the gaze *qua* object in the continuous flow of images? Our thesis is that this void constitutes the necessary leftover of *montage,* so that pornography, nostalgia, and montage form a kind of quasi-Hegelian "triad" in relation to the status of the gaze *qua* object.

The Hitchcockian Cut

MONTAGE

Montage is usually conceived as a way of producing from fragments of the real—pieces of film, discontinuous individual shots—an effect of "cinematic space," i.e., a specific cinematic reality. That is to say, it is universally acknowledged that "cinematic space" is never a simple repetition or imitation of external, "effective" reality, but an effect of montage. What is often overlooked, however, is the way this transformation of fragments of the real into cinematic reality produces, through a kind of structural necessity, a certain leftover, a surplus that is radically heterogeneous to cinematic reality but nonetheless implied by it, part of it.[10] That this surplus of the real is, in the last resort, precisely the gaze *qua* object, is best exemplified by the work of Hitchcock.

We have already pointed out that the fundamental constituent of the Hitchcockian universe is the so-called "spot": the stain upon which reality revolves, passes over into the real, the mysterious detail that "sticks out," that does not "fit" into the symbolic network of reality and that, as such, indicates that "something is amiss." The fact that this spot ultimately coincides with the threatening gaze of the other is confirmed in an almost too obvious way by the famous tennis court scene from *Strangers on a Train,* in which Guy watches the crowd watching the game. The camera first gives us a long shot of the crowd; all heads turn alternately left and right, following the path of the ball, all except one, which stares with a fixed gaze into the camera, i.e., at Guy. The camera then quickly approaches this motionless head. It is Bruno, linked to Guy by a murderous pact. Here we have in pure, distilled form the stiff, motionless gaze, sticking out like a strange body and thus disturbing the harmony of the image by introducing a threatening dimension.

The function of the famous Hitchcockian "tracking shot" is precisely to produce a spot: in the tracking shot, the camera moves from an establishing shot to a close-up of a detail that remains a blurred spot, the true form of which is accessible only to an anamorphotic "view from aside." The shot slowly isolates from its surroundings the element that cannot be integrated into the symbolic reality, that must remain a strange body if the depicted reality is to retain its consistency. But what interests us here is the fact that under certain conditions, montage *does* intervene in the tracking shot, i.e., the continuous approach of the camera is interrupted by cuts.

What, more precisely, are these conditions? Briefly, the tracking shot must be interrupted when it is "subjective," when the camera shows us the subjective view of a person approaching the object-spot. That is to say, whenever, in a Hitchcock film, a hero, a person around whom the scene is structured, approaches an object, a thing, another person, anything that can become "uncanny" (*unheimlich*) in the Freudian sense, Hitchcock as a rule alternates the "objective" shot of this person in motion, his/her approach toward the uncanny Thing, with a subjective shot of what this person sees, i.e., with a subjective view of the Thing. This is, so to speak, the elementary procedure, the zero degree of Hitchcockian montage.

Let us take a few examples. When, toward the end of *Psycho,* Lilah climbs up the rise to the mysterious old house, the presumed home of "Norman's mother," Hitchcock alternates the objective shot of Lilah climbing with her subjective view of the old house. He does the same in *The Birds,* in the famous scene analyzed in detail by Raymond Bellour,[11] when Melanie, after crossing the bay in a small rented boat, approaches the house where Mitch's mother and sister live. Again, he alternates an objective shot of the uneasy Melanie, aware of intruding on the privacy of a home, with her subjective view of the mysteriously silent house.[12] Of innumerable other examples, let us mention merely a short, trivial scene between Marion and a car dealer in *Psycho.* Here, Hitchcock uses his montage procedure several times (when Marion approaches the car dealer; when, toward the end of the scene, a policeman approaches who has already stopped her on the highway the same morning, etc.). By means of this purely formal procedure, an entirely trivial, everyday incident is given an uneasy, threatening dimension that cannot be sufficiently explained by its diegetic contents (i.e., by the fact that Marion is buying a new car with stolen money and thus fears exposure). Hitchcockian montage elevates an everyday, trivial object into a sublime Thing. By purely formal manipulation, it succeeds in bestowing on an ordinary object the aura of anxiety and uneasiness.[13]

In Hitchcockian montage, two kinds of shots are thus permitted and two forbidden. Permitted are the objective shot of the person approaching a Thing and the subjective shot presenting the Thing as the person sees it. Forbidden are the objective shot of the Thing, of the "uncanny" object, and—above all—the subjective shot of the approaching person from the perspective of the "uncanny" object itself. Let us refer again to the above-mentioned scene from *Psycho* depicting Lilah approaching the house on the top of the hill. It is crucial that Hitchcock shows the threatening Thing (the house) exclusively from the point of view of Lilah. If he were to have added a "neutral" objective shot of the house, the whole mysterious effect would have been lost. We (the spectators) would have to endure a radical desublimation;

we would suddenly become aware that there is nothing "uncanny" in the house as such, that the house is—like the "black house" in the Patricia Highsmith short story—just an ordinary old house. The effect of uneasiness would be radically "psychologized"; we would say to ourselves, "This is just an ordinary house; all the mystery and anxiety attached to it are just an effect of the heroine's psychic turmoil!"

The effect of "uncanniness" would also be lost if Hitchcock had immediately added a shot "subjectifying" the Thing, i.e., a subjective shot from inside the house. Let us imagine that as Lilah approached the house, there had been a trembling shot showing Lilah through the curtains of the house window, accompanied by the sound of hollow breathing, thus indicating that somebody was watching her from inside the house. Such a procedure (used regularly in standard thrillers) would, of course, intensify the strain. We would say to ourselves, "This is terrible! There is somebody in the house (Norman's mother?) watching Lilah; she is in mortal danger without knowing it!" But such a subjectification would again suspend the status of the gaze *qua object,* reducing it to the subjective point of view of another diegetic personality. Sergei Eisenstein himself once risked such a direct subjectification, in a scene from *The Old and the New,* a film that celebrated the successes of the collectivization of Soviet agriculture in the late '20s. It is a somewhat Lysenkoist scene demonstrating the way nature finds pleasure in subordinating itself to the new rules of collective farming, the way even cows and bulls mate more ardently once they are included in *kilkhozes.* In a quick tracking shot, the camera appproaches a cow from behind, and in the next shot it becomes clear that this view of the camera was the view of a bull mounting a cow. Needless to say, the effect of this scene is so obscenely vulgar that it is almost nauseating. What we have here is a kind of Stalinist pornography.

It would be wiser, then, to turn away from this Stalinist obscenity to the Hollywood decency of Hitchcock. Let us return to the scene from *Psycho* in which Lilah approaches the house where "Norman's mother" presumably lives. In what does its "uncanny" dimension consist? Could we not best describe the effect of this scene by paraphrasing the words of Lacan: in a way, *it is already the house that gazes at Lilah*? Lilah sees the house, but nonetheless she cannot see it at the point from which it gazes back at her. Here the situation is the same as that which Lacan recollects from his youth and reports in *Seminar XI*: as a student on holiday, he joined a fishing expedition. Among the fishermen on the boat, there was a certain Petit-Jean who, pointing out an empty sardine can glittering in the sun, asked Lacan: *"You see the can? Do you see it? Well, it doesn't see you!"* Lacan's comment: "If what Petit-Jean said to me, namely that the can did not see me, had any meaning, it was because in a sense, it was looking at me, all the same." It was looking at him because, as Lacan explains, using a key notion of the Hitchcockian universe, "I functioned somewhat like a spot in the picture."[14] Among these uneducated fishermen earning their living with great difficulty, he was effectively out of place, "the man who knew too much."

The examples we have analyzed thus far were purposely elementary; let us conclude then with an analysis of a scene in which the Hitchcockian montage is part of a more complex whole. The scene from *Sabotage* in which Sylvia Sidney kills Oscar Homolka. The two characters are dining together at home; Sylvia is still in a state of shock, having learned recently that Oscar, her husband, is a "saboteur" guilty of the death of her younger brother who was blown up by a bomb on a bus. When Sylvia brings the vegetable platter to the table, the knife on the platter acts as a magnet. It is almost as if her hand, against her will, were compelled to grab it, yet she cannot resolve herself finally to do so. Oscar, who up till now has pursued banal, everyday table conversation, perceives that she is spellbound by the knife and what this augurs for him. He stands up and walks round the table toward her. When they are face to face, he reaches for the knife but, unable to complete the gesture, lets *her* grab it. The camera then moves in closer, showing only their faces and shoulders, so that it is not clear what is happening with their hands. Suddenly Oscar utters a short cry and falls down, without our knowing whether she stabbed him or he, in a suicidal gesture, impaled himself on the blade.

The first thing that deserves notice is the way the act of murder results from the encounter of two thwarted threatening gestures.[15] Both Sylvia's move forward with the knife and Oscar's move toward it correspond to the Lacanian definition of the threatening gesture: it is not an interrupted gesture, i.e., a gesture that is intended to be carried out, to be completed, but is thwarted by an external obstacle. It is, on the contrary, something that was already begun in order *not* to be accomplished, not to be brought to its conclusion.[16] The very structure of the threatening gesture is thus that of a theatrical, hysterical act, a split, self-hindered gesture: a gesture that cannot be accomplished not because of some external obstacle but because it is in itself the expression of a contradictory, self-conflicting desire—in this case, Sylvia's desire to stab Oscar and at the same time the prohibition that blocks the realization of this desire. Oscar's move (when, after becoming aware of her intention, he stands up and comes forward to meet her) is again contradictory, split into his "self-preserving" desire to snatch the knife from her and master her, and his "masochistic" desire to offer himself to the stab of the knife, a desire conditioned by his morbid feeling of guilt. The successful act (the stabbing of Oscar) results thus from the encounter of two failed, hindered, split acts. Her desire to stab him is met by his own desire to be punished and, ultimately, killed. Apparently, Oscar moves forward to defend himself, but this move is at the same time supported by the desire to be stabbed, so that, in the end, it is of no importance which of the two "really" carried out the crucial gesture (did she push the knife in or did he throw himself on the blade?). The "murder" results from the overlap, the coincidence of her desire with his.

In relation to the structural place of Oscar's "masochistic" desire, we should refer to the logic of fantasy elaborated by Freud in "A Child Is Being Beaten."[17] Freud explains here how the final form of the fantasy scene ("a child is being beaten") presupposes two previous phases. The first, "sadistic" phase is "my father is beating the child (my brother, somebody who is my rival double)"; the second is its "masochistic" inversion: "I am being beaten by my father"; while the third and final form of the fantasy renders indistinct, neutralizes the subject (who is doing the beating?) as well as the object (what child is being beaten?) in the impersonal "a child is being beaten." According to Freud, the crucial role belongs to the *second,* "masochistic" phase: this is where the real trauma lies, this is the phase that is radically "repressed." We find no trace of it in the child's fantasizing, we can only *construct* it retroactively on the basis of "clues" pointing to the fact that *there is something missing* between "my father is beating the child," and "a child is being beaten." Because we cannot transform the first form into the third, definite one, Freud reasons that intermediate form must intervene:

> This second phase is the most important and the most momentous of all. But we may say of it that in a certain sense it has never had a real existence. It is never remembered, it has never succeeded in becoming conscious. It is a construction of analysis, but it is no less a necessity on that account.[18]

The second form of the fantasy is thus the Lacanian real: a point that never took place "in (symbolic) reality," that has never been inscribed in the symbolic texture, but that must nonetheless be presupposed as a kind of "missing link" guaranteeing the consistency of our symbolic reality. Our thesis is that Hitchcockian murders (in addition to Oscar's death in *Sabotage,* let us mention at least the final fall of the saboteur from the Statue of Liberty in *Saboteur* and Gromek's murder in *Torn Curtain*) are governed by a homologuous fantasy logic. The first phase is always "sadistic," it consists in our identification with the hero who finally gets the opportunity to have done with the villain. We cannot wait to see Sylvia finish the evil Oscar, to see the decent American push the Nazi saboteur over the railing, to see Paul Newman get rid of Gromek, etc. The final phase is, of course, the compassionate inversion. When we see that the "villain" is really a helpless, broken being, we are overwhelmed with compassion and guilt, we are punished for our previous "sadistic" desire. In *Saboteur,* the hero tries desperately to *save* the villain suspended by his sleeve, the seams of which tear one by one; in *Sabotage,* Sylvia compassionately embraces the dying Oscar, preventing him from hitting the floor; in *Torn Curtain,* the very long duration of the act of murder, the clumsiness of Paul Newman, and the desperate resistance of the victim render the whole affair extremely painful, barely supportable.

At first it may seem that it is possible to pass directly from the first to the final phase of the fantasy, i.e., from sadistic pleasure at the imminent destruction of the villain to a sense of guilt and compassion. But if this were all, Hitchcock would be simply a kind of moralist presenting us with the price to be paid for our "sadistic" desire: "You wanted the villain to be killed, now you've got it and must suffer the consequences!" There is in Hitchcock, however, always an intermediate phase. The "sadistic" desire for the villain to be killed is followed by a sudden awareness that it is actually the "villain" himself who is in a stifled but nonetheless unequivocal way disgusted with his own corruption and wants to be "delivered" from this unbearable pressure through his own punishment and death. This is the delicate moment in which we become aware that the hero's (and thus our, the spectators') desire to annihilate the "villain" *is already the desire of the "villain" himself.* In *Sabotage,* for example, it is the moment at which it becomes clear that Sylvia's desire to stab Oscar overlaps with Oscar's desire to exculpate himself via his own death. This constant implicit presence of a tendency to self-annihilation, of an enjoyment found in provoking one's own ruin, in short of the death drive, is what bestows upon the Hitchcockian "villain" his ambiguous charm, and it is at the same time what prevents us from passing immediately from the initial "sadism" to a final compassion for the villain. This compassion is based upon an awareness that the villain himself experiences his guilt and wants to die. In other words, our compassion arises only when we become aware of the *ethical* attitude contained in the villain's subjective position.

What, however, has all this to do with Hitchcockian montage? In this final scene of *Sabotage,* although Sylvia is its emotional center, she is, nevertheless, the scene's object—Oscar is its subject. That is to say, it is *his* subjective perspective that articulates the rhythm of the scene. In the beginning, Oscar pursues the usual dinner conversation and entirely fails to notice Sylvia's extreme inner tension. When she becomes transfixed by the knife, the astonished Oscar glances at her and becomes aware of her desire. This introduces the first scansion: the empty chatter comes to a halt as it becomes clear to Oscar what Sylvia is contemplating. Thereupon he stands up and steps forward to meet her. This part of the action is shot in the manner of Hitchcockian montage, i.e., the camera first shows us Oscar approaching Sylvia around the table and then Oscar's view of the paralyzed, inflexible Sylvia, staring at him in desperation, as if asking him to help her make up her mind. When they find themselves face to face, he is himself paralyzed and lets *her* grab the knife. Then we are given a shot of their exchange of glances, i.e., we do not see what is going on below their waists. Suddenly, he utters an incomprehensible cry. Next shot: a close-up of her hand holding the knife stabbed deep into his chest. Thereupon she embraces him, as in an act of compassion, before he collapses to the floor. So he helped her indeed: by moving close to her, he let her know that he has accepted her desire as his own, i.e., that he also wants to die. No wonder, then, that afterward Sylvia embraces him compassionately. He has, so to speak, met her halfway, he has delivered her from unbearable tension.[19]

The moment of Hitchcockian montage—the moment at which Oscar advances toward Sylvia—is thus the moment at which Oscar accepts her desire as his own or, to refer to the Lacanian definition of the hysteric's desire as the desire of the other, the moment at which Oscar is hystericized. When we see Sylvia through Oscar's eyes, in the subjective shot of the camera approaching her, we witness the moment at which Oscar becomes aware that her desire overlaps his own, i.e., that he himself yearns to die—the moment at which he takes upon himself the lethal gaze of the other.

III   Fantasy, Bureaucracy, Democracy

Gaze and Voice as Objects

THE DIMENSION OF *ACOUSMATIQUE*

The reader well-schooled in contemporary theory is likely to view the "gaze" and the "voice" as primary targets of the Derridean effort of deconstruction: what is the gaze if not *theoria* grasping the "thing itself" in the presence of its form or in the form of its presence; what is voice if not the medium of pure "auto-affection" enabling the presence-to-itself of the speaking subject? The aim of "deconstruction" is precisely to demonstrate how the gaze is always already determined by the "infra-structural" network, which delimits what can be seen from what remains unseen and thus necessarily escapes capture by the gaze, i.e., by the margin or frame, which can-not be accounted for by an "auto-reflexive" reappropriation. Correspondingly, deconstruction demonstrates the way the self-presence of the voice is always already split/deferred by the trace of writing. Here, however, we must note the radical incom-mensurability between poststructuralist deconstruction and Lacan, who describes the function of the gaze and voice in an almost exactly opposite way. For Lacan, these objects are not on the side of the *subject* but on the side of the *object*. The gaze marks the point in the object (in the picture) from which the subject viewing it is already *gazed at,* i.e., it is the object that is gazing at me. Far from assuring the self-presence of the subject and his vision, the gaze functions thus as a stain, a spot in the picture disturbing its transparent visibility and introducing an irreducible split in my relation to the picture: I can never see the picture at the point from which it is gazing at me, i.e., the eye and the gaze are constitutively asymmetrical. The gaze as object is a stain preventing me from looking at the picture from a safe, "objective" distance, from enframing it as something that is at my grasping view's disposal. The gaze is, so to speak, a point at which the very frame (of my view) is already inscribed in the "con-tent" of the picture viewed. And it is, of course, the same with the voice as object: this voice—the superegoic voice, for example, addressing me without being attached to any particular bearer—functions again as a stain, whose inert presence interferes like a strange body and prevents me from achieving my self-identity.

To clarify this, let us again recall the classical Hitchcockian procedure we articulated in the previous chapter: how does Hitchcock shoot a scene in which the subject is approaching some mysterious, "uncanny" object, generally a house? By alternating the subjective view of the approaching object (house) and an objective shot of the subject in motion. Why does this formal procedure as such generate anxiety, why does the approaching object (the house) become "uncanny"? What we have here is precisely the above-mentioned dialectic of eye and gaze: the subject sees the house, but what provokes anxiety is the indefinable feeling that the house itself is somehow already gazing at her, gazing at her from a point that totally escapes her view and thus makes her utterly helpless. This situation is rendered perfectly by Lacan's phrase "You never look at me from the place from which I see you."[1]

The corresponding status of the voice as object was developed by Michel Chion apropos of the notion of *la voix acousmatique,* the voice without bearer, which cannot be attributed to any subject and thus hovers in some indefinite interspace. This voice is implacable precisely because it cannot be properly placed, being part neither of the diegetic "reality" nor of the sound accompaniment (commentary, musical score), but belonging, rather, to that mysterious domain designated by Lacan as "between two deaths." The first association that comes to mind here is again Hitchcock's *Psycho.* As was demonstrated by Chion in his brilliant analysis, the central problem of *Psycho* is to be located on a formal level, it concerns the relation of a certain voice (the "mother's voice") to the body for which it searches.[2] In the end, the voice finds a body, but not that of the mother; rather it "sticks" artificially onto the body of Norman. The tension created by the errant voice could also explain the effect of relief, even the poetic beauty of "*désacousmatisation,*"—of the moment when the voice finally finds its bearer—as in George Miller's *Mad Max II* (*The Road Warrior*). At the beginning of the film, an old man's voice introduces the story while we are shown an unspecified view of Mad Max alone on the road. Only at the very end does it become clear to whom this voice and this gaze belong: to the little wild boy with a boomerang who later became chief of his tribe and recounted the story to his descendants. The beauty of the final inversion lies in its unexpectedness: both elements—the gaze-voice and the person who is its bearer—are given from the beginning, but it is only at the very end that the connection between them is established, i.e., that the gaze-voice is "pinned" to one of the persons of the diegetic reality.[3]

Insofar as it is not anchored to a specific source, localized in a specific place, the *voix acousmatique* functions as a threat that lurks everywhere (Michel Chion pointed out with perspicacity that the whole effect of the "mother's voice" in *Psycho* would be ruined if the film's soundtrack were to be recorded in Dolby-stereo[4]—its free-floating presence is the all-pervasive presence of a *nonsubjectivized object,* i.e., of a voice-object without support in a subject serving as its source. It is in this way that *désacousmatisation* equals *subjectivization,* as is exemplified by the unde-servedly underrated *When a Stranger Calls,* perhaps the best variation on the theme of a stranger molesting and terrifying somebody by phone. The first part of the film is narrated from the point of view of a young baby-sitter on duty in a big suburban home. The two children are sound asleep on the second floor, while she watches TV in a sitting room downstairs. When a stranger starts to telephone again and again, always repeating the same question, "Did you check the children?" she calls the police, who advise her to close all the doors and windows and to try to engage the molester in a prolonged conversation next time he calls, so that they can trace the call. Later, after the molester has made a few more calls, the police call her back: they have succeeded in tracing the calls to another phone in the same house. The molester has been in the house the whole time, close to her; he has already brutally killed the children and was calling from their room. The unknown murderer is until this point figured as a shapeless threat, present only in the form of a bodiless *voix acousmatique,* an object with which no identification is possible. But the film then performs a clever switch by giving us the narrative perspective of the pathological murderer himself. The entire central part of the film depicts the miserable everyday life of this solitary, forlorn individual spending the night among Salvation Army ref-ugees, wandering around desolate coffee bars, and trying desperately to establish contact with fellow-creatures, so that when the detective hired by the dead children's parents corners him and is ready to stab him, all our sympathy is already on his side. In itself, each of these two narrative perspectives is quite common: if the whole film had been narrated from the point of view of the young baby sitter, we would have just another story of "terror on the line," of an unknown stranger terrorizing an inno-cent victim. If, on the other hand, the point of view had been that of the molester, we would again have a customary psychological thriller transposing us into the pathological universe of the murderer. The entire subversive effect results from the switch in perspective, from the fact that we find ourselves transposed into the point of view of the murderer *after* he has been presented to us as a horrifying point of the real, a point with which it is impossible to identify. This switch brings about a stirring experience: all of a sudden the object itself which, up till then, appeared to us as unattainable-impossible, begins to speak, subjectivizes itself.[5]

The case of *voix acousmatique* with the most far-reaching consequences for a "criticism of ideology" is Terry Gillian's *Brazil.* "Brazil" is the stupid song from the 1950s that resounds compulsively throughout the film. This music, whose status is never quite clear (when it is part of the diegetic reality and when it is just part of the musical score), embodies, by means of its painfully noisy repetition, the superego imperative of idiotic enjoyment. "Brazil," to put it briefly, is the content of the fantasy of the film's hero, the support, the point of reference structuring his enjoyment, and it is precisely for this reason that it allows us to demonstrate the fantasy's fundamental ambiguity. Throughout the film, it seems that the idiotic, intrusive rhythm of "Brazil" serves as a support for totalitarian enjoyment, i.e., that it condenses the fantasy frame of the "crazy" totalitarian social order that the film depicts. But at the very end, when his resistance is apparently broken by the savage torture to which he has been subjected, the hero escapes his torturers by beginning to whistle "Brazil!" Although functioning as a support for the totalitarian order, fantasy is then at the same time the leftover of the real that enables us to "pull ourselves out," to preserve a kind of distance from the socio-symbolic network. When we become crazed in our obsession with idiotic enjoyment, even totalitarian manipulation cannot reach us.

We come across the same phenomenon of the *voix acousmatique* in Fassbinder's *Lili Marleen*: during the film, the popular love song of the German soldiers is replayed to exhaustion, and this endless repetition changes a lovely melody into a painfully disgusting parasite that fails to release us even for a moment. Here, again, its status is unclear: totalitarian power (personified by Goebbels) tries to manipulate it, to use it to capture the imagination of the tired soldiers, but the song escapes its grasp like a genie released from a bottle. It begins to lead a life of its own—nobody can master its effects. The crucial feature of Fassbinder's film is this insistence on the utter ambiguity of "Lili Marleen": a Nazi love song promulgated by all sorts of propaganda devices, certainly, but at the same time, on the verge of transforming itself into a subversive element that could burst from the very ideological machine by which it is supported, and thus always in danger of being prohibited. Such a fragment of the signifier permeated with idiotic enjoyment is what Lacan, in the last stage of his teaching, called *le sinthome. Le sinthome* is not the symptom, the coded message to be deciphered by interpretation, but the meaningless letter that immediately procures *jouis-sense,* "enjoyment-in-meaning," "enjoy-meant."[6] If we consider the role of the *sinthome* in the construction of the ideological edifice, we are compelled to rethink the "criticism of ideology." Ideology is usually conceived as a discourse: as an enchainment of elements the meaning of which is overdetermined by their specific articulation, i.e., by the way some "nodal point" (the Lacanian master-signifier) totalizes them into a homogeneous field. We could refer here to the already classic Laclauian analyses of the way particular ideological elements function like "floating signifiers," whose meanings are fixed retroactively by the operation of hegemony ("Communism," for example, operates as a "nodal point" that specifies the meaning of all other ideological elements: "freedom" becomes "effective freedom" as opposed to "formal bourgeois freedom," "state" becomes "the means of class oppression," etc.).[7] But when we take into account the dimension of the *sinthome,* it is no longer sufficient to denounce the "artificial" character of the ideological experience, to demonstrate the way the object experienced by ideology as "natural" and "given" is effectively a discursive construction, a result of a network of symbolic overdetermination; it is no longer enough to locate the ideological text in its context, to render visible its necessarily overlooked margins. What we must do (what Gillian or Fassbinder do), on the contrary, is to *isolate* the *sinthome* from the context by virtue of which it exerts its power of fascination in order to expose the *sinthome*'s utter stupidity. In other words, we must carry out the operation of changing the precious gift into a gift of shit (as Lacan put it in his *Seminar XI*),[8] of experiencing the fascinating, mesmerizing voice as a disgusting, meaningless fragment of the real. This kind of "estrangement" is perhaps even more radical than is Brechtian *Verfremdung*: the former produces a distance not by locating the phenomenon in its historical totality, but by making us experience the utter nullity of its immediate reality, of its stupid, material presence that escapes "historical mediation." Here we do not *add* the dialectical mediation, the context bestowing meaning on the phenomenon, instead we *subtract* it. The spectacle of *Brazil* or *Lili Marleen* does not therefore stage any sort of "repressed truth of totalitarianism," it does not confront totalitarian logic with its "truth." It simply dissolves totalitarianism as an effective social bond by isolating the heinous kernel of its idiotic enjoyment.

It is on this very borderline that the sublime and, at the same time, painful scene from Spielberg's *Empire of the Sun* is placed. Little Jim, imprisoned in a Japanese camp near Shanghai, watches the *kamikaze* performing their rituals before the final flight. He joins their song with his own hymn, sung in Chinese as he learned it in church. This canto, incomprehensible to everybody present, Japanese as well as

English, is a fantasy voice. Its effect is obscene, not because there is something "dirty" in it, but because through it Jim discloses his innermost self, the most intimate sphere of his being. Through the hymn he publicly reveals the object in himself, the *agalma* or hidden treasure that supports his identity. Which is why everyone who hears this voice is in a way embarrassed—as when somebody discloses "too much" of himself to us—even as they listen to it with a kind of undefined respect. What is crucial is the change in the quality of Jim's voice: at a certain point, his hoarse, thirsty, lone voice changes into a voice that vibrates harmoniously and comes accompanied by organ and choir. It is clear that we have shifted perspective from the way others hear him to the way Jim hears himself, from reality to fantasy space.

It is no accident that all three films depict a totalitarian universe in which the subject can survive only by clinging to some superego voice enabling him to elude the complete "loss of reality" (the title songs "Brazil" and "Lili Marleen," Jim's hymn). As Lacan has already pointed out, our "sense of reality" is never supported by a "reality test (*Realitätsprufung*)" alone; to sustain itself, reality always requires a certain superego command, a certain "So be it!" The status of the voice uttering this command is neither imaginary nor symbolic, it is *real*.

"Love Thy Sinthome *as Thyself"*

A Letter beyond Discourse

We have thus arrived at the most radical dimension of the break that separates the last Lacan from the "standard" version of his theory. The limit in "classical" Lacan is the limit of *discourse*; discourse is the very field of psychoanalysis and the unconscious is defined as the "discourse of the Other." Toward the end of the 1960s, Lacan gave definite form to his theory of discourse by means of the four discourses (master, university, hysteric, analyst), i.e., the four possible types of social bond or four possible articulations of the network regulating intersubjective relations.[9] The first is the *discourse of the master*: a certain signifier (S_1), represents the subject (8) for another signifier or, more precisely, for all other signifiers (S_2). The problem is, of course, that this operation of signifying representation never comes off without producing some disturbing surplus, some leftover or "excrement," designated by a small *a*. The other discourses are simply three different attempts to "come to terms" with this remnant (the famous *objet petit a*), to "cope" with it:

• The *discourse of the university* immediately takes this leftover for its object, its "other," and tries to transform it into a "subject" by applying to it the network of "knowledge" (S_2). This is the elementary logic of the pedagogical process: out of an "untamed" object (the "unsocialized" child), we produce a subject by means of an implantation of knowledge. The "repressed" truth of this discourse is that behind the semblance of the neutral "knowledge" that we try to impart to the other, we can always locate the gesture of the master.

• The *discourse of the hysteric* begins from the opposite side. Its basic constituent is the question addressed to the master: "Why am I what you are saying that I am?" This question arises as the hysteric's reaction to what Lacan, in the early '50s, called the "founding word," the act of conferring a symbolic mandate that, by naming me, defines, establishes my place in the symbolic network: "You are my master (my wife, my king . . .)." Apropos of this "founding word," the question always arises "What is it in me that makes me the master (the wife, the king)?" In other words, the hysterical question articulates the experience of a fissure, of an irreducible gap between the signifier that represents me (the symbolic mandate that determines my place in the social network) and the nonsymbolized surplus of my being-there. There is an abyss separating them; the symbolic mandate can never be founded in, accounted for by my "effective properties" insofar as its status is by definition that of a "performative." The hysteric embodies this "question of being": his/her basic problem is *how to justify, how to account for his/her existence* (in the eyes of the big Other).[10]

• The *discourse of the analyst* is the inverse of that of the master. The analyst occupies the place of the surplus object; he identifies himself directly with the leftover of the discursive network. Which is why the discourse of the analyst is far more paradoxical than it may appear at first sight: it attempts to knit a discourse starting precisely from the element that escapes the discursive network, that "falls out" from it, that is produced as its "excrement."

What we must not forget is that the matrix of the four discourses is a matrix of the four possible positions in the intersubjective network of communication. We are here situated within the field of *communication* qua *meaning,* in spite of—or, rather, because of—all the paradoxes implied by the Lacanian conceptualization of these terms. Communication is, of course, structured like a paradoxical circle in which the sender receives from the receiver his own message in its reverse, true form, i.e., it is the decentered Other that decides the true meaning of what we have said (in this sense it is the S_2 that is the true master-signifier conferring meaning retroactively upon S_1). What circulates between subjects in symbolic communication is of course ultimately the lack, absence itself, and it is this absence that opens the space for "positive" meaning to constitute itself. But all these are paradoxes immanent to the field of communication *qua* meaning: the very signifier of nonsense, the "signifier without signified," is the condition of the possibility of the meaning of all the other signifiers, i.e., we must never forget that the "nonsense" with which we are here concerned is strictly internal to the field of meaning, that it "truncates" it from within.[11]

All the effort of Lacan's last years is directed, however, at breaking through this field of communication *qua* meaning. After establishing the definitive, logically purified structure of communication, of the social bond, via the matrix of the four discourses, Lacan undertook to delineate the outlines of a certain "free-floating" space in which signifiers find themselves prior to their discursive binding, to their *articulation*. This is the space of a certain "prehistory" preceding the "story" of the social bond, i.e., of a certain psychotic kernel evading the discursive network. This helps us to explain another unexpected feature of Lacan's *Seminar XX (Encore)*: a shift, homologous to that from signifier to sign, from the Other to the One. Up to his last years, all Lacan's effort was directed toward delineating a certain otherness preceding the One: first, in the field of the signifier as differential, every One is defined by the bundle of its differential relations to its Other, i.e., every One is in advance conceived as "one-among-the-others"; then, in the very domain of the great Other (the symbolic order), Lacan tried to isolate, to "separate" its *ex-timé*, its impossible-real kernel (the *objet petit a* is in a way "the other in the midst of the Other itself," a foreign body in its very heart). But all of a sudden, in *Seminar XX*, we stumble upon a certain One (from *There Is One, Y a de l'Un*) that is not one-among-the-others, that does not yet partake of the articulation proper to the order of the Other. This One is of course precisely the One of *jouis-sense*, of the signifier insofar as it is not yet enchained but rather freely floating, permeated with enjoyment: it is this enjoyment that prevents it from being articulated into a chain. To indicate the dimension of this One, Lacan coined the neologism *le sinthome*. This point functions as the ultimate support of the subject's consistency, the point of "thou art that," the point marking the dimension of "what is in the subject more than himself" and what he therefore "loves more than himself," the point that is nonetheless neither symptom (the coded message in which the subject receives its own message from the Other in reverse form) nor fantasy (the imaginary scenario that, by means of its fascinating presence, curtains the lack in the Other, the symbolic order, its inconsistency, i.e., a certain fundamental impossibility implied by the very act of symbolization, "the impossibility of the sexual relationship").

To render more palpable the contours of this concept, let us refer to the work of Patricia Highsmith who, in her short stories, often varies the motif of nature's pathological "tic" or deformation which, as such, materializes the subject's enjoyment, i.e., serves as its objective counterpart and support. In "The Pond," a recently divorced mother with a small son moves to a country house with a deep, dark pond in the backyard. This pond, out of which strange roots sprout, exerts a strange attraction on her son. One morning the mother finds her son drowned, entangled in its roots; desperate, she calls the garden service. Their men arrive and spread all around the pond a poison designed to kill the weeds. This does not seem to work: the roots grow even stronger, until, finally, the mother herself tackles the task, cutting and sawing the roots with an obsessive determination. They now appear to her to be alive, to be reacting to her. The more she attacks them, the more she gets caught in their web. Eventually she stops resisting and yields to their embrace, recognizing in their power of attraction the call of her dead son. Here we have an example of the *sinthome*: the pond is the "open wound of nature," the kernel of enjoyment that simultaneously attracts and repels us. We find an inverted variation on the same motif in "The Mysterious Cemetery": in a small Austrian town, doctors of the local hospital perform strange radioactive experiments on their dying patients. In the cemetery behind the hospital, where the patients are buried, strange things begin to happen: extraordinary protuberances shoot out from the graves, red spongy sculptures whose growth cannot be stopped. After an initial unease, the townspeople resign themselves to these outgrowths, which become a tourist attraction. Poems are then written about these "sprouts of enjoyment."

It would, however, be a theoretical mistake to equate these strange protuberances with the Lacanian *objet petit a,* the object-cause of desire. The "object small *a*" would be rather the "black house" in another Patricia Highsmith story (cf. chapter 1): a quite ordinary, everyday object that, as soon as it is "elevated to the status of the Thing," starts to function as a kind of screen, an empty space on which the subject projects the fantasies that support his desire, a surplus of the real that propels us to narrate again and again our first traumatic encounters with *jouissance*. The example of the "black house" demonstrates clearly the purely *formal* nature of the "object small *a*": it is an empty form filled out by everyone's fantasy. In contrast, the protuberances at the Austrian cemetery are almost too present, they are in a way a formless content forcing upon us the massive, inert presence, their nauseous, glutinous bulk. It is not difficult to recognize, in this opposition, the opposition between *desire* and *drive*: the object small *a* names the void of that unattainable surplus that sets our desire in motion, while the pond exemplifies the inert object, the embodiment of the enjoyment around which the drive circulates. The opposition between desire and drive consists precisely in the fact that desire is by definition caught in a certain dialectic, it can always turn into its opposite or slide from one object to another, it never aims at what appears to be its object, but always "wants something else." The drive, on the other hand, is inert, it resists being enmeshed in a dialectical movement; it circulates around its object, fixed upon the point around which it pulsates.

But even this opposition does not exhaust the range of objects that we encounter in psychoanalysis: there is a third kind, perhaps the most interesting, which escapes the opposition between the object of desire and the object of drive described above. Such an object would be, for example, the button in the story of the same name by Patricia Highsmith. This is a story of a Manhattan family with a mongoloid child, a small, fat freak who is unable to understand anything—it just laughs stupidly and spews out its food. The father cannot get accustomed to this mongoloid child, even long after its birth: it appears to him as an intrusion of the senseless real, as a caprice of God or Destiny, a totally undeserved punishment. The idiotic cooing of the child reminds him daily of the inconsistency and indifferent contingency of the universe, i.e., of its ultimate senselessness. Late one evening, fed up with the child (and with his wife who, in spite of her aversion, tries to conceive an affection for the little freak), the father takes a walk through the lonely streets. In a dark corner, he runs into a drunk, has a scuffle with him, and kills him in a frustrated rage, fed by the perceived injustice of fate. The father notices that he is in possession of a button from the drunk's overcoat; rather than throw it away, he keeps it as a kind of souvenir. It is a little piece of the real, a reminder both of the absurdity of fate and of the fact that at least once, he has been able to take his revenge by means of a no less meaningless act. The button confers on him the power to keep his temper in the times to come, it is a kind of token guaranteeing his ability to cope with the everyday misery of life with a freak.

How then does this button function? In contrast to the object small *a,* there is nothing metonymic-unattainable about it: it is just a little piece of the real that we can hold in our hands and manipulate like any other object. And in contrast to the cemetery protuberances, is it not a terrifying object of fascination: on the contrary, it reassures and comforts, its very presence serves as a guarantee that we will be able to endure the inconsistency and absurdity of the universe. Its paradox is then the following: it is a little piece of the real attesting to the ultimate nonsense of the universe, but insofar as this object allows us to condense, to locate, to materialize the nonsense of the universe in it, insofar as the object serves to represent this nonsense, it enables us to sustain ourself in the midst of inconsistency. The logic of these four types of object (the "black house," the cemetery protuberances, the button, the pond) can be articulated by means of the schema found at the beginning of chapter 7 of Lacan's *Encore*:[12]

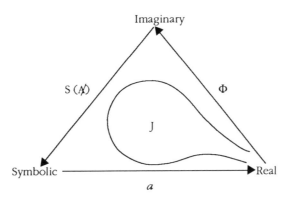

As Jacques-Alain Miller has pointed out, the three vectors in this schema do not indicate a relation of causality: I→S does not mean "the imaginary determines the symbolic," it marks rather the process of the symbolization of the imaginary. The object small *a* is thus the "hole in the real" that sets symbolization in motion (the "black house," for example: the screen for the projection of our fantasy narrations); capital phi, the "imaginarization of the real," is a certain image that materializes the nauseous enjoyment (the protuberances at the Austrian cemetery, for example); and finally S(A), the signifier of the lack in the big Other (the symbolic order), of its inconsistency, the mark of the fact that "the Other (as a closed, consistent totality) doesn't exist," is the little bit of the real functioning as the signifier of the ultimate senselessness of the (symbolic) universe (the button, for example). The abyss in the middle (the balloon encircling the letter J—*jouissance*) is of course the whirlpool of enjoyment threatening to swallow us all, like the pond in Patricia Highsmith's story: the pothole exerting its fatal attraction. The three objects on the sides of the triangle are perhaps nothing but the three ways to maintain a kind of distance toward this traumatic central abyss; we could thus repeat Lacan's schema by inserting in it the names of the objects found in Patricia Highsmith's stories:[13]

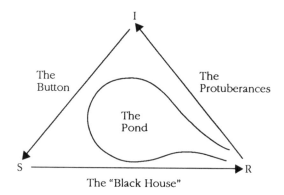

The "Black House"

IDENTIFICATION WITH THE SYMPTOM
The ontological status of such excrescences of the real sticking out from common reality (S(A̶), Φ, or *a*) is utterly ambiguous: when confronted with them, we cannot avoid the simultaneous sentiment of their "reality" and their "irreality." It is as if, at the same time, they "exist" and "do not exist." This ambiguity overlaps perfectly with the two opposed meanings of the term *existence* in Lacan:

• First, existence in the sense of a "judgment of existence," by which we symbolically affirm the existence of an entity: existence is here synonymous with symbolization, integration into the symbolic order—only what is symbolized fully "exists." Lacan uses *existence* in this sense when maintaining that "Woman does not exist" or that "there is no sexual relation." Neither Woman nor the sexual relationship possess a signifier of their own, neither can be inscribed into the signifying network, they resist symbolization. What is at stake here is what Lacan, alluding to both Freud and Heidegger, calls "the primordial *Bejahung*," an affirmation prior to denial, an act that "allows the thing to be," that sets the real free into the "clearance of its being."[14] According to Lacan, the famous "sensation of irreality" that we experience in the face of certain phenomena is to be located precisely at this level: it indicates that the object in question has lost its place in the symbolic universe.

• Second, existence in the opposite sense, i.e., as ex-sistence: as the impossible-real kernel resisting symbolization. The first traces of such a notion of existence are already visible in *Seminar II,* where Lacan emphasizes that "there is something so improbable about all existence that one is in effect perpetually questioning oneself about its reality."[15] It is, of course, this ex-sistence of the real, of the Thing embodying impossible enjoyment, that is excluded by the very advent of the symbolic order. We could say that we are always caught in a certain *vel,* that we are always forced to choose between meaning and ex-sistence: the price we have to pay for access to meaning is the exclusion of ex-sistence. (Herein lies perhaps the hidden economy of the phenomenological *epoche*: to gain access to the realm of meaning by suspending, by putting ex-sistence in parenthesis.) And if we refer to this notion of ex-sistence, we could say that it is precisely woman that "exists," i.e., that persists as a leftover of enjoyment beyond meaning, resisting symbolization, which is why, as Lacan puts it, woman is "the *sinthome* of man."

This dimension of ex-sisting *sinthome* is thus more radical than that of symptom or fantasy: *sinthome* is a psychotic kernel that can neither be interpreted (as symptom) nor "traversed" (as fantasy)—what to do with it, then? Lacan's answer (and at the same time the last Lacanian definition of the final moment of the psychoanalytic process) is to *identify with the sinthome.* The *sinthome,* then, represents the final limit of the psychoanalytic process, the reef on which psychoanalysis is grounded. But, on the other hand, is not this experience of the radical impossibility of the *sinthome* the ultimate proof that the psychoanalytic process is brought to its end? This is the proper accent of Lacan's thesis on the "symptom Joyce":

> The reference to the psychosis of Joyce in no way indicated a kind of applied psychoanalysis: what was at stake, on the contrary, was the effort to call into question the very discourse of the analyst *by means of* the symptom Joyce, insofar as the subject, identified with his symptom, is closed to its artifice. And perhaps there is no better end of an analysis.[16]

We reach the end of the psychoanalytic process when we isolate this kernel of enjoyment which is, so to speak, immune to the symbolic efficacy, the operating mode of the discourse. This would also be the last Lacanian reading of Freud's motto *Wo es war, soll Ich werden*: in the real of your symptom, you must recognize the ultimate support of your being. There where your symptom already was, with this place you must identify, in its "pathological" singularity you must recognize the element that guarantees your consistency. We can see, now, how great a distance from the "standard" version of his theory Lacan covered in the last decade of his teaching. In the '60s, he still conceived the symptom as "a way, for the subject, to give way on his desire," as a compromise formation bearing witness to the fact that the subject did not persist in his desire, which is why access to the truth of the desire was possible only via the interpretative dissolution of the symptom. Generally speaking, we could say that the formula "going through the fantasy—identification with the symptom" reverses what we spontaneously consider to be an "authentic existential position," i.e., "dissolution of the symptoms—identification with the fantasy." Is not the "authenticity" of a given subjective position measured precisely by how far we have delivered ourselves from pathological "tics" and identified with the fantasy, with our "fundamental existential project"? In the last Lacan, in contrast, the analysis is over when we take a certain distance toward the fantasy and identify with the pathological singularity on which the consistency of our enjoyment depends.

It is only at this final stage that it becomes clear how we have to conceive the Lacanian thesis—found in the very last page of his *Seminar XI*—that "the analyst's desire is not a pure desire."[17] All previous Lacanian determinations of the final moment of the analytic process, i.e., of the "passage (*passe*)" of analysand into analyst, still implied a kind of "purification" of desire, a kind of breakthrough to the "desire in its pure state." First, we had to get rid of the symptoms as compromise formations, then, we had to "traverse" the fantasy as the frame determining the coordinates of our enjoyment: the "desire of the analyst" was thus conceived as a desire purified of enjoyment, i.e., our access to "pure" desire is always paid for by the loss of enjoyment. In the last stage, however, the whole perspective is reversed: we have to identify precisely with the particular form of our enjoyment.

But how does *this* identification with the symptom differ from what we usually conceive under this term, i.e., from the typical hysterical reversal into "madness," when the only way to get rid of the element that hystericizes us is to identify with it; a kind of "if you can't beat them, join them" approach? To exemplify this second, hysterical mode of identification with the symptom, let us refer again to Ruth Rendell, to her brilliant short story "Convolvulus Clock." During a visit to her friend in a small town, Trixie, an old spinster, steals a fine old clock from the local antique shop. But once she has taken it, the clock continually incites unease and guilt. Trixie begins to read allusions to her little crime in every passing remark. When a friend mentions that a similar clock has recently been stolen from the antique shop, the panicked Trixie pushes her under an approaching tube train. The ticking of the clock continues to obsess her. Unable to take it any longer, she goes into the countryside and throws the clock from a bridge into a stream. The stream is shallow, however, and it seems to Trixie that anyone glancing down from the bridge can clearly see the clock; so she enters the water, grabs the clock, crushes it with stones, and throws the broken bits all around. But the more she scatters the pieces, the more it appears to her that the entire stream is overflowing with clock. When, after a while, a neighboring farmer pulls her from the water, all wet, quivering and bruised, Trixie waves her arms about like the hands of a clock and repeats: "Tick-tock. Tick-tock. Convolvulus clock."[18]

To differentiate this kind of identification from that marking the final moment of the psychoanalytic process, we must introduce the distinction between *acting out* and what Lacan calls *passage à l'acte*. Broadly speaking, acting out is still a symbolic act, an act addressed to the big Other, whereas a "passage to act" suspends the dimension of the big Other as the act is transposed into the dimension of the real. In other words, acting out is an attempt to break through a symbolic deadlock (an impossibility of symbolization, of putting into words) by means of an act, even though this act still functions as the bearer of some ciphered message. Through this act we attempt (in a "crazy" way, true) to honor a certain debt, to wipe out a certain guilt, to embody a certain reproach to the Other, etc. By means of her final identification with the clock, the unfortunate Trixie tries to attest her innocence to the Other, i.e., to get rid of the unbearable burden of her guilt. The "passage to act" entails in contrast an exit from the symbolic network, a dissolution of the social bond. We could say by *acting out,* we identify ourselves with the symptom as Lacan conceived it in the '50s (the ciphered message addressed to the Other), whereas by *passage à l'acte,* we identify with the *sinthome* as the pathological "tic" structuring the real kernel of our enjoyment, like the "harmonica man" (played by Charles Bronson) in Sergio Leone's *Once Upon a Time in the West.* As a young man, he was witness (more precisely, an involuntary collaborator) to a traumatic scene: robbers forced him to support on his shoulders his older brother, around whose neck a noose had been tied. The younger brother was at the same time ordered to play a harmonica. When he collapsed from fatigue, his brother was suspended in the air, hanged, and died. The younger brother goes through life as a kind of "living dead," incapable of "normal sexual relations," beyond the circle of ordinary human passions and fears. The only thing that allows him to preserve some consistency, i.e., that prevents him from "going nuts," from falling into an autistic catatonia, is precisely his personal "nut," his specific form of "madness," identification with his symptom-harmonica. "He plays the harmonica when he should speak and he speaks when he should better play the harmonica," his friend Cheyenne says of him. Nobody knows his name, he is always called simply "Harmonica," and when Frank—the robber responsible for the original traumatic scene—asks him about his name, he can only answer him by quoting the names of dead men he wants to avenge. To use Lacanian terminology: the harmonica man has undergone a "subjective destitution," he has no name (it is perhaps no accident that the last of Leone's westerns is called *My Name Is Nobody*), no sig-

nifier to represent him, which is why he retains his consistency only through identification with his symptom. With this "subjective destitution," his very relation to
truth undergoes a radical change: in hysteria (and obsessional neurosis, its "dialect")
we always partake in the dialectical movement of truth,[19] which is why the acting out
at the climax of the hysterical crisis remains throughout determined by the coordinates of truth, whereas the *passage à l'acte,* so to speak, suspends the dimension
of truth. Insofar as truth has the structure of a (symbolic) fiction, truth and the real
of enjoyment are incompatible.

There is, perhaps, an experience in the field of politics that entails a kind of
"identification with the symptom": the well-known pathetic experience "We are all
that!," the experience of identification when we are confronted with a phenomenon
that functions as an intrusion of unbearable truth, as an index of the fact that the social
mechanism "doesn't work." Let us take, for example, Jew-baiting riots. A whole network of strategies—simple ignorance; treating it as some deplorable horror that
does not, however, really concern us, since it is some savage ritual from which we
can distance ourselves; "sincere compassion" for the victims—allow us to evade the
fact that the persecution of Jews pertains to a certain repressed truth of our civilization. We attain an authentic attitude only when we arrive at the experience that—
in a sense that is far from being simply metamorphical—"we are all Jews." And it is
the same for all traumatic moments of the intrusion into the social field of some
"impossible" kernel that resists integration: "We all live in Chernobyl!," "We are all
boat people!," and so on. Apropos of these cases, it should also be clear how "identification with the symptom" is correlated with "going through the fantasy": by means
of such an identification with the (social) symptom, we traverse and subvert the fantasy frame that determines the field of social meaning, the ideological self-under-
standing of a given society, i.e., the frame within which, precisely, the "symptom"
appears as some alien, disturbing intrusion, and not as the point of eruption of the
otherwise hidden truth of the existing social order.

The Postmodernist Break

MODERNISM VERSUS POSTMODERNISM

When the topic of "postmodernism" is discussed in "deconstructivist" circles, it is obligatory—a sign of good manners, so to speak—to begin with a negative reference to Habermas, with a kind of distancing from him. In complying with this custom, we would like to add a new twist: to propose that Habermas is himself postmodernist, although in a peculiar way, without knowing it. To sustain this thesis, we will question the very way Habermas constructs the opposition between modernism (defined by its claim to a universality of reason, its refusal of the authority of tradition, its acceptance of rational argument as the only way to defend conviction, its ideal of a communal life guided by mutual understanding and recognition and by the absence of constraint) and postmodernism (defined as the "deconstruction" of this claim to universality, from Nietzsche to "poststructuralism"; the endeavor to prove that this claim to universality is necessarily, constitutively "false," that it masks a particular network of power relations; that universal reason is as such, in its very form, "repressive" and "totalitarian"; that its truth claim is nothing but an effect of a series of rhetorical figures.[1] This opposition is simply false: for what Habermas describes as "postmodernism" is the immanent obverse of the modernist project itself; what he describes as the tension between modernism and postmodernism is the immanent tension that has defined modernism from its very beginning. Was not the aestheticist, antiuniversalist ethics of the individual's shaping his life as a work of art always part of the modernist project? Is the genealogic unmasking of universal categories and values, the calling into question of the universality of reason not a modernist procedure par excellence? Is not the very essence of theoretical modernism, the revelation of the "effective contents" behind the "false consciousness" (of ideology, of morality, of the ego), exemplified by the great triad of Marx-Nietzsche-

Freud? Is not the ironic, self-destructive gesture by means of which reason recognizes in itself the force of repression and domination against which it fights—the gesture at work from Nietzsche to Adorno and Horkheimer's *Dialectic of Enlightenment*—is not this gesture the supreme act of modernism? As soon as fissures appear in the unquestionable authority of tradition, the tension between universal reason and the particular contents escaping its grasp is inevitable and irreducible.

The line of demarcation between modernism and postmodernism must, then, lie elsewhere. Ironically, it is Habermas himself who, on account of certain crucial features of his theory, belongs to postmodernism: the break between the first and the second generation of the Frankfurt school, that is, between Adorno, Horkheimer, and Marcuse on the one side and Habermas on the other, corresponds precisely to the break between modernism and postmodernism. In Adorno and Horkheimer's *Dialectic of Enlightenment,*[2] in Marcuse's *One-Dimensional Man,*[3] in their unmasking of the repressive potential of "instrumental reason," aiming at a radical revoluton in the historical totality of the contemporary world and at the utopian abolition of the difference between "alienated" life spheres, between art and "reality," the modernist project reaches its zenith of self-critical fulfillment. Habermas is, on the other hand, postmodern precisely because he recognizes a positive condition of freedom and emancipation in what appeared to modernism as the very form of alienation: the autonomy of the aesthetic sphere, the functional division of different social domains, etc. This renunciation of the modernist utopia, this acceptance of the fact that freedom is possible only on the basis of a certain fundamental "alienation," attests to the fact that we are in a postmodernist universe.

This confusion concerning the break between modernism and postmodernism comes to a critical point in Habermas's diagnosis of poststructuralist deconstructionism as the dominant form of contemporary philosophical postmodernism. The use of the prefix "post-" in both cases should not lead us astray (especially if we take into account the crucial but usually overlooked fact that the very term "poststructuralism," although designating a strain of French theory, is an Anglo-Saxon and German invention. The term refers to the way the Anglo-Saxon world perceived and located the theories of Derrida, Foucault, Deleuze, etc.—in France itself, nobody uses the term "poststructuralism"). Deconstructionism is a modernist procedure par excellence; it presents perhaps the most radical version of the logic of "unmasking" whereby the very unity of the experience of meaning is conceived as the effect of signifying mechanisms, an effect that can take place only insofar as it ignores the textual movement that produced it. It is only with Lacan that the "postmodernist" break occurs, insofar as he thematizes a certain real, traumatic kernel whose status remains deeply ambiguous: the real resists symbolization, but it is at the same time its own retroactive product. In this sense we could even say that deconstructionists are basically still "structuralists" and that the only "poststructuralist" is Lacan, who affirms enjoyment as "the real Thing," the central impossibility around which every signifying network is structured.

HITCHCOCK AS POSTMODERNIST

In what, then, does the postmodernist break consist? Let's begin with Antonioni's *Blow Up,* perhaps the last great modernist film. As the hero develops photographs shot in a park, his attention is attracted to a stain that appears on the edge of one of the photographs. When he enlarges the detail, he discovers the contours of a body there. Though it is the middle of the night, he rushes to the park and indeed finds the body. But on returning to the scene of the crime the next day, he finds that the body has disappeared without leaving a trace. The first thing to note here is that the body is, according to the code of the detective novel, the object of desire *par excellence,* the cause that starts the interpretive desire of the detective (and the reader): How did it happen? Who did it? The key to the film is only given to us, however, in the final scene. The hero, resigned to the cul-de-sac in which his investigation has ended, takes a walk near a tennis court where a group of people—without a tennis ball—mime a game of tennis. In the frame of this supposed game, the imagined ball is hit out of bounds and lands near the hero. He hesitates a moment and then accepts the game: bending over, he makes a gesture of picking up the ball and throwing it back into the court. This scene has, of course, a metaphorical function in relation to the rest of the film. It indicates the hero's consenting to the fact that "the game works without an object": even as the mimed tennis game can be played without a ball, so his own adventure proceeds without a body.

"Postmodernism" is the exact reverse of this process. It consists not in demonstrating that the game works without an object, that the play is set in motion by a central absence, but rather in displaying the object directly, allowing it to make visible its own indifferent and arbitrary character. The same object can function successively as a disgusting reject and as a sublime, charismatic apparition: the difference, strictly structural, does not pertain to the "effective properties" of the object, but only to its place in the symbolic order.

One can grasp this difference between modernism and postmodernism by analyzing the effect of horror in Hitchcock's films. At first, it seems that Hitchcock simply respects the classical rule (already known by Aeschylus in *The Oresteia*) according to which one must place the terrifying object or event outside the scene and show only its reflections and its effects on the stage. If one does not see the object directly, one fills out its absence with fantasy projections (one sees it as more horrible than it actually is). The elementary procedure for evoking horror would be, then, to limit oneself to reflections of the terrifying object in its witnesses or victims.

As is well known, this is the crucial axis of the revolution in horror movies accomplished in the 1940s by the legendary producer Val Lewton (*Cat People, The Seventh Victim,* etc.). Instead of directly showing the terrifying monster (vampire, murderous beast), its presence is indicated only by means of off-screen sounds, by shadows, and so on, and thus rendered all the more horrible. The properly Hitchcockian approach, however, is to *reverse* this process. Let's take a small detail from *Lifeboat,* from the scene where the group of Allied castaways welcome on board their boat a German sailor from the destroyed submarine: their surprise when they find out that the person saved is an enemy. The traditional way of filming this scene would be to let us hear the screams for help, to show the hands of an unknown person gripping the side of the boat, and then *not* to show the German sailor, but to move the camera to the shipwrecked survivors: it would then be the perplexed expression on their faces that would indicate to us that they had pulled something unexpected out of the water. What? When the suspense was finally built up, the camera would finally reveal the German sailor. But Hitchcock's procedure is *the exact contrary* of this: what he does not show, precisely, is the shipwrecked survivors. He shows the German sailor climbing on board and saying, with a friendly smile, "*Danke schön!*" Then he *does not* show the surprised faces of the survivors; the camera remains on the German. If his apparition provoked a terrifying effect, one can only detect it by *his* reaction to the survivor's reaction: his smile dies out, his look becomes perplexed. This demonstrates what Pascal Bonitzer[4] calls the Proustian side of Hitchcock, for this procedure corresponds perfectly to that of Proust in *Un amour de Swann* when Odette confesses to Swann her lesbian adventures. Proust only describes Odette— that her story has a terrifying effect on Swann is evident only in the change in the tone of her story when she notices its disastrous effect. One shows an ordinary object or an activity, but suddenly, through the reactions of the milieu to this object, *reflecting themselves in the object itself,* one realizes that one is confronting the source of an inexplicable terror. The terror is intensified by the fact that this object is, in its appearance, completely ordinary: what one took only a moment ago for a totally common thing is revealed as evil incarnate.

Such a postmodernist procedure seems to us much more subversive than the usual modernist one, because the latter, by not showing the Thing, leaves open the possibility of grasping the central emptiness under the perspective of an "absent God." The lesson of modernism is that the structure, the intersubjective machine, works as well if the Thing is lacking, if the machine revolves around an emptiness; the postmodernist reversal shows *the Thing itself as the incarnated, materialized emptiness*. This is accomplished by showing the terrifying object directly and then by revealing its frightening effect to be simply the effect of its place in the structure. The terrifying object is an everyday object that has started to function, by chance, as that which fills in the hole in the Other (the symbolic order). The prototype of a modernist text would be Samuel Beckett's *Waiting for Godot*. The whole futile and senseless action of the play takes place while waiting for Godot's arrival when, finally, "something might happen"; but one knows very well that "Godot" can never arrive because he is just a name for nothingness, for a central absence. What would the "postmodernist" rewriting of this same story look like? One would have to put Godot himself on stage: he would be someone exactly like us, someone who lives the same futile, boring life that we do, who enjoys the same stupid pleasures. The only difference would be that, not knowing it himself, he has found himself by chance at the place of the Thing; he would be the incarnation of the Thing whose arrival was awaited.

A less-known film by Fritz Lang, *Secret Beyond the Door,* stages in pure (one is almost tempted to say *distilled*) form this logic of an everyday object found in the place of *das Ding*. Celia Barrett, a young businesswoman, travels to Mexico after her older brother's death. She meets Mark Lamphere there, marries him, and moves in with him. A little later, the couple receives his intimate friends and Mark shows them his gallery of historical rooms, reconstituted in the vault of his mansion. But he forbids their entrance into room number seven, which is locked. Fascinated by the taboo placed on it, Celia gets a key made and enters the room, which turns out to be an exact replica of her room. The most familiar things take on a dimension of the uncanny when one finds them in another place, a place that "is not right." And the thrill effect results precisely from the familiar, domestic character of what one finds in this Thing's forbidden place—here we have the perfect illustration of the fundamental ambiguity of the Freudian notion of *das Unheimliche*.

The opposition between modernism and postmodernism is thus far from being reducible to a simple diachrony; we are even tempted to say that postmodernism in a way *precedes* modernism. Like Kafka—who logically, not only temporally, precedes Joyce—the postmodernist *inconsistency* of the Other is retroactively perceived by the modernist gaze as its *incompleteness*. If Joyce is the modernist par excellence, the writer of the symptom ("the symptom Joyce," as Lacan puts it), of the interpretive delirium taken to the infinite, of the *time* (to interpret) where each stable moment reveals itself to be nothing but a "condensation" of a plural signifying process, Kafka is in a certain way already postmodernist, the antipode of Joyce, the writer of fantasy, of the *space* of a nauseous inert presence. If Joyce's text provokes interpretation, Kafka's blocks it.

It is precisely this dimension of a nondialecticizable, inert presence that is misrecognized by a modernist reading of Kafka, with its accent on the inaccessible, absent, transcendent agency (the Castle, the Court), holding the place of the lack, of the absence as such. From this modernist perspective, the secret of Kafka would be that in the heart of the bureaucratic machinery, there is only an emptiness, nothing: bureaucracy would be a mad machine that "works by itself," as in *Blow Up* where the game is played without a body-object. One can read this conjunction in two opposed ways, which nevertheless share the same theoretical frame: theological and immanentist. One reading takes the elusive, inaccessible, transcendent character of the center (of the Castle, of the Court) as a mark of an "absent God" (the universe of Kafka as an anguished universe, abandoned by God); the other reading takes the emptiness of this transcendence as an "illusion of perspective," as a reverse form of the apparition of the immanence of desire (the inaccessible transcendence, the central lack, is then only the negative form of the apparition of the surplus of desire, of its productive movement, over the world of objects *qua* representations).[5]

These two readings, although opposed, miss the same point: the way this absence, this empty place, is always already filled out by an inert, obscene, revolting *presence*. The Court in *The Trial* is not simply absent, it is indeed present under the figures of the obscene judges who, during night interrogations, glance through pornographic books; the Castle is indeed present under the figure of subservient, lascivious, and corrupt civil servants. Which is why the formula of the "absent God" in Kafka does not work at all: for Kafka's problem is, on the contrary, that in this universe God is *too present,* in the guise of various obscene, nauseous phenomena. Kafka's universe is a world in which God—who up to now had held himself at an assured distance—has gotten too close to us. Kafka's universe is a "universe of anxiety," why not?—on condition, however, that one takes into account the Lacanian definition of anxiety (what provokes anxiety is not the loss of the incestuous object but, on the contrary, its very *proximity*). We are too close to *das Ding,* that is the theological lesson of postmodernism: Kafka's mad, obscene God, this "Supreme Being of Evil," is exactly the same as God *qua* Supreme Good—the difference lies only in the fact that we have gotten too close to Him.

Bureaucracy and Enjoyment

TWO DOORS OF THE LAW

To specify further the status of the Kafkaesque obscene enjoyment, let's take as a starting point the famous apologue concerning the door of the law in *The Trial,* the anecdote told to K. by the priest in order to explain to him his situation vis-à-vis the law. The patent failure of all the major interpretations of this apologue seems only to confirm the priest's thesis that "the comments often enough merely express the commentator's bewilderment." There is, however, another way to penetrate the anecdote's mystery: instead of seeking its meaning directly, it would be preferable to treat it in the way Claude Lévi-Strauss treats a myth: by establishing its relations to a series of other myths and elaborating the rules of their transformation. Where can we find, then, in *The Trial,* another "myth" that functions as a variation, as an inversion, of the apologue concerning the door of the law?

We do not have far to look: at the beginning of the second chapter ("First interrogation"), Josef K. finds himself in front of another door of the law (the entrance to the interrogation chamber); here also, the doorkeeper lets him know that this door is intended only for him. The washerwoman says to him, "I must shut this door after you, nobody else must come in," which is clearly a variation of the last words of the doorkeeper to the man from the country in the priest's apologue: "No one but you could gain admittance through this door, since this door was intended only for you. I am now going to shut it." At the same time, the apologue concerning the door of the law (let's call it, in the style of Lévi-Strauss, m^1) and the first interrogation (m^2) can be opposed through a whole series of distinctive features. In m^1 we are in front of the entrance to a magnificent court of justice, in m^2 we are in a block of workers' flats, full of filth and crawling obscenities; in m^1 the doorkeeper is an employee of the court, in m^2 it is an ordinary woman washing children's clothes; in m^1 it's a man, in m^2 a woman; in m^1 the doorkeeper prevents the man from the country from passing through the door and entering the court, in m^2 the washerwoman pushes him into the interrogation chamber half against his will. In short, the frontier separating everyday life from the sacred place of the law cannot be transgressed in m^1, but in m^2 it is easily transgressed.

The crucial feature of m^2 is already indicated by its location: the Court is located in the middle of the vital promiscuity of worker's lodgings. Reiner Stach is quite justified in recognizing in this detail a distinctive trait of Kafka's universe, "the trespassing of the frontier that separates the vital domain from the judicial domain."[6] The structure here, of course, is that of the Moebius strip: if we progress far enough in our descent to the social underground, we find ourselves suddenly on the other side, in the middle of the sublime and noble law. The place of transition from one domain to the other is a door guarded by an ordinary washerwoman of a provocative sensuality. In m¹, the doorkeeper doesn't know anything, whereas here the woman possesses a kind of advance knowledge. Ignoring the naive cunning of K., the excuse that he is looking for a joiner called Lanz, she makes him understand that his arrival has been awaited for a long time, even though K. himself only chose to enter her room quite by chance, as a last desperate attempt after a long and useless ramble:

> The first thing he saw in the little room was a great pendulum clock which already pointed to ten. "Does a joiner called Lanz live here?" he asked. "Please go through," said a young woman with sparkling black eyes, who was washing children's clothes in a tub, and she pointed her damp hand to the open door of the next room. . . . "I asked for a joiner, a man called Lanz." "I know," said the woman, "just go right in." K. might not have obeyed if she had not come up to him, grasped the handle of the door, and said: "I must shut this door after you, nobody else must come in."[7]

The situation here is exactly the same as in the well-known incident from *The Arabian Nights*: one enters a place quite by chance and learns that one's arrival has been long expected. The paradoxical foreknowledge of the washerwoman has nothing whatsoever to do with so-called "feminine intuition"—it is based on the simple fact that she is connected with the law. Her position regarding the law is far more crucial than that of a minor functionary; K. discovers this for himself soon afterward when his passionate argumentation before the tribunal is interrupted by an obscene intrusion:

> Here K. was interrupted by a shriek from the end of the hall; he peered from beneath his hand to see what was happening, for the reek of the room and the dim light together made a whitish dazzle of fog. It was the washerwoman, whom K. had recognized as a potential cause of disturbance from the moment of her entrance. Whether she was at fault now or not, one could not tell. All K. could see was that a man had drawn her into a corner by the door and was clasping her in his arms. Yet it was not she who had uttered the shriek but the man; his mouth was wide open and he was gazing up at the ceiling.[8]

What is the relation, then, between this woman and the Court of the law? In Kafka's work, the woman as a "psychological type" is wholly consistent with the anti-

feminist ideology of an Otto Weininger: the woman is a being without a proper self;
she is incapable of assuming an ethical attitude (even when she appears to act on
ethical grounds, she is calculating the enjoyment she will derive from her actions);
she is a being without any access to the dimension of truth (even when what she is
saying is literally true, she lies as a consequence of her subjective position). It is insuf-
ficient to say of such a being that she feigns her affections to seduce a man, for the
problem is that there is nothing behind this mask of simulation . . . nothing but a
certain glutinous, filthy enjoyment that is her very substance. Confronted with such
an image of woman, Kafka does not succumb to the usual critical-feminist temptation
(of demonstrating that this figure is the ideological product of specific social conditions; of contrasting it with the outlines of another type of femininity). In a much
more subversive gesture, Kafka wholly accepts this Weiningerian portrait of woman
as a "psychological type," while making it occupy an unheard of, unprecedented
place, the place of the law. This is, perhaps, as has already been pointed out by Stach,
the elementary operation of Kafka: this *short circuit between the feminine "substance" ("psychological type") and the place of the law.* Smeared by an obscene vitality, the law itself—traditionally, a pure, neutral universality—assumes the features of
a heterogeneous, inconsistent *bricolage* penetrated with enjoyment.

The Obscene Law

In Kafka's universe, the Court is—above all—lawless, in a formal sense: it is as
if the chain of "normal" connections between causes and effects were suspended, put
in parenthesis. Every attempt to establish the Court's mode of functioning by logical
reasoning is doomed in advance to fail. All the oppositions noted by K. (between the
anger of the judges and the laughter of the public on the benches; between the merry
right side and the severe left side of the public) prove false as soon as he tries to base
his tactics on them; after an ordinary answer by K. the public bursts into laughter:

> "Well, then," said the Examining Magistrate, turning over the leaves and
> addressing K. with an air of authority, "you are a house-painter?" "No,"
> said K., "I'm the junior manager of a large Bank." This answer evoked
> such a hearty outburst of laughter from the Right party that K. had to laugh
> too. People doubled up with their hands on their knees and shook as if
> in spasms of coughing.[9]

The other, positive side of this inconsistency is, of course, enjoyment: it erupts
openly when the argument of K. is disturbed by a public act of sexual intercourse.
This act, difficult to perceive because of its overexposure (K. has to "peer beneath

his hands to see what was happening"), marks the moment of the eruption of the traumatic real, and the error of K. consists in overlooking the *solidarity* between this obscene disturbance and the Court. He thinks that everybody will be anxious to have order restored and the offending couple ejected from the meeting. But when he tries to rush across the room, the crowd obstructs him. Someone seizes him from behind, by the collar—at this point, the game is over: puzzled and confused, K. loses the thread of his argument; filled with impotent rage, he leaves the room.

The fatal error of K. was to address the Court, the Other of the law, as a homogeneous entity, attainable by means of consistent argument, whereas the Court can only return him an obscene smile, mixed with signs of perplexity. In short, K. expects *action* from the Court (legal deeds, decisions), but what he gets instead is an *act* (a public copulation). Kafka's sensitivity to this "trespassing of the frontier that separates the vital domain from the judicial domain" depends upon his Judaism: the Jewish religion marks the moment of the most radical separation of these domains. In all previous religions, we encounter a place, a domain of sacred enjoyment (in the form of ritual orgies, for example), whereas in Judaism the sacred domain is evacuated of all traces of vitality and the living substance is subordinated to the dead letter of the Father's law. Kafka trespasses the divisions of his inherited religion, flooding the judicial domain, once again, with enjoyment.

Which is why Kafka's universe is eminently that of the *superego*. The Other as the Other of the symbolic law is not only dead, it doesn't even know that it is dead (like the terrible figure in Freud's dream); it couldn't know it insofar as it is totally insensible to the living substance of enjoyment. The superego presents, on the contrary, the paradox of a law that, according to Jacques-Alain Miller, "proceeds from the time when the Other was not yet dead, evidenced by the superego, a surviving remainder of that time." The superego imperative "Enjoy!," the inversion of the dead law into the obscene figure of the superego, implies a disquieting experience: suddenly we become aware that what a minute ago appeared to us a dead letter is really alive, breathing, pulsating. Let us recall a short scene from the film *Aliens*. The group of heroes is advancing through a long tunnel the stone walls of which are twisted like interlaced plaits of hair. All at once the plaits start to move and to secrete a glutinous mucus, the petrified corpse comes alive again.

We must, then, reverse the usual metaphor of "alienation" whereby the dead, formal letter, a kind of parasite or vampire, sucks out the living, present force. Living subjects can no longer be considered prisoners of a dead cobweb. The dead, formal character of the law becomes now the sine qua non of our freedom, and the real totalitarian danger arises only when the law no longer wants to stay dead.

The result of m^1 is, then, that there is no truth about truth. Every warrant of the law has the status of a semblance; the law is *necessary* without being *true*. To quote the words of the priest in m^1, "it is not necessary to accept everything as true; one must only accept it as necessary." The meeting of K. with the washerwoman adds to this the obverse, usually passed over in silence: insofar as the law is not grounded in truth, it is impregnated with enjoyment. Thus, m^1 and m^2 are complementary, representing the two modes of lack: the lack of incompleteness and the lack of inconsistency. In m^1, the Other of the law appears as *incomplete*. In its very heart, there is a certain gap; we can never reach the last door of the law. It is the reference to m^1 that supports the interpretation of Kafka as a "writer of absence," that is, the negative theological reading of his universe as a crazy bureaucratic machine turning blindly around the central void of an absent God. In m^2, the Other of the law appears on the contrary, as *inconsistent*: nothing is wanting in it, nothing is lacking, but for all that it still is not "whole/all," it remains an inconsistent *bricolage,* a collection following a kind of aleatory logic of enjoyment. This provides the image of Kafka as a "writer of presence"—the presence of what? Of a blind machinery to which nothing is lacking insofar as it is the very surfeit of enjoyment.

If modern literature can be characterized as "unreadable," then Kafka exemplifies this characteristic in a way that is different from James Joyce. *Finnegan's Wake* is, of course, an "unreadable" book; we cannot read it the way we read an ordinary "realist" novel. To follow the thread of the text, we need a kind of a "reader's guide," a commentary that enables us to see our way through the inexhaustible network of ciphered allusions. Yet this "illegibility" functions precisely as an invitation to an unending process of reading, of interpretation (recall Joyce's joke that with *Finnegan's Wake,* he hopes to keep literary scientists occupied for at least the next four hundred years). Compared to this, *The Trial* is quite "readable." The main outlines of the story are clear enough. Kafka's style is concise and of proverbial purity. But it is this very "legibility" that, because of its overexposed character, produces a radical opacity and blocks every essay of interpretation. It is as if Kafka's text were a coagulated, stigmatized, signifying chain repelling signification with an excess of sticky enjoyment.

THE SUPEREGO KNOWS TOO MUCH

The *bureaucracy* depicted in Kafka's novels—the immense machinery of totally useless, superfluous knowledge, running blindly and provoking an unbearable feeling of "irrational" guilt—functions as a superegoic knowledge (S_2 in Lacan's mathemes). This fact runs counter to our spontaneous understanding. Nothing seems more obvious than the connection between the superego and the Lacanian S_1, the master signifier. Is the superego not the very model of an "irrational" injunction founded solely in its own process of enunciation, demanding obedience without further justification? Lacanian theory, however, runs counter to this spontaneous intuition: the opposition between S_1 and S_2, that is, between the master signifier and the chain of knowledge, overlaps the opposition of ego-ideal (the "unitary trait," the point of symbolic identification) and the superego. The superego is on the side of S_2; it is a fragment of the chain of knowledge whose purest form of apparition is what we call the "irrational feeling of guilt." We feel guilty without knowing why, as a result of acts we are certain we did not commit. The Freudian solution to this paradox is, of course, that this feeling is well-founded: we feel guilty because of our repressed unconscious desires. Our conscious ego does not (want to) know anything about them, but the superego "sees all and knows all" and thus holds the subject responsible for its unacknowledged desires: "the superego knew more than the ego about the unconscious id."[10]

We should, then, renounce the usual notion of the unconscious as a kind of "reservoir" of wild, illicit drives: the unconscious is also (one is even tempted to say: above all) fragments of a traumatic, cruel, capricious, "unintelligible" and "irrational" law text, a set of prohibitions and injunctions. In other words, we must "put forward the paradoxical proposition that the normal man is not only far more immoral than he believes but also far more moral than he knows."[11] What is the precise meaning of this distinction between belief and knowledge, produced as if by a kind of slip and lost already in the note accompanying the quoted phrase from *The Ego and the Id*? In this note Freud rephrases his proposition by saying that it "simply states that human nature has a far greater extent, both for good and for evil, than it thinks [*glaubt*: believes] it has, i.e., than ego is aware of through conscious perceptions."[12] Lacan taught us to be extremely attentive to such distinctions that emerge momentarily and are forgotten immediately afterward, for it is through them that we can detect Freud's crucial insights, the whole dimension of which he himself failed to notice (let us recall only what Lacan has been able to derive from a similar "slippery" distinction between ego-ideal and ideal ego). What, then, is the import of that ephemeral distinction between belief and knowledge? Ultimately, only one answer is possible: if man is more immoral than he (consciously) believes and more moral than he (consciously) knows, in other words, if his relation toward the id (the illicit drives) is that of (dis)belief, and his relation toward the superego (its traumatic prohibitions and injunctions) that of (non)knowledge, i.e., of ignorance, must we not conclude that *the id in itself already consists of unconscious, repressed beliefs*, and that *the superego consists of an unconscious knowledge,* of a paradoxical knowledge unbeknown to the subject? As we have seen, Freud himself treats the superego as a kind of knowledge ("the superego *knew* more than the ego about the unconscious id"). But where can we grasp this knowledge in a palpable way, where does it acquire—so to speak—a material, external existence? In *paranoia,* in which this agency that "sees all and knows all" is embodied in the real, in the person of the all-knowing persecutor, able to "read our thoughts." Concerning the id, we only have to remember the famous challenge made by Lacan to his audience that they show him one single person who did not unconsciously believe in his own immortality, in God. According to Lacan, the true formula of atheism is "God is unconscious." There is a certain fundamental belief—a belief in the Other's basic consistency—that belongs to language as such. By the mere act of speaking, we *suppose* the existence of the big Other as guarantor of our meaning. Even in the most ascetic analytical philosophy, this fundamental belief is maintained in the form of what Donald Davidson called "the principle of charity," conceiving it as the condition for successful communication.[13] The only subject who can effectively renounce the "charity principle," that is, whose relation to the big Other of the symbolic order is characterized by a fundamental disbelief, is the *psychotic,* a paranoiac, for example, who sees in the symbolic network of meaning around him a plot staged by some evil persecutor.

Toward an Ethic of Fantasy

Violations of the Fantasy Space

"The Stuff of Madness," a short story by Patricia Highsmith, reads like a variation on the motif of the "pet cemetery." Christopher Waggoner's wife Penelope is pathologically attached to her pets: in the garden behind the house, all her deceased cats and dogs are exhibited, stuffed. Learning about this peculiarity, journalists petition her for a visit so that they can write an article on her and, of course, take photos of the garden. Christopher vigorously rejects this intrusion into the privacy of his home; at last forced to give way to his wife's resolution, he devises a cruel vengeance. He secretly manufactures an exact wax replica of Louise, his former lover, and puts the statue on a stone bench in the center of the garden. When, next morning, Penelope takes the journalists on a tour of the garden and sees the statue of Louise, she collapses from a heart attack (she knew only too well that Chris had never loved her and that Louise was his only true love). After she has been taken to the hospital, Chris remains alone in the house. The following morning, he is found dead in the garden—stiff as a doll in the lap of his Louise. The fantasy around which this story turns is, of course, Penelope's, not Chris's: the garden space, the fantasy universe of the stuffed pets, is a construction by means of which Penelope masks the ultimate failure of her marriage. The inconsiderate cruelty of Christopher's act consists in including in this fantasy space the very object that must be excluded, that is, the object whose presence disintegrates the fantasy: the figure of the Other Woman who embodies the miscarriage of the sexual relationship between Chris and Penelope. The effect of Christopher's act is, of course, that Penelope breaks down: the whole economy of her desire is disturbed, the very support that gave consistency to her personality, the frame of coordinates enabling her to live her life as "meaningful," is taken from her. This is, perhaps, the only possible psychoanalytic definition of sin: an intrusion into the fantasy space of the other whereby we "ruin his dreams." This is why Christopher's final act is of a strictly ethical nature, that is, by placing the statue of his lover in his wife's fantasy space, he also opens a niche for himself, a place beside Louise's statue. His ill-considered act does not simply place him in the position of a manipulator who would control the game from a kind of objective distance, because within the space he manipulates, he involuntarily designates a place for himself. The only thing that remains to be done, therefore, is to *take his place in his own picture*, to fill out its vacancy with his own body, and he must, so to speak, pay for it in kind— by his own death. This helps us to clarify, perhaps, what Lacan meant when he said that suicide is ultimately the only authentic act.

We encounter this same sort of ethical suicide in Max Ophuls's *Letter from an Unknown Woman*, a film based on Stephan Zweig's short story of the same name. It is the story of a Viennese pianist, a man of pleasure, who returns home late one evening and orders his servant to prepare his luggage quickly so that they can leave the city early the next morning. He has been challenged to a duel but intends, as usual, to run away. While the servant is busy with the packing, the pianist finds on his desk a letter from an unknown woman, addressed to him; he starts to read it. It is the tragic confession of a woman who has loved him without his knowing the central role he played in her life. She began to admire him in her teens, when he took her love to be an adolescent infatuation; later, to get close to him, she posed as a *fille de joie* and he failed even to recognize in her his former love—to him, she was just one in a series of conquests. After having an affair with him, she became pregnant, entrusted the child to the care of nuns, and committed suicide, so that now, as he reads her letter, she is already dead. The pianist is so shaken by the letter that, at dawn, he tells his servant to unpack the luggage: he will go to the duel, although he knows this means his certain death. What is especially interesting here is the difference between the film and Zweig's story, a difference that confirms the superiority of the film (and thus refutes the commonplace about the Hollywood "vulgarization" of literary masterpieces). In the story, the pianist receives the letter, reads it, and remembers the woman only in a few hazy flashes—she simply didn't mean anything to him. The entire framing plot of the challenge to a duel and the pianist's suicidal acceptance is added by the film. The hero's final gesture is profoundly consistent from an ethical point of view: after becoming aware of the crucial role he played in another person's universe and of the unbearable suffering he must have caused, the only way he can redeem his sin is by means of his suicide.[1]

Sydney Pollack's thriller *Yakuza* presents another variation of the same motif: here the redemption is not directly suicidal, but rather a respectful act of ritualized sacrifice. Robert Mitchum plays an American detective who falls in love with a beautiful Japanese woman who lives alone with her brother. Soon after becoming her lover, he learns that the man posing as her brother is really her husband, who has played the role of brother because he needed Mitchum's help and was afraid of losing his support if Mitchum were prevented from satisfying his desire. When Mitchum recognizes the suffering and humiliation he must have caused by his inconsiderate love, he apologizes to the husband in a traditional Japanese way: by cutting off a knuckle of his little finger and giving it to the husband, wrapped up in a handkerchief. By this gesture Mitchum does not indicate his acceptance of the Japanese ethical code as his own; the Japanese universe continues to seem to him as strange as it did before. The gesture simply expresses his regret for the terrible humiliation and suffering he caused by his inconsiderate ignorance of the other's symbolic universe.

Perhaps we could risk making of this a maxim of the psychoanalytic ethic, a kind of intersubjective supplement to the famous Lacanian maxim "do not cede your desire": avoid as much as possible any violation of the fantasy space of the other, i.e., respect as much as possible the other's "particular absolute," the way he organizes his universe of meaning in a way absolutely particular to him. Such an ethic is neither imaginary (the point is not to love our neighbor as ourselves, insofar as he resembles ourselves, i.e., insofar as we see in him an image of ourselves) nor symbolic (the point is also not to respect the other on account of the dignity bestowed on him by his symbolic identification, by the fact that he belongs to the same symbolic community as ourselves, even if we conceive this community in the widest possible sense and maintain respect for him "as a human being"). What confers on the other the dignity of a "person" is not any universal-symbolic feature but precisely what is "absolutely particular" about him, his fantasy, that part of him that we can be sure we can never share. To use Kant's terms: we do not respect the other on account of the universal moral law inhabiting every one of us, but on account of his utmost "pathological" kernel, on account of the absolutely particular way every one of us "dreams his world," organizes his enjoyment.

But is not the very aim of the psychoanalytic process to shake the foundations of the analysand's fundamental fantasy, i.e., to bring about the "subjective destitution" by which the subject acquires a sort of distance toward his fundamental fantasy as the last support of his (symbolic) reality? Is not the psychoanalytic process itself, then, a refined and therefore all the more cruel method of humiliation, of removing the very ground beneath the subject's feet, of forcing him to experience the utter nullity of those "divine details" around which all his enjoyment is crystallized? Fantasy as a "make-believe" masking a flaw, an inconsistency in the symbolic order, is always particular—its particularity is absolute, it resists "mediation," it cannot be made part of a larger, universal, symbolic medium. For this reason, we can acquire a sense of the dignity of another's fantasy only by assuming a kind of distance toward our own, by experiencing the ultimate contingency of fantasy as such, by apprehending it as the way everyone, in a manner proper to each, conceals the impasse of his desire. The dignity of a fantasy consists in its very "illusionary," fragile, helpless character.

THE IMPASSE OF LIBERALISM

In his *Contingency, Irony and Solidarity*, Richard Rorty faces the same problem by attempting to answer the question: how, upon what, can we build a liberal-democratic ethic after the failure of its universal-rationalistic foundations?[2] According to Rorty, we are today witnessing the final breakdown of the Enlightenment's efforts to base human rights and freedoms on some transcendent or transcendental support, exempted from the radical contingency of the historical process (the "natural rights" of man, universal reason, etc.), on some ideal—a kind of Kantian regulative idea—that would guide the historical process (the Habermasian ideal of a communication without constraints, for example). Even the very historical course of events can no longer be grasped as a unitary process by some controlling meta-narration (the Marxist narrative of history as the history of the class struggle no longer holds). History is always being rewritten backward, every new narrative perspective restructures the past, changes its meaning, and it is a priori impossible to assume a neutral position from which it would be possible to coordinate and totalize the diverging narrative symbolizations. Are we not then led to the unavoidable conclusion that all ethical projects, including those that are openly antidemocratic, racist, etc., are ultimately equivalent, insofar as we can give preference to one of them only by assuming a certain narrative perspective that is contingent, i.e., insofar as every argument in its favor is by definition circular, presupposing in advance its own point of view? What would be the ethical attitude proper to the "ironist," in Rorty's sense of the term, as opposed to the "metaphysician" ("I use 'ironist' to name the sort of person who faces up to the contingency of his or her own most central beliefs and desires")[3]?

> Whereas the metaphysician takes the morally relevant feature of other human beings to be their relation to a larger shared power—rationality, God, truth, or history, for example—the ironist takes the morally relevant definition of a person, a moral subject, to be "something that can be

humiliated." Their sense of human solidarity is based on a sense of common danger, not on a common possession or a shared power. . . . He
thinks that the task of the intellectual is to preserve and defend liberalism
by backing it up with some true propositions about large subjects, but she
thinks that this task is to increase our skill at recognizing and describing
the different sorts of little things around which individuals or communities center their fantasies and their lives.[4]

These "different sorts of little things," what Nabokov calls the "divine details,"
designate of course the fundamental fantasy, that "particular absolute" functioning
as a frame within which things and events are meaningful to us. Therefore Rorty proposes as a basis of solidarity not the possession of some common properties, values,
beliefs, ideals, not the recognition of the other as somebody who believes and
desires what we believe and desire, but rather the recognition of the other as somebody who can suffer, who can be in pain. Pain is here not primarily physical but above
all "mental pain,"[5] humiliation brought about by the intrusion into another's fantasy.
In Orwell's *1984*, O'Brien breaks Winston when, by means of the threat of rats, he
disturbs Winston's relation to Julia: by uttering the desperate cry "Do it to Julia!" Winston does something that shatters the very foundation of his being. "Each of us stands
in the same relation to some sentence, and to some thing"[6]—Lacan tried to designate
this very relation by his formula for fantasy, $\$ \lozenge a$.

At this precise point, however, some of Rorty's formulations become problem-
atically imprecise. When he says that the "ultimate humiliation" consists in finding
ourselves in a state in which "the story I have been telling myself about myself—my
picture of myself as honest, or loyal, or devout—no longer makes sense,"[7] Rorty
reduces "mental pain" to the breakdown of the subject's symbolic and/or imaginary
identification. What we have here is simply an instance in which one of our actions
cannot be integrated into the (contingent) symbolic narration that delineates the
horizon of our self-apprehension; this failure precipitates the collapse of the image
in which we appeared likable to ourselves. That somewhat mysterious "relation to
some sentence, and to some thing" is, however, located on a level more radical than
that of symbolic and/or imaginary identification: it concerns the relation to the
object-cause of desire, i.e., the basic coordinates regulating our "desiring faculty." Far
from being of no consequence, this confusion plays a positive role in Rorty's theoretical edifice: it is only on its basis that he is able to formulate his project of a "liberal utopia: one in which ironism . . . is universal."[8]

In what does this "liberal utopia" consist? Rorty's fundamental premise is that we must "drop the demand for a theory which unifies the public and private" and be "content to treat the demands of self-creation and of human solidarity as equally valid, yet forever incommensurable."[9] The ideal, utopian society would be then a society in which the domains of "public" and "private" are clearly differentiated, a society making possible to every individual and community the free pursuit of "the different sorts of little things around which [they] center their fantasies and their lives," a society in which the role of social law is reduced to a set of neutral rules guarding this freedom of self-creation by protecting each individual from violent intrusions into his private space. The problem with this liberal dream is that the split between the public and private never comes about without a certain remainder. Here, we are not proposing the usual Marxist repudiation of liberalist individualism, which would demonstrate with bravura the way the very split public/private is socially conditioned, a product of a specific social structure, and the way even the most intimate modes of subjective self-experience are already "mediated" by the predominant form of social relations. A liberal could easily concede these points and still maintain his position. The real impasse runs in the opposite direction: the very social law that, as a kind of neutral set of rules, should limit our aesthetic self-creation and deprive us of a part of our enjoyment on behalf of solidarity, is always already penetrated by an obscene, "pathological," surplus enjoyment. The point is thus not that the split public/private is not possible, but that it is possible only on condition that the very domain of the public law is "smeared" by an obscene dimension of "private" enjoyment: public law draws the "energy" for the pressure it exerts on the subject from the very enjoyment of which it deprives him by acting as an agency of prohibition. In psychoanalytic theory, such an obscene law has a precise name: the *superego*.

Freud himself pointed out that the superego feeds on the forces of the id, which it suppresses and from which it acquires its obscene, malevolent, sneering quality—as if the enjoyment of which the subject is deprived were accumulated in the very place from which the superego's prohibition is enunciated.[10] The linguistic distinction between the subject of the statement and the subject of the enunciation finds here its perfect use: behind the statement of the moral law that imposes on us the renunciation of enjoyment, there is always hidden an obscene subject of enunciation, amassing the enjoyment it steals. The superego is, so to speak, an agency of the law exempted from its authority: it does itself what it prohibits us from doing. We can explain its fundamental paradox thus: the more innocent we are, i.e., the more we follow the superego's order and renounce enjoyment, the more guilty we feel, for the more we obey the superego, the greater is the enjoyment accumulated in it and, thus, the greater the pressure it exerts on us.[11] To get an idea of what a social agency functioning like the superego would be like, one has only to recall the bureaucratic machinery with which the subject is confronted in Kafka's great novels (*The Castle, The Trial*); this immense apparatus is penetrated with obscene enjoyment.

KANT WITH MCCULLOUGH

We can now locate in a precise manner the flaw of Rorty's "liberal utopia": it presupposes the possibility of a universal social law *not* smudged by a "pathological" stain of enjoyment, i.e., delivered from the superego dimension. In other words, it presupposes a duty that would *not* be the "most indecent of all obsessions" (to borrow a phrase from a contemporary kitsch bestseller). What Kant did not know, this philosopher of unconditional duty, the vulgar sentimental literature, the kitsch of today knows very well. This is not surprising, if one realizes that it is precisely in the universe of such a literature that the tradition of "courtly love," which considers the love of the Lady a supreme duty, still survives. An exemplary case of the courtly love genre is to be found in *An Indecent Obsession* by Colleen McCullough, a novel completely unreadable and for that reason published in France in the collection of *J'ai lu* (I've Read It). It is the story of a nurse in charge of mental patients in a small hospital of the Pacific around the end of World War II who is divided between her professional duty and her love for one of her patients. At the end of the novel she figures out her desire, gives up love, and goes back to her duty. At first glance, then, the most insipid moralism: the victory of duty over passionate love, the renunciation of "pathological" love for the sake of duty. The presentation of the motives for this renunciation is nevertheless a little more subtle; here are the last sentences of the novel:

> She had a duty here. . . . This wasn't just a job—her heart was in it, fathoms deep in it! This was what she truly wanted. . . . Nurse Langtry began to walk again, briskly and without any fear, understanding herself at last. And understanding that duty, the most indecent of all obsessions, was only another name for love.[12]

One is dealing then with a true dialectical Hegelian inversion: the opposition of love and duty is "sublated" (*aufgehoben*) when one feels duty itself to be "only another name for love." By means of this reversal—the "negation of the negation"—

duty, at first the negation of love, coincides with a supreme love that abolishes all other "pathological" loves of worldly objects, or, to use Lacanian terms, functions as the "quilting point" (*point de capiton*) of all other "ordinary" loves. The tension between duty and love—between the purity of duty and the indecency or pathological obscenity of passionate love—is resolved at the moment when one experiences the radically obscene character of duty itself.

At the beginning of the novel, it is duty that is pure, universal, while passionate love appears pathological, particular, indecent; at the end, however, it is duty that is revealed to be "the most indecent of all obsessions." This is the way one should understand the Lacanian thesis according to which Good is only the mask of radical, absolute Evil, the mask of "indecent obsession" by *das Ding*, the atrocious, obscene Thing. Behind Good, there is radical Evil: Good is "another name for an Evil" that does not have a particular, "pathological" status. Insofar as it obsesses us in an indecent way, insofar as it functions as a traumatic, strange body that disturbs the ordinary course of things, *das Ding* makes it possible for us to untie ourselves, to free ourselves from our "pathological" attachment to particular worldly objects. The "Good" is only a way of maintaining a distance toward this evil Thing, a distance that makes it bearable.

This is what Kant, unlike the kitsch literature of our century, does not know: the other, obscene side of duty itself. This is why it was only possible for Kant to evoke the concept of *das Ding* in its negative form, as an absurd (im)possibility—in his treatise on negative quantities, for example, apropos of the difference between logical contradiction and real opposition. Contradiction is a logical relationship that does not have any real existence, while real opposition is a relationship between two poles that are equally positive. The latter relationship is not between something and its lack, but between two positive givens. An example—which is not at all accidental, insofar as it reveals the level at which we are when we speak of real opposition, namely that of the pleasure principle—is pleasure and pain: "Pleasure and pain are not compared to each other like gain and absence of gain ($+$ and $-$). In other words, they are not opposed simply as contradictory (*contradictoire s. logice oppositum*), but also as contraries (*contrarie s. realiter oppositum*)."[13]

Pleasure and pain are poles of a real opposition, in themselves positive facts. One is negative only in relation to the other, while Good and Evil are contradictory, their relation being that of $+$ and 0. That is why Evil is not a positive entity. It is only the lack, the absence of Good. It would be an absurdity to take the negative pole of a contradiction as something positive, "to think of a particular sort of object and to call it a negative thing."[14] *Das Ding* is, however, in its Lacanian conceptualization, *pre-*

cisely such a "negative thing," a paradoxical Thing that is nothing but the materialization, the embodiment of a lack, of a hole in the Other or the symbolic order. *Das
Ding* as "incarnated Evil" is indeed an object that escapes the pleasure principle, the
opposition between pleasure and pain: it is a "nonpathological" object in the strict
Kantian sense of the term and as such an unthinkable paradox for Kant. Which is
why Kant is to be thought along "with Sade," as Lacan suggests—or at least with
McCullough.

The Nation-Thing

THE DEMOCRATIC ABSTRACTION

All this has, of course, far-reaching consequences for the very notion of democracy. Even in the '60s, Lacan predicted a new rise of racism for the coming decades,
an aggravation of ethnic tensions and of aggressive affirmations of ethnic particularities. Although Lacan aimed above all at Western societies, the recent flare of
nationalism in the countries of "real socialism" bears out his premonition more fully
than he could have anticipated. From what does this sudden impact of the ethnic
Cause, the ethnic Thing (this term is to be conceived here in its precise Lacanian
sense as a traumatic, real object fixing our desire), draw its strength? Lacan locates
its strength as the reverse of the striving after universality that constitutes the very
basis of our capitalist civilization: it was Marx himself who conceived the dissolution
of all particular, "substantial" ethnic, hereditary ties as a crucial feature of capitalism.
In recent decades, the striving for universality has been given a new thrust by a whole
series of economic, technological, and cultural processes: the overcoming of
national frontiers in the economic domain; technological, cultural, and linguistic
homogenization by means of new media (the computer revolution, satellite trans-
mission of information); the rise of "planetary" political issues (concern for human
rights, the ecological crisis), etc. In all these different forms of the movement toward
planetary "integration," the very notions of a sovereign nation state, of a national culture, etc., seem slowly but unavoidably to lose their weight. All the so-called "ethnic
particularities" are of course preserved, but precisely as submerged in the medium
of universal integration—no longer independently grown, they are posited as particular aspects of the universal many-sidedness. Such, for example, is the fate of
"national cuisines" in a contemporary megalopolis: behind every corner lurk
Chinese, Italian, French, Indian, Mexican, Greek restaurants, which fact only confirms the loss of the proper ethnic roots of these cuisines.

This is, of course, a commonplace of contemporary conservative "cultural criticism." Does Lacan, then, by linking the rise of racism to the process of universalization, range himself with this ideological argument which warns that contemporary civilization, by causing people to lose their anchoring, their sense of belonging to some particular community, precipitates a violent backlash of nationalism? While Lacan (a follower, in this respect, of Marx) does recognize a moment of truth in this nostalgic, conservative attitude, he nonetheless radically subverts its whole perspective.

We should begin with an elementary question: who is the subject of democracy? The Lacanian answer is unequivocal: the subject of democracy is not a human person, "man" in all the richness of his needs, interests, and beliefs. The subject of democracy, like the subject of psychoanalysis, is none other than the Cartesian subject in all its abstraction, the empty punctuality we reach after subtracting all its particular contents. In other words, there is a structural homology between the Cartesian procedure of radical doubt that produces the *cogito*, an empty point or reflective self-reference as a remainder, and the preamble of every democratic proclamation "all people *without regard to* (race, sex, religion, wealth, social status)." We should not fail to notice the violent act of abstraction at work in this "without regard to"; it is an abstraction of all positive features, a dissolution of all substantial, innate links, which produces an entity strictly correlative to the Cartesian *cogito* as a point of pure, nonsubstantial subjectivity. Lacan likened the subject of psychoanalysis to this entity, to the great surprise of those used to the "psychoanalytic image of man" as a wealth of "irrational" drives; he denotes the subject by a crossed-out S, indicating thereby a constitutive lack of any support that would offer the subject a positive, substantial identity. It is because of this lack of identity, that the concept of *identification* plays such a crucial role in psychoanalytic theory: the subject attempts to fill out its constitutive lack by means of identification, by identifying itself with some master-signifier guaranteeing its place in the symbolic network.

This violent act of abstraction does not express an ideologically overstretched image of democracy, an "exaggeration never met in real life," it pertains on the contrary to the very logic we follow as soon as we accept the principle of formal democracy: "democracy" is fundamentally "antihumanistic," it is not "made to the measure of (concrete, actual) men," but to the measure of a formal, heartless abstraction. There is in the very notion of democracy no place for the fullness of concrete human content, for the genuineness of community links: democracy *is* a formal link of abstract individuals. All attempts to fill out democracy with "concrete contents" succumb sooner or later to the totalitarian temptation, however sincere their motives may be.[15] Critics of democracy are thus correct in a way: democracy implies a split between the abstract *citoyen* and the *bourgeois* bearer of particular, "pathological" interests, and any reconciliation between the two is structurally impossible. Or, to refer to the traditional opposition between *Gesellschaft* (society, as a mechanical, external agglomeration of atomized individuals) and *Gemeinschaft* (society as a community held together by organic links): democracy is definitely bound up with *Gesellschaft*; it literally lives on the split between the "public" and "private," it is possible only within the framework of what was once, when the voice of Marxism was still heard, called "alienation."

Today, we can perceive this affinity of democracy with "alienated" *Gesellschaft* in the so-called "new social movements": ecology, feminism, the peace movement. They differ from traditional political movements (parties) by a certain self-limitation, the reverse side of which is a certain surplus; they want at the same time "less" and "more" than the traditional parties. That is to say, the "new social movements" are reluctant to enter the routine political struggle, they continually emphasize their unwillingness to become political parties like the others, they exempt themselves from the sphere of the struggle for power. At the same time, however, they make it clear that their aim is much more radical than that of the ordinary political parties: what they are striving after is a fundamental transformation of the entire mode of action and belief, a change in the "life paradigm" affecting our most intimate attitudes. They offer, for example, a new attitude toward nature, which would no longer be that of domination but rather that of a dialogic interplay; against aggressive "masculine" reason, they stand for a pluralistic, "soft," "feminine" rationality, etc. In other words, it is not possible to be an ecologist or feminist in quite the same way as one can be a conservative or a social democrat in a Western formal democracy. What is at stake in the former case is not just a political belief but an entire life attitude. And such a project of radical change in the "life paradigm," once formulated as a political program, necessarily undermines the very foundations of formal democracy. The antagonism between formal democracy and the "new social movements" is irreducible, which is why this antagonism has to be fully assumed and not eluded by means of utopian projects for a "concrete democracy" which would absorb the whole diversity of the so-called "life-world."

The subject of democracy is thus a pure singularity, emptied of all content, freed from all substantial ties; and, according to Lacan, the problem with this subject does not lie where neoconservatism sees it. The problem is not that this abstraction proper to democracy dissolves all concrete substantial ties, but rather that *it can never dissolve them*. The subject of democracy is, in its very blankness, smeared with a certain "pathological" stain. The "democratic break"—the casting away of the wealth of particular contents constitutive of the democratic subject, homologous to the "epistemological break" through which science constitutes itself by freeing itself from the realm of ideological notions—never comes about without a certain remainder. This remainder is, however, not to be conceived as an empirical limitation, that which causes the break to fail. Instead this remainder possesses an a priori status, it is a positive condition of the "democratic break," its very support. Precisely insofar as it claims to be "pure," "formal," democracy remains forever tied to a contingent moment of positivity, of material "content": by losing this material support, the very form dissolves itself.

. . . AND ITS LEFTOVER

This leftover to which formal democracy clings, that which renders possible the subtraction of all positive contents, is of course the ethnic moment conceived as "nation": democracy is always tied to the "pathological" fact of a nation-state. Every attempt to inaugurate a "planetary" democracy based upon the community of all people as "citizens of the world" soon attests its own impotence, fails to arouse political enthusiasm. Here we have again an exemplary case of the Lacanian logic of not-all where the universal function is founded upon an exception: the ideal leveling of all social differences, the production of the citizen, the subject of democracy, is possible only through an allegiance to some particular national Cause. If we apprehend this Cause as the Freudian Thing (*das Ding*), materialized enjoyment, it becomes clear why it is precisely "nationalism" that is the privileged domain of the eruption of enjoyment into the social field: the national Cause is ultimately the way subjects of a given nation organize their collective enjoyment through national myths. What is at stake in ethnic tensions is always the possession of the national Thing: the "other" wants to steal our enjoyment (by ruining our "way of life") and/or it has access to some secret, perverse enjoyment. In short, what gets on our nerves, what really bothers us about the "other," is the peculiar way he organizes his enjoyment (the smell of his food, his "noisy" songs and dances, his strange manners, his attitude to work—in the racist perspective, the "other" is either a workaholic stealing our jobs or an idler living on our labor). The basic paradox is that our Thing is conceived as something inaccessible to the other and at the same time threatened by him; this is similar to castration which, according to Freud, is experienced as something that "really cannot happen," but whose prospect nonetheless horrifies us.

The eruption of the national Thing in all its violence has always taken the devotees of international solidarity by surprise. Perhaps the most traumatic case of this was the debacle of the international workers' movement in the face of "patriotic" euphoria at the outbreak of World War I. Today, it is difficult to imagine what a traumatic shock it was to the leaders of all currents of social democracy, from Edouard Bernstein to Lenin, when the social democratic parties of all countries (with the exception of the Bolsheviks in Russia and Serbia) gave way to chauvinist outbursts and "patriotically" stood behind "their" respective governments, oblivious to the proclaimed solidarity of the working class "without country": this shock bears witness to an encounter of the real of enjoyment. Yet in some ways these chauvinist outbursts of "patriotic feeling" were far from unexpected: years before the actual outbreak of the war, social democracies drew the attention of workers to the fact that imperialist forces were preparing for a new world war, and warned against yielding to "patriotic" chauvinism. Even at the outbreak of the war, i.e., in the days following the Sarajevo assassination, the German social democrats cautioned workers that the ruling class would use the assassination as an excuse to declare war. Furthermore, the Socialist International adopted a formal resolution obliging all its members to vote against war credits in case of war—but with the outbreak of the war, internationalist solidarity vanished into thin air. This overnight reversal took Lenin by surprise: when he read in the daily newspaper that the social democratic deputies had voted for the war credits, he was at first convinced that this issue was fabricated by German police to lead workers astray!

Consequently, it is not sufficient to say that "pure" democracy is not possible: the crucial point is where we locate this impossibility. "Pure" democracy is not impossible because of some empirical inertia that prevents its full realization but which may be gradually abolished by democracy's further development; rather, democracy is possible only on the *basis* of its own impossibility; its limit, the irreducible "pathological" remainder, is its positive condition. At a certain level, this was already known to Marx (which is why, according to Lacan, the origin of the notion of the symptom is to be found in Marx): the "formal democracy" of the market, its equivalent exchange, implies "exploitation," appropriation of the surplus value, but this imbalance is not an indication of an "imperfect" realization of the principle of equivalent exchange, rather equivalent market exchange is *the very form of "exploitation,"* of the appropriation of surplus value. That is to say, formal equivalence is the form of a nonequivalence of contents. Herein lies the connection between the *objet petit a*, surplus enjoyment, and the Marxian notion of surplus value (Lacan himself coined the term *suplus enjoyment* on the model of *surplus value*): surplus value is the "material" remainder, the surplus contents, appropriated by the capitalist through the very form of the equivalent exchange between capital and the labor force.

One need not wait for Marx, however, to discover the imbalance, the paradoxes of the bourgeois principle of formal equality; difficulties had already arisen with the Marquis de Sade. His project for a "democracy of enjoyment"—as articulated in his pamphlet "Frenchmen, yet another effort if you want to be republicans . . . ," included in *Philosophy in the Bedroom*[16]—stumbles upon the fact that democracy can only be a democracy of the subject (of the signifier): *there is no democracy of the object*. The respective domains of fantasy and symbolic law are radically incommensurable. That is to say, it is in the very nature of fantasy to resist universalization: fantasy is the absolutely particular way every one of us structures his/her "impossible" relation to the traumatic Thing. It is the way every one of us, by means of an imaginary scenario, dissolves and/or conceals the fundamental impasse of the inconsistent big Other, the symbolic order. The field of the law, of "rights" and "duties," on the other hand, pertains by its very nature to the dimension of universality, it is a field of universal equalization brought about by equivalent exchange and reciprocity. We could thus define *objet petit a*, the object-cause of desire embodying surplus enjoyment, precisely as the surplus that escapes the network of universal exchange, which is why the formula of fantasy as irreducible to the dimension of universality is $\$\Diamond a$, i.e., the subject confronted with this "impossible" surplus.

The "heroism" of Sade's project consists in its impossible endeavor to confer upon the very field of enjoyment (of the fantasy structuring enjoyment) the bourgeois form of universal legality, of equivalent exchange, of the reciprocity of equal rights and duties. To the list of the "rights of man" proclaimed by the French revolution, Sade adds the "right to enjoyment," an embarrassing supplement that secretly subverts the universal field of rights in which it purports to place itself. Again we witness the logic of the not-all: the field of the universal "rights of man" is based upon the exclusion of a certain right (the right to enjoyment); as soon as we include this particular right, the very field of universal rights is thrown off balance. Sade starts from the statement that the French revolution got stuck halfway: in the domain of enjoyment, it remained prisoner of prerevolutionary, patriarchal, nonemancipated values. But as Lacan demonstrated in "Kant with Sade," any attempt to give to the "right to enjoyment" the form of a universal norm in conformity with the "categorical imperative" necessarily ends in a deadlock. Such a Sadian norm would affirm that anybody—irrespective of his/her sex, age, social status, etc.—has a right to dispose freely of any part of my body in order to satisfy in any conceivable way his/her desires. In Lacan's fictional reconstruction, this reads: "I have the right of enjoyment over your body, anyone can say to me, and I will exercise this right, without any limit stopping me in the capriciousness of the exactions that I might have the taste to satiate."[17] Lacan points out that such a universal norm, although satisfying the criterion of Kant's categorical imperative, is self-defeating insofar as it excludes reciprocity: ultimately, one always gives more than one takes, i.e., everybody finds himself occupying the position of the victim. For that reason, it is not possible to sanction the right to enjoyment in the form "Everyone has a right to exert his/her particular fantasy!" Sooner or later, we entangle ourselves in a kind of self-obstruction; by definition, fantasies cannot coexist peacefully" in some neutral medium. For example, since there is no sexual relationship, man can develop an endurable relation with a woman only insofar as she enters the frame of his peculiarly perverted fantasy. What can we say, then, about somebody with whom a sexual relation is possible only when the clitoris is cut out? Moreover, what can we say about *the woman* who accepts this and demands the right to undergo the painful ritual of cutting out her clitoris? Is this part of her "right to enjoyment," or are we supposed to liberate her in the name of Western values from this "barbaric" way of organizing her enjoyment? This point is, there is no way out: even if we say a woman can humiliate herself as long as she does so of her own free will, we can imagine the existence of a fantasy that consists in being humiliated *against* her will.

What to do, then, once we are confronted with this fundamental impasse of democracy? The "modernist" procedure (the one to which Marx is attached) would be to conclude—from such an "unmasking" of formal democracy, i.e., from the disclosure of the way the democratic form always conceals an imbalance of contents—that formal democracy as such has to be abolished, replaced by a superior form of concrete democracy. The "postmodernist" approach would require us, on the contrary, to assume this constitutive paradox of democracy. We must assume a kind of "active forgetfulness" by accepting the symbolic fiction even though we know that "in reality, things are not like that." The democratic attitude is always based upon a certain fetishistic split: *I know very well* (that the democratic form is just a form spoiled by stains of "pathological" imbalance), *but just the same* (I act as if democracy were possible). Far from indicating its fatal flaw, this split is the very source of the strength of democracy: democracy is able to take cognizance of the fact that its limit lies in itself, in its internal "antagonism." This is why it can avoid the fate of "totalitarianism," which is condemned ceaselessly to invent external "enemies" to account for its failures.

Freud's "Copernican turn," his subversion of the self-centered image of man, is thus not to be conceived as a renunciation of the Enlightenment, as a deconstruction of the notion of the autonomous subject, i.e., of the subject freed from the constraint of external authority. The point of Freud's "Copernican turn" is *not* to demonstrate that the subject is ultimately a puppet in the hands of unknown forces that escape his grasp (unconscious drives, etc.). It does not improve things to exchange this naive, naturalist notion of the unconscious for a more sophisticated notion of the unconscious as "discourse of the great Other" that makes the subject the place where language itself speaks, i.e., an agency subjected to decentered signifying mechanisms. Despite some Lacanian propositions that echo this structuralist notion, this sort of "decentering" does not capture the objective of Lacan's "return to Freud." According to Lacan, Freud is far from proposing an image of man as a victim of "irrational" drives, proper to *Lebensphilosophie*; he assumes without restraint the fundamental gesture of the Enlightenment: a refusal of the external authority of tradition and a reduction of the subject to an empty, formal point of negative self-relation. The problem is that, by "circulating around itself," as its own sun, this autonomous subject encounters in itself something "more than itself," a strange body in its very center. This is what Lacan's neologism *extimité* aims at, the designation of a stranger in the midst of my intimacy. Precisely by "circulating only around itself," the subject circulates around something that is "in itself more than itself," the traumatic kernel of enjoyment that Lacan refers to by the German word *das Ding*. The subject is perhaps nothing but a name for this circular movement, for this distance toward the Thing which is "too hot" to be approached closely. It is because of this Thing that the subject resists universalization, that it cannot be reduced to a place—even if it is an empty place—in the symbolic order. It is because of this Thing that at a certain point, love for the neighbor necessarily turns into destructive hatred, in accordance with the Lacanian motto *I love you, but there is in you something more than you*, objet petit a, *which is why I mutilate you.*

Notes

1.   Jean-Claude Milner, *Détections fictives,* Paris, Editions du Seuil, 1985, pp. 45-71.

2.   "When you entrust someone with a mission, the *aim* is not what he brings back, but the itinerary he must take. The *aim* is the way taken. . . . If the drive may be satisfied without attaining what, from the point-of-view of a biological totalization of function, would be the satisfaction of its end of reproduction, it is because it is a partial drive, and its aim is simply this return into circuit." (Jacques Lacan, *The Four Fundamental Concepts of Psycho-Analysis,* London, Hogarth Press, 1977, p. 179.)

3.   In other words, we could pin down the ultimate paradox of Zeno's paradoxes by means of the Hegelian distinction between what the subject "intends to say" and what he "effectively says" (the distinction that, incidentally, coincides with the Lacanian distinction between *signification* and *signifiance*). What Zeno "wants to say," his intention, is to exclude the paradoxical nature of our relationship to object small *a* by proving its nonexistence; what he effectively does (more properly: says) is to articulate the very paradoxes that define the status of this object as impossible-real.

4.   Jacques Lacan, "Réponses à des étudiants en philosophie," in *Cahiers pour l'analyse* 3, Paris, Graphe, 1967, p. 7.

5.   For an articulation of such a notion of fantasy in regard to cinema, see Elizabeth Cowie, *Sexual Difference and Representation in the Cinema,* London, Macmillan, 1990.

6.   In this respect, the role of the cleared cornfield, transformed into a baseball diamond in Phil Robinson's *Field of Dreams* is exactly homologous to the "black house": it is a clearance opening the space where the fantasy figures can appear. What we must not overlook apropos of *Field of Dreams* is the purely formal aspect: all we have to do is to cut out a square in the field and enclose it with a fence, and already phantoms start to appear in it, and the ordinary corn behind it is miraculously transformed into the mythical thicket giving birth to the phantoms and guarding their secret—in short, an ordinary field becomes a "field of dreams." In this it is similar to Saki's famous short story "The Window": a guest arrives at a country house and looks through the spacious French window at the field behind the house; the daughter of the family, the only one to receive him upon his arrival, tells him that all other members of the family had died recently in an accident; soon afterward, when the guest looks through the window again, he sees them approaching slowly across the field, returning from the hunt. Convinced that what he sees are ghosts of the deceased, he runs away in horror . . . (The daughter is of course a clever pathological liar. For her family, she quickly concocts another story to explain why the guest left the house in a panic.) So, a few words encircling the window with a new frame of reference suffice to transform it miraculously into a fantasy frame and to transubstantiate the muddy tenants into frightful ghostly apparitions.

What is especially indicative in *Field of Dreams* is the content of the apparitions: the film culminates in the apparition of the ghost of the hero's father (the hero remembers him only from his later years, as a figure broken by the shameful end of his baseball career)—now he sees him young and full of ardor, ignorant of the future that awaits him. In other words, he sees his father in a state where the father *doesn't know that he is already dead* (to repeat the well-known formula of a Freudian dream) and the hero greets his arrival with the words "Look at him! He's got his whole life in front of him and I'm not even a gleam in his eye!," which offer a concise definition of the elementary skeleton of the fantasy scene: to be present, as a pure gaze, before one's own conception or, more precisely, at the very act of one's own conception. The Lacanian formula of fantasy ($ \$ \Diamond a$) is to be conceived precisely as such a paradoxical conjunction of the subject and the object *qua* this impossible gaze; i.e., the "object" of fantasy is not the fantasy scene itself, its content (the parental coitus, for example), but the impossible gaze witnessing it. This impossible gaze involves a kind of time paradox, a "travel into the past" enabling the subject to be present before its beginning. Let us simply recall the famous scene from David Lynch's *Blue Velvet,* where the hero watches through a fissure in the closet door the sado-masochistic sexual play between Isabella Rossellini and Denis Hopper in which he relates to her now as son, now as father. This play is the "subject," the content of the fantasy, whereas the hero himself, reduced to the presence of a pure gaze, is the object. The basic paradox of the fantasy consists precisely in this temporal short circuit where the subject *qua* gaze *precedes itself* and witnesses its own origin. Another example is found in Mary Shelley's *Frankenstein,* where Dr. Frankenstein and his bride are interrupted in a moment of intimacy by their sudden awareness that they are being watched by the artificially created monster (their "child"), a mute witness of its own conception: "Therein lies the statement of the fantasy that impregnates the text of *Frankenstein:* to be the gaze that reflects the enjoyment of one's own parents, a lethal enjoyment.... What is the child looking at? The primal scene, the most archaic scene, the scene of his own conception. Fantasy is this impossible gaze." (Jean-Jacques Lecercle, *Frankenstein: Mythe et Philosophie,* Paris, Presses Universitaires de France, 1988, pp. 98-99)

7.   Cf. the classical study of Ernst Kantorowicz, *The King's Two Bodies,* Princeton, Princeton University Press, 1965.

8.   Cf. Brian Rotman, *Signifying Zero,* London, Macmillan, 1986.

9.   Lacan, *The Four Fundamental Concepts of Psycho-Analysis,* pp. 75-76.

10.   Like Jim in Steven Spielberg's *Empire of the Sun* who is really an airplane dreaming to be Jim, or like the hero of Terry Gillian's *Brazil* who is really a giant butterfly dreaming that he is a human bureaucrat.

2   *The Real and Its Vicissitudes*

1.   With regard to this relation between drive and desire, we could perhaps risk a small rectification of the Lacanian maxim of the psychoanalytic ethic "not to cede one's desire": is not desire as such already a certain yielding, a kind of compromise formation, a metonymic displacement, retreat, a defense against intractable drive? "To desire" *means* to give way on the drive—insofar as we follow Antigone and "do not give way on our desire," do we not precisely step out of the domain of desire, do we not shift from the modality of desire into the modality of pure drive?

2.   As a rule, these embodiments of pure drive *wear a mask*—why? We could perhaps obtain the answer via one of Lacan's somewhat enigmatic definitions of the real: in *Television,* he speaks of the "grimace of the real" (Jacques Lacan, *Television,* in *October* no. 40 [Spring 1987], p.10). The real is thus not an inaccessible kernel hidden beneath layers of symbolizations, it is *on the surface*— it is just a kind of excessive disfiguration of reality, like the fixed grimace of a smile on Joker's face in *Batman.* Joker is, so to speak, a slave of his own mask, condemned to obey its blind compulsion— the death drive resides in this surface deformation, not in what is beneath it. The real horror is a stupid laughing mask, not the distorted, suffering face it conceals. An everyday experience with a child confirms it: if we put on a mask in its presence, it is horrified, although it knows that beneath, there is just our familiar face—as if some unspeakable evil pertains to the mask itself. The status of

a mask is thus neither imaginary nor symbolic (denoting a symbolic role we are supposed to play), it is strictly *real*—if, of course, we conceive the real as a "grimace" of reality.

3.   We encounter the same motif of "subjectivization" of a cyborg in Ridley Scott's *Bladerunner,* where the hero's android girlfriend "becomes subject" by (re)inventing her personal history; here, the Lacanian thesis that woman is "a symptom of man" acquires an unexpected *literal* value: she is effectively the hero's *sinthome,* "synthetic complement," i.e., the sexual difference coincides with the difference human/android.

4.   Cf. Sigmund Freud, *Totem and Taboo,* in *The Standard Edition of the Complete Psychological Works of Sigmund Freud* (hereafter *SE*), vol. 13, London, Hogarth Press, 1953.

5.   Cf. Catherine Millot, *Nobodaddy,* Paris, Le Point Hors-Ligne, 1988.

6.   Cf. Gilles Deleuze and Felix Guattari, *Anti-Oedipus,* New York, Viking Press, 1977.

7.   Jacques Lacan, *Le séminaire, livre VII: L'éthique de la psychanalyse,* Paris, Seuil, 1986, p. 305.

8.   Ibid., p. 319.

9.   Cf. Sigmund Freud, "Notes upon a Case of Obsessional Neurosis", in *SE,* vol. 10.

10.   Sigmund Freud, *The Question of Lay Analysis,* in *SE,* vol. 20, p. 257.

11.   Cf. Jacques-Alain Miller, "Les réponses du réel," in *Aspects du malaise dans la civilisation,* Paris, Navarin, 1988.

12.   The ironic-perverse achievement of *Empire of the Sun* consists undoubtedly in its presenting us—who live in an epoch of postmodern nostalgia, when a multitude of images of lost time offer themselves as the object-cause of desire—with the concentration camp, the traumatic point of the real/impossible of our history, as a nostalgic object. Think of the way *Empire of the Sun* depicts every-day life in the camp: children coming happily down the slope on handcarts, elderly gentlemen playing improvised golf, ladies chattering merrily while ironing their washing, and Jim going on errands between them, delivering the linen, trading shoes and vegetables, resourceful and feeling like a fish in its element—all accompanied by music that, according to traditional Hollywood codes, illustrates the vivacious idyll of everyday small-town life. Such is the image of the *concentration camp,* of the phenomenon that undoubtedly functions as the traumatic "real" of the twentieth century, i.e., as that which "returns as the same" in all different social systems. It was invented at the turn of the century by Englishmen during their war against the Boers, it was practiced not only by the two main total-itarian powers (Nazi Germany, Stalinist USSR), but also by such a "pillar of democracy" as the USA (the isolation of the Japanese during World War II). Which is why every attempt to render the con-centration camp as something "relative," to reduce it to one of its forms, to conceive it as a result of some specific set of social conditions—to prefer the term "Gulag" or "holocaust" to that of "con-centration camp," for example—already indicates an escape from the unbearable weight of the real.

13.   At the same time, we should not forget that there is also a comical-benevolent side to the big Other as the mechanism regulating the chaos of contingent intersections of parallel narrative lines. Note two at first sight totally discrepant films, *Desperately Seeking Susan* and *Family Plot,* Hitch-cock's last—what do they have in common? In both cases, two lines intermingle accidentally and this apparently chaotic "intermixture" is guided by an ironically benevolent, invisible hand guar-anteeing the happy final outcome. (*Desperately Seeking Susan* is of special interest since the cross-ing of the two lines is caused by a sudden transformation of an ordinary "tame" girl [Rosanna Arquette] into a "wild" Madonna character. The two literally "change places" and a subtle game of identification takes place.)

14.   Octave Mannoni, "Je sais bien, mais quand même...," in *Clefs pour l'imaginaire,* Paris, Seuil, 1968.

15.   In other words, the falsity of the subjective position of the obsessive ecologist consists in the fact that in warning us constantly against the impending catastrophe, in accusing us of indifference, etc., what really worries him is that the catastrophe *will not* arrive. The proper answer to him is a simple reassuring tap on the shoulder: "Calm yourself, you don't have to worry about it, the catas-trophe will certainly arrive!"

16.   Cf. Sigmund Freud, "The Moses of Michelangelo", in *SE,* vol. 13.

17.   Cf. chapter 5 of James Gleick, *Chaos: Making of a New Science,* New York, Viking Press, 1987, and chapter 13 of Ian Stewart, *Does God Play Dice? The Mathematics of Chaos,* Cambridge, Mass., Basil Blackwell, 1989.

18.   Cf. Jacques Lacan, *Le seminaire, livre XX: Encore,* Paris, Seuil, 1975.

19.   Jacques Lacan, *Ecrits: A Selection,* London, Tavistock, 1977, p. 319.

20.   Cf. Michel Chion, "Revolution douce," in *La toile trouée,* Paris, Cahiers du Cinema / Editions de l'Etoile, 1988.

21.   It should therefore be clear why Nazism, in its psychotic libidinal economy, was inclined to the cosmological theory according to which Earth is not a planet with an infinity of empty space around it, but on the contrary a round hold in the middle of eternal ice: an island of the symbolic, surrounded by coagulated enjoyment.

22.   In the domain of painting, it is "action painting" as practiced by abstract expressionism that corresponds to *rendu:* the spectator is supposed to view the painting from close up so that he loses his "objective distance" toward it and is immediately "drawn" into it. The painting neither imitates reality nor represents it via symbolic codes, it "renders" the real by "seizing" the spectator.

23.   The clearest case of *rendu* in Hitchcock's work is of course the famous backward tracking shot in *Frenzy,* where the very movement of the camera (serpentine, then straight backward), by following the line of a necktie, tells us what is happening behind the doors of the apartment from which the movement started: another "necktie murder." In his text on Hitchcock "Système formel d'Hitchcock," in *Cahiers du cinema,* hors-série 8: Alfred Hitchcock, Paris 1980), François Regnault even risked the hypothesis that such a relation between "form" and "content" offers us a clue to the entire Hitchcock opus: the "content" is always rendered by a certain formal feature (*Vertigo:* the spiral circles; *Psycho:* the intersected lines, etc.).

        On another level, a similar transposition of accent from content to its frame is characteristic of the entire history of Hollywood up to this time, by which the frame consists in the form of subjectivity proper to the Hollywood hero through whose perspective we see the action. This transposition is most easily perceived when Hollywood sets out to handle some traumatic contemporary social theme (racism, Third World wars, etc.): all three representative films about "Western journalism and the Third World" (*Salvador, Under Fire, The Year of Living Dangerously*), although sympathetic to the Third World's hardships, are nevertheless ultimately not about Third World problems, but about the maturing of the (American) hero in which the great Third World turmoils (the fall of Somoza, the military coup d'etat in Indonesia) serve as a kind of background. This formula was brought to its peak in all representative Vietnam films, from *Apocalypse Now* to *Platoon,* where the war itself is just an exotic stage for the hero's Oedipal "inner journey" and where, to recall the publicity spot for *Platoon,* the first war victim is (the hero's) innocence. The latest case of it is *Mississippi Burning,* in which the search for the Ku Klux Klan murderers of civil rights workers functions as a dramatic backdrop to the "real theme" of the film, the tension between its two heroes, the crudely bureaucratic liberal antiracist (Dafoe) and his more down-to-earth, comprehending colleague (Hackmann). The crucial moment of the film is at its end, when Dafoe calls Hackmann by his Christian name for the first time. In the style of eighteenth-century novels, the film could be subtitled "a story of how two policemen who at first dislike each other were finally able to call each other by their first names."

        This specific form of subjectivity within which historical reality is reduced to a kind of background for (or metaphor of) the hero's "inner conflicts" is carried to the extreme in Warren Beatty's *Reds.* From the perspective of American ideology, what is the most traumatic event of the twentieth century? The October revolution, beyond all doubt. And Warren Beatty invented a way, the only possible way, to "rehabilitate" the October revolution, to integrate it into the Hollywood universe: by staging it as a metaphorical background for the sexual act between the movie's main characters, John Reed (Beatty) and his companion (Diane Keaton). In the film, the October revolution takes place immediately after a crisis in their relationship. While he is delivering a fierce revolutionary oration to the aroused crowd, Beatty and Keaton exchange passionate glances—the cries of the crowd serve as a metaphor of the renewed outburst of passion between the lovers. The crucial, mythical scenes of the Revolution (street demonstrations, the storming of the Winter Palace) alternate with the depiction of their passionate lovemaking. These mass scenes function as vulgar metaphors of the sexual act. Lenin himself, addressing the deputies in a great hall, appears as a kind of paternal figure, guaranteeing the success of the sexual act, while the whole scene is accompanied by the singing of the Internationale. Here we have the exact opposite of Soviet socialist realism where the lovers experience their love as a contribution to the struggle for socialism, making a vow to sacrifice all for the success of the revolution and to drown themselves in the masses. In *Reds,* on the contrary, revolution itself appears as a metaphor for the successful sexual encounter.

24.   Sigmund Freud, *The Interpretation of Dreams,* in *SE,* vols. 4–5, p. 430.

25.   Cf. Stephen Hawking, *A Brief History of Time,* New York, Bantam Press, 1988.

3   Two Ways to Avoid the Real of Desire

1.   It is needless to add that attempts at a pseudo-"dialectical" synthesis conceiving the figure of the detective as the contradictory fusion of bourgeois rationality and its reverse, irrational intuition, fare no better: both sides together fail to procure what each of them lacks.

2.   Freud, *The Interpretation of Dreams,* pp. 277–278.

3.   Jacques-Alain Miller, "Action de la structure," in *Cahiers pour l'Analyse* 9, Paris, Graphe, 1968, pp. 96–97.

4.   Richard Alewyn, "Anatomie des Detektivromans," in Jochen Vogt, ed., *Der Kriminalroman,* Munich, UTB-Verlag, 1971, vol. 2, p. 35.

5.   Freud, *The Interpretation of Dreams,* p. 104.

6.   Victor Shklovsky, "Die Kriminalerzaehlung bei Conan Doyle," in Jochen Vogt, ed., *Der Kriminalroman,* Munich, UTB-Verlag, 1971, vol. 1, p. 84.

7.   It is on the basis of this structural necessity of the false solution that we can explain the role of one of the standard figures of the classical detective story: the detective's naive, everyday companion who is usually also the narrator (Holmes's Watson, Poirot's Hastings, etc.). In one of Agatha Christie's novels, Hastings asks Poirot of what use he is to him in his work of detection, insofar as he is just an ordinary, average person, full of everyday prejudices. Poirot answers that he needs Hastings *precisely on that account,* i.e., precisely because he is an ordinary man who embodies what we could call the field of *doxa,* spontaneous common opinion. That is to say, after accomplishing his crime, the murderer must efface its traces by composing an image that conceals its true motive and points toward a false culprit (a classical topos: the murder is accomplished by a victim's close relative who arranges things to give the impression that the act was performed by a burglar surprised by the unexpected arrival of the victim). *Whom,* precisely, does the murderer want to deceive by means of this false scene? What is the "reasoning" of the murderer when he stages the false scene? It is of course the very field of *doxa,* of "common opinion" embodied in the detective's faithful companion. Consequently, the detective does not need his Watson in order to point out the contrast between his dazzling perspicacity and the companion's ordinary humanity; instead Watson, with his commonsense reactions, is necessary in order to exhibit in the clearest possible way the effect that the murderer intended to produce by his staging of a false scene.

8.   Miller, "Action de la structure," p. 96.

9.   Lacan, *The Four Fundamental Concepts of Psycho-Analysis,* pp. 139–140 (the quotation is, of course, slightly changed to suit our purposes).

10.   Which is why the "retired colourman" in one of the late Sherlock Holmes stories, although ingenious enough, does not really take advantage of all the ruses of deception proper to the order of the signifier. This old official, whose wife was missing and presumed to have escaped with a young lover, suddenly started to repaint his house—why? In order that the strong smell of fresh paint would prevent the visitors from detecting another smell, that of the decaying bodies of his wife and

her lover whom he killed and hid in the house. An even more ingenious deception would have been to paint the walls in order to provoke the impression that the smell of paint is meant to cover up another smell, i.e., to provoke the impression that we are hiding something, while in reality there is nothing to hide.

11.   Apropos of the "subject supposed to know," it is absolutely crucial to grasp this link between knowledge and the stupid, senseless *presence* of the subject embodying it. The "subject supposed to know" is someone who, *by his mere presence,* guarantees that the chaos will acquire meaning, i.e., that "there is a method in this madness." Which is why the title of Hal Ashby's film about the effects of transference, *Being There,* is thoroughly adequate: it is enough for the poor gardener Chance, played by Peter Sellers, to find himself—by means of a purely contingent misapprehension—at a certain place, to occupy the place of transference for the others, and already he operates as the wise "Chauncey Gardener." His stupid phrases, scraps of his gardening experience and of what he remembers from watching TV incessantly, are all of a sudden supposed to contain another, metaphorical, "deeper" meaning. His childish utterances about how to take care of a garden in winter and spring, for example, are read as profound allusions to the thawing of relations between the superpowers. Those critics who saw in the film a eulogy of the simple man's commonsense, its triumph over the artificiality of experts, were totally wrong. In this respect, the film is definitely not spoiled by any compromise, Chance is depicted as completely and painfully idiotic, the whole effect of his "wisdom" results from his "being there," at the place of transference. Even though the American psychoanalytical establishment has been unable to swallow Lacan, Hollywood, happily, has been more accommodating.

12.   Agatha Christie's *Murder on the Orient-Express* confirms this by way of an ingenious exception: here, the murder is accomplished by the entire group of suspects, and it is precisely for this reason that they cannot be guilty, so the paradoxical although necessary outcome is that *the culprit coincides with the victim,* i.e., the murder proves to be a well-deserved punishment.

13.   Jacques Lacan, *The Ego in Freud's Theory and in the Technique of Psychoanalysis,* New York, Norton, 1988, p. 204.

14.   We have of course left out of consideration the extremely interesting rise of the postwar "crime novel," which shifts the attention from the detective (either as the "subject supposed to know" or as the first-person narrator) to the victim (Boileau-Narcejac) or the culprit (Patricia Highsmith, Ruth Rendell). The necessary consequence of this shift is that the entire temporal structure of the narrative is changed. The story is presented in the "usual" linear way, with the accent placed on what goes on *before* the crime, i.e., we are no longer concerned with the *aftermath* of crime and with attempts to reconstruct the course of events leading up to it. In Boileau-Narcejac's novels (*Les Diaboliques,* for example), the story is usually told from the perspective of the future victim, a woman to whom strange things seem to happen, foreboding a horrible crime, though we are not sure until the final denouement if all this is true or just her hallucination. On the other hand, Patricia Highsmith depicts the whole diversity of contingencies and psychological impasses that could induce an apparently "normal" person to commit a murder. Even in her first novel, *Strangers on a Train,* she established her elementary matrix: that of a transferential relationship between a psychotic murderer capable of performing the act and a hysteric who organizes his desire by means of a reference to the psychotic, i.e., who literally *desires by proxy* (no wonder Hitchcock recognized immediately the affinity between this matrix and his motif of the "transference of guilt"). Incidentally, an interesting case in respect to this opposition between the "victim" novel and the "culprit" novel is Margaret Millar's masterpiece *Beast in View,* in which the two coincide: the culprit turns out to be the victim of the crime itself, a pathologically split personality.

15.   The fact that this is a matter of a postfantasy "purification" of desire is attested by an ingenious detail: in the final scene, the wardrobe of Jane Greer unmistakably resembles that of a nun.

4   How the Non-duped Err

1.   Sigmund Freud, *The Future of an Illusion,* in *SE,* vol. 21, p. 34.

2.   In both *The Thirty-Nine Steps* and *North by Northwest,* we find scenes homologous to the one in *Saboteur*: in *The Thirty-Nine Steps,* it is the political reunion where Hannay, mistaken for the expected speaker, improvizes a nonsensical political address; in *North by Northwest,* it is the auction scene in which Thornhill acts rudely and senselessly to provoke the arrival of the police.

3.   Cf. Eric Rohmer and Claude Chabrol, *Hitchcock: The First Forty-Four Films,* New York, Ungar, 1979.

4.   Gilles Deleuze, *L'image-mouvement,* Paris, Editions de Minuit, 1983, p. 273, translated as *The Movement-Image,* Minneapolis, University of Minnesota Press, 1986.

5.   Cf. Jon Elster, *Sour Grapes,* Cambridge, Cambridge University Press, 1982.

6.   For the notion of "acousmatique", cf. chapter 7 below.

7.   It would be interesting to articulate a detailed parallel between *A Letter to Three Wives* and Offenbach's *Hoffmann's Tales,* where the three stories told by Hoffman to his drinking partners present three modes of disharmony in the sexual relation: the poet's first love turns out to be a mechanical doll; the second is a deceitful woman of easy virtue; and the third gives preference to her vocation as a singer (she sings her last song, knowing that, because of her illness, it will mean her death). The crucial constituent of the opera is, however, the frame uniting these three stories: Hoffman tells them to his audience while waiting for his great love, a capricious primadonna. Through this narration, he in a way organizes the failure of his amorous undertaking, so that his final defeat (when the primadonna comes for him after her performance, she finds him dead drunk and leaves with his rival) gives expression to his true desire.

8.   Lacan, *Le séminaire, livre VII: L'éthique de la psychanalyse,* p. 133.

9.   Lesley Brill, *The Hitchcock Romance,* Princeton, Princeton University Press, 1988, p. 220.

10.   Just before the end of the film, it seems for a moment that Scottie (James Stewart) is prepared to accept Judy "as she is," not as Madeleine reincarnated, and to acknowledge the depth of her suffering love for him. But this prospect of a happy ending is immediately cut short by the emergence of a ghostlike mother superior whose sudden apparition causes Judy to retreat in panic and fall from the church tower—needless to add that the very term "mother superior" evokes the maternal superego.

11.   G. W. F. Hegel, *Gesammelte Werke,* vol. 8, Hamburg, Meiner, 1976, p. 187; English translation quoted from D. Ph. Verene, *Hegel's Recollection,* Albany, SUNY Press, 1985, pp. 7–8.

5   The Hitchockian Blot

1.   From this perspective, the denouement of *Dial M for Murder* is extremely interesting insofar as it *reverses* the usual situation of Hitchcock's films: "the man who knew too much" is not the hero foreboding some terrifying secret behind the idyllic surface, but *the murderer himself.* That is to say, the inspector traps the murderous husband of Grace Kelly through a certain surplus knowledge— the murderer is caught knowing something that it would not be possible for him to know if he were innocent (the hiding place of the other key to his apartment). The irony of the denouement is that what provokes the downfall of the murderer is precisely his quick and clever reasoning. If he had been just a little bit more slow-witted, i.e., if, after the key in his jacket had failed to open the door to his apartment, he had been unable to deduce quickly what must have happened, he would have been forever safe from the hand of justice. In the way he sets the trap for the murderer, the inspector acts like a real Lacanian analyst: the crucial ingredient of his success is not his ability to "penetrate the other," to understand him, to adapt to his reasoning, but rather his capacity to take into account the structuring role of a certain object that circulates among the subjects and entangles them in a network that they cannot dominate—the key in *Dial M for Murder* (and in *Notorious*), the letter in Edgar Allan Poe's "The Purloined Letter," etc.

2.   Cf., for example, Lacan, *The Four Fundamental Concepts of Psycho-Analysis,* p. 92.

3.   We must be attentive to the diversity of the ways this motif of the "uncanny" detail is at work in Hitchcock's films. Note just five of its variations:

- *Rope*: here, we have the spot *first* (the traumatic act of murder) and *then* the idyllic everyday situation (the party) constructed to conceal it.
- *The Man Who Knew Too Much*: in a short scene in which the hero (James Stewart) makes his way to the taxidermist Ambrose Chappell, the street the hero traverses is depicted as charged with a sinister atmosphere; but in fact things are precisely what they seem to be (the street is just an ordinary suburban London street, etc.), so that the only "stain" in the picture is *the hero himself,* his suspicious gaze that sees threats everywhere.
- *The Trouble with Harry*: a "stain" (a body) smears the idyllic Vermont countryside, but instead of provoking traumatic reactions, people who stumble upon it merely treat it as a minor inconvenience and pursue their daily affairs.
- *Shadow of a Doubt*: the "stain" here is uncle Charlie, the film's central character, a pathological murderer who rejoins his sister's family in a small American town. In the eyes of the townsfolk, he is a friendly, rich benefactor; it is only his niece Charlie who "knows too much" and sees him as he is—why? The answer is found in the identity of their names: the two of them constitute two parts of the same personality (like Marion and Norman in *Psycho,* where the identity is indicated by the fact that the two names reflect each other in an inverted form).
- And finally *The Birds,* where—in what is surely Hitchcock's final irony—the "unnatural" element that disturbs everyday life is the birds, i.e., *nature itself.*

4.   Cf. Michel Chion, "Le quatrième côté," in *Cahiers du cinéma* 356 (1984), pp. 6–7.

5.   Jacques Lacan, *Ecrits,* Paris, Seuil, 1966, p. 554.

6.   Jacques-Alain Miller, "Montré à Premontré," in *Analytica* 37, (1984), pp. 28–29.

7.   The anal level is the locus of metaphor—one object for another, give the faeces in place of the phallus" (Lacan, *The Four Fundamental Concepts of Psycho-Analysis,* p. 104).

8.   See note 23 to chapter 2, above.

9.   This scene, creating as it does a phantasmatic effect, also illustrates the thesis that the subject is not necessarily inscribed in the phantasmatic scene as observer, but can be one of the objects observed. The birds' subjective view of the town creates a menacing effect, even though our view—the camera's view—is that of the birds and not that of their prey, because we are inscribed in the scene as inhabitants of the town, i.e., we identify with the menaced inhabitants.

10.   Robin Wood, *Hitchcock's Films,* New York, A. S. Barnes and Co., 1977, p. 116.

11.   Lacan, *Le séminaire, livre XX: Encore,* p. 23.

12.   Lacan, *Ecrits,* pp. 54–59.

13.   Christopher Lasch, *The Culture of Narcissism,* London, Abacus, 1980, p. 176.

14.   Here it is crucial to grasp the logic of the connection between the woman's perspective and the figure of the resigned, impotent Master. Lacan's answer to Freud's famous question "*Was will das Weib?* What does the (hysterical) woman want?" is: *a Master, but one whom she could dominate.* The perfect figuration of this hysterical fantasy is Charlotte Brontë's *Jane Eyre* where, at the end of the novel, the heroine is happily married to the blinded, helpless fatherlike figure (*Rebecca,* of course, belongs to the same tradition).

15.   Lasch, *The Culture of Narcissism,* p. 12.

16.   Cf. Saul Kripke, *Naming and Necessity,* Cambridge, Mass., Harvard University Press, 1972.

17.   It is against the background of this problem that we could perhaps locate the lesson to be drawn from Stanley Cavell's *Pursuits of Happiness: The Hollywood Comedies of Remarriage* (Cambridge, Mass., Harvard University Press, 1981), namely a version of the Hegelian theory of repetition in history: the only proper marriage is the second one. First we marry the other *qua* our narcissistic complement; it is only when his/her delusive charm fades that we can engage in marriage as an attachment to the other beyond his/her imaginary properties.

18.   It is because *North by Northwest* repeats the logic of the Oedipal journey that it offers us a kind of spectral analysis of the function of the father, dividing it into three figures: Roger Thornhill's *imaginary* father (the UN diplomat stabbed in the hall of the General Assembly), his *symbolic* father (the CIA "Professor" who invented the *name* "Kaplan" to which Thornhill is tied), and his *real* father, i.e., the resigned, perverse villain Van Damm.

19   Cf. François Regnault, "Système formel d'Hitchcock," in *Cahiers du cinéma,* hors-série 8.

6 Pornography, Nostalgia, Montage: A Triad of the Gaze

1.   Jacques Lacan, "God and the *Jouissance* of The Woman," in *Feminine Sexuality: Jacques Lacan and the Ecole Freudienne,* ed. Juliet Mitchell and Jacqueline Rose, New York, Norton, 1982, p. 147.

2.   In this respect, the pervert's subjective position differs clearly from those of the obsessional neurotic and the psychotic. Both the pervert and the obsessional are caught in frenetic activity in service of the big Other; the difference is, however, that the aim of the obsessional's activity is to *prevent* the big Other from enjoying (i.e., the "catastrophe" he fears will erupt if his activity ceases is ultimately the enjoyment of the Other), whereas the pervert works precisely *to ensure* that the big Other's "will to enjoyment" will be satisfied. This is why the pervert is free of the eternal doubt and oscillation that characterize the obsessional: he simply takes for granted that his activity serves the enjoyment of the Other. The psychotic, on the other hand, is himself the *object* of the Other's enjoyment, his "complement" (like Schreber, who conceived himself as God's sexual partner): it is the Other who works on him, in contrast to the pervert, who is just an instrument, a neutral tool working for the Other.

3.   Cf. Lacan, *Ecrits,* pp. 774–775.

4.   The other, in some way complementary determination of "totalitarianism" (more specifically, far-right totalitarianism), also consists in a kind of short circuit, not this time between subject and object (the subject being reduced to the object-instrument of the Other), but between the ideological signification produced by the symbolic code (the big Other) and the fantasies by means of which the big Other of ideology conceals its inconsistency, its lack. To refer to the mathemes in the Lacanian "graph of desire," this short circuit takes place between $s(A)$ and $\$ \Diamond a$. (Cf. Lacan, *Ecrits: A Selection,* p. 313). Let us take the case of neoconservativism: on the level of the signified—$s(A)$—this ideology offers us a field of meaning structured around the opposition between secular, egalitarian humanism and the values of family, law and order, responsibility, and self-reliance. Within this field, freedom is supposed to be menaced not only by Communism, but also by the welfare state bureaucracy, etc., etc. At the same time, however, this ideology works "between the lines," on an unspoken level, i.e., by not directly mentioning these menaces but by implying them as a silent surmise of its discourse. A whole series of fantasies are in play without which we cannot explain the efficacy of neoconservatism, the fact that it can capture subjects in such a passionate way: sexist fantasies about the menace that unruly "liberated" female sexuality presents for men; the racist fantasy that the WASP is the embodiment of Man *qua* Man and that beneath every black, yellow, etc., there is a white American longing to emerge; the fantasy that the "other"—the enemy—endeavors to rob us of our enjoyment, that he has access to some hidden enjoyment, inaccessible to us; and so on. Neoconservativism lives on this difference, it relies on fantasies that it cannot put into words, integrate into the field of its ideological signification. The frontier that divides neoconservativism from rightist totalitarianism is trespassed precisely at the moment there is a short circuit between the field of signification and these fantasies, i.e., when fantasies directly invade the field of signification, when they are directly referred to—as, for example, in Nazism, which openly articulates (includes in the field of its ideological meaning) the whole texture of sexual and other fantasies that serve as support of anti-Semitism. Nazi ideology openly states that Jews seduce our innocent daughters, that they are capable of perverse pleasures, etc.; this ideology does not leave it up to the addressee to surmise these "facts." Herein lies the grain of truth of the common wisdom according to which the difference

between the "moderate" and "radical" right consists merely in the fact that the latter says openly what the former thinks without daring to say.

5.   Lacan, *The Four Fundamental Concepts of Psycho-Analysis,* p. 109.

6.   It is precisely because in pornography, the picture does *not* gaze back at us, because it is "flat," without any mysterious "spot" needing to be looked at "awry" in order to assume distinct form, that the fundamental prohibition determining the direction of the gaze of actors on the screen is suspended: in a pornographic movie, the actor—as a rule, the woman—in the moment of intense sexual pleasure looks directly into the camera, addressing us, the spectators.

7.   This paradox of "impossible knowledge" that is inscribed in the way persons react on screen is far more interesting than it appears at first sight; for example, it offers us a way of explaining the logic of the *cameo appearances* of Hitchcock in his own films. What is his worst film? *Topaz.* In it, Hitchcock appears in a wheelchair in an airport lounge, as if wishing to inform us that his creative power is definitely crippled. In his last film, *Family Plot,* he appears as a shadow on the windowpane of the registry office, as if wishing to inform us that he is already close to death. Every one of his cameo appearances reveals such an "impossible knowledge," as if Hitchcock were capable of assuming for an instant a position of pure metalanguage, of taking an "objective look" at himself and locating himself in the picture.

8.   Cf. Fredric Jameson, "Postmodernism, or the Cultural Logic of Late Capitalism," in *New Left Review* 146 (1984).

9.   Lacan, *The Four Fundamental Concepts of Psycho-Analysis,* p. 74.

10.   This problem was first articulated by Noël Burch in his theory of off-screen space, i.e., of a specific exterior implied, constituted by the very interplay of the shot and counter-shot; cf. Noël Burch, *The Theory of Film Practice,* New York, Praeger, 1973.

11.   Cf. Raymond Bellour, *L'analyse du film,* Paris, Edition Albatros, 1979.

12.   It is no coincidence that in both cases, the object approached by the hero is a *house*—apropos of *Notorious,* Pascal Bonitzer developed a detailed theory of the house as the location of an incestuous secret in Hitchcock's work; cf. Pascal Bonitzer, "Notorious," in *Cahiers du cinéma* 358 (1980).

13.   In his ironic, amiably sadistic teasing of the spectator, Hitchcock takes into account precisely this gap between the formal procedure and the content to which it is applied, i.e., the fact that anxiety results from a purely formal procedure. First, by means of formal manipulation, he bestows upon an everyday, trivial object an aura of mystery and anxiety; it then becomes manifest that this object effectively *is* just an everyday object. The best-known case of this is found in the second version of *The Man Who Knew Too Much.* On a suburban London street, James Stewart approaches a lonely stranger. Silently, they exchange glances as an atmosphere of tension and anxiety is created; it seems that the stranger is threatening Stewart. But we soon discover that Stewart's suspicion is entirely unfounded—the stranger is just an accidental passerby.

14.   Lacan, *The Four Fundamental Concepts of Psycho-Analysis,* pp. 95–96.

15.   Cf. Mladen Dolar, "L'agent secret: le spectateur qui en savait trop," in Slavoj Žižek, ed., *Tout ce que Vous avez toujours voulu savoir sur Lacan sans jamais oser le demander à Hitchcock,* Paris, Navarin, 1988.

16.   "What is a gesture? A threatening gesture, for example? It is not a blow that is interrupted. It is certainly something that is done in order to be arrested and suspended." (Lacan, *The Four Fundamental Concepts of Psycho-Analysis,* p. 116.)

17.   Cf. Sigmund Freud, "A Child Is Being Beaten," *SE,* vol. 10.

18.   Ibid., p. 185.

19.   François Truffaut not only pointed out that this scene "almost suggests suicide rather than murder," but also drew the parallel between Oscar's and Carmen's death: "It's as if Oscar Homolka were allowing himself to be killed by Sylvia Sidney. Prosper Merimée staged Carmen's death on the same dramatic principle, with the victim thrusting her body forward to meet the slayer's fatal stab." (François Truffaut, *Hitchcock,* London, Panther Books, 1969, p. 120.)

7 *The Ideological Sinthome*

1.   Lacan, *The Four Fundamental Concepts of Psycho-Analysis,* p. 104. Since the gaze is on the side of the object, it cannot be subjectified: as soon as we attempt to do so, as soon as we try to add a subjective shot from the house itself, for example (the trembling camera looking at the approaching Lilah from behind the curtains), we fall to the level of the ordinary thriller, i.e., we would be concerned with the point of view of another *subject,* not with the gaze as *object.* Apropos of the gaze and voice as objects in film, cf. Joan Copjec, *Apparatus and Umbra,* Cambridge, MIT Press, forthcoming.

2.   Cf. Michel Chion, *La voix au cinéma,* Paris, Cahiers du cinema/Editions de l'Etoile, 1982, pp. 116–123.

3.   One of Roald Dahl's stories ("Genesis and Catastrophe") is based upon a similar effect; it takes place around 1880 in Germany and describes an extremely difficult birth. The doctors themselves wonder fearfully whether the child will survive or not. We read the story with great compassion and fear for the child's life, but happily all ends well; the doctor holds out the crying baby to the mother and says: "It's all right, Frau Hitler, your little Adolf will be fine!" Eric Frank Russell's science fiction story "The Sole Solution" draws this logic to its extreme: it describes the inner feelings of somebody filled with doubt, someone who cannot reach a decision, who makes all kinds of plans, switches from one plan to another, etc. Finally, he makes up his mind and says: "Let there be light!" What we took, all through the story, for the groaning of some confused idiot, turns out to be the hesitation of God immediately before the act of creation. Which, incidentally, confirms Schelling's theory that the only consistent answer to the question "Why did God create the world?" is "To save himself from madness." To use contemporary psychiatric terminology, the Creation was a kind of Divine "creative therapy."

4.   Cf. Chion, *La voix au cinéma,* p. 122.

5.   In the domain of the crime novel, the undisputed master of this sort of transposition into the point of view of the "impossible" object is Patricia Highsmith. Let us just mention *A Dog's Ransom,* probably her definitive novel, in which a middle-class New York couple's everyday life is derailed when their dog is stolen and a ransom is demanded for it. Soon after, we are transposed into the position of the blackmailer himself—another helpless creature, full of futile rage.

6.   Apropos of the notion of ideological *jouis-sense,* cf. Slavoj Žižek, *The Sublime Object of Ideology,* London, Verso Books, 1989.

7.   Cf. Ernesto Laclau and Chantal Mouffe, *Hegemony and Socialist Strategy,* London, Verso Books, 1985.

8.   "I give myself to you, . . . but this gift of my person . . . is changed inexplicably into a gift of shit" (Lacan, *The Four Fundamental Concepts of Psycho-Analysis,* p. 268).

9.   Cf., among the published seminars, Lacan, *Le séminaire, livre XX: Encore.*

10.   In contrast to *perversion,* which is defined precisely by the lack of a question. The pervert possesses an immediate certainty that his activity serves the enjoyment of the Other. Hysteria and obsessional neurosis, its "dialect," differ concerning the way the subject attempts to justify his existence: the hysteric by offering himself to the Other as the object of its love, the obsessional by striving to comply with the demand of the Other via his frenetic activity. The answer of the hysteric is thus love, while that of the obsessional is work.

11.   "Communication *qua* meaning" because the two of them ultimately overlap: it is not only that the circulating "object" is always meaning (and in the negative form of nonsense, of lack of meaning), the point is rather that meaning itself is always intersubjective, constituted through the circle of communication (it is the other, the addressee, who retroactively determines the meaning of what I have said).

12.   Lacan, *Le seminaire, livre XXI. Encore,* p. 83.

13.   The most famous object small *a* in popular culture is, of course, Hitchcock's McGuffin, the "secret" that sets in motion the action but that is in itself totally indifferent, "nothing at all," just a certain void (a coded melody, a secret formula, etc.). The whole triad of objects described above

could moreover be perfectly exemplified by the three types of objects found in Hitchcock's films: the McGuffin as the object small *a*; the terrifying embodiment of enjoyment (the birds, the gigantic statues, etc.) as the capital phi; the circulating "fragment of the real" (the wedding ring, cigarette lighter, etc.) as S(A̶). Cf. chapter 5 in Žižek, *The Sublime Object of Ideology.*

By means of this triad of objects, we could also formalize the relation between three types of "ladies that vanish": Attie Ross in *A Letter to Three Wives,* the "Other Woman" exhibiting the failure and deadlock of an "ordinary" marriage, isn't she a kind of embodiment of S(A̶), signifier of the Other's inconsistency? The charming old lady that disappears in *The Lady Vanishes,* doesn't she function as *objet a,* the object-cause propelling our desire to symbolize the mystery, to unravel the secret? Madeleine in *Vertigo,* isn't she Φ, a fascinating image of lethal enjoyment? And, finally, aren't the three of them precisely the three ways to keep our distance from the central J, i.e., to keep clear of being engulfed by its abyss?

14.   Lacan, *Ecrits,* pp. 387–388.

15.   Lacan, *The Seminar of Jacques Lacan, Book II: The Ego in Freud's Theory and in the Technique of Psychoanalysis,* p. 229.

16.   Jacques-Alain Miller, "Preface," in *Joyce avec Lacan,* Paris, Navarin, 1988, p. 12.

17.   Lacan, *The Four Fundamental Concepts of Psycho-Analysis,* p. 276.

18.   One of the Donald Duck cartoons possesses a homologous structure. Donald Duck comes with a group of tourists to a clearing in the midst of a virgin forest; the guide calls their attention to the lovely view, but at the same time warns them against a certain mean bird who strolls around this clearing—her specialty is to ruin the tourist's snapshots. Just as they point their cameras at the view, she enters the frame, croaking the same idiotic refrain each time. This intrusive bird of course ruins all Donald Duck's shots. Donald gets mad, tries first to drive her out, then to destroy her, but the bird escapes all his traps; Donald becomes more and more desperate, until, finally, he breaks down and starts to cry helplessly. The final scene of the cartoon: a new group of tourists enters the clearing, the guide again warns them against the intrusive bird, and just as the first tourist points the camera and is about to snap a shot, Donald Duck himself enters the frame, waving wildly and croaking the idiotic refrain he has learned from the bird.

19.   The original hysterical position is characterized by the paradox of "telling the truth in the form of a lie": in terms of the literal "truth" (of a correspondence between "words" and "things"), the hysteric undoubtedly "lies," but it is precisely through this factual "lie" that the truth about his desire is articulated. Insofar as obsessional neurosis is a "dialect of hysteria" (Freud), it implies a kind of inversion of this relation: the obsessional "lies in the form of a truth." The obsessional always "sticks to facts"; in this way, he strives to blur the traces of his subjective position. He is "hystericized," i.e., his desire erupts, when, finally, he "succeeds in lying," when, in the form of a slip, for example, he "falsifies the facts."

8   *The Obscene Object of Postmodernity*

1.   Cf. Jürgen Habermas, *The Philosophical Discourse of Modernity,* Cambridge, Mass., MIT Press, 1987.

2.   Theodor Adorno and Max Horkheimer, *Dialectic of Enlightenment,* London, Allen Lane, 1973.

3.   Herbert Marcuse, *One-Dimensional Man,* Boston, Beacon Press, 1964.

4.   Pascal Bonitzer, "Longs feux," in *L'Ane* 16 (1984).

5.   Cf. Gilles Deleuze and Felix Guattari, *Kafka: Toward a Minor Literature,* Minneapolis, University of Minnesota Press, 1986.

6.   Reiner Stach, *Kafkas erotischer Mythos,* Frankfurt, Fischer Verlag, 1987, p. 38.

7.   Franz Kafka, *The Trial,* New York, Schocken, 1984, p. 37.

8.   Ibid., p. 46.

9.   Ibid., p. 50.

10.   Sigmund Freud, "The Ego and the Id," in *SE,* vol. 19, p. 51. The nicest irony of the title of Freud's "The Ego and the Id" is that it leaves out the third crucial notion that contains the real theoretical innovation of this essay: its title should be "The Superego in Its Relations to the Ego and the Id."

11.   Ibid., p. 52.

12.   Ibid.

13.   Cf. Donald Davidson, "Mental Events," in *Essays on Actions and Events,* New York, Oxford University Press, 1980.

9   Formal Democracy and Its Discontents

1.   In Hitchcock's *Vertigo,* the situation is somewhat similar: although, here, the hero (James Stewart) does not ignore the woman but is, on the contrary, obsessed by her, he excludes totally from consideration her own perspective—she counts for him only insofar as she enters his fantasy frame. The only way for Judy, who really loves him, to gain his love is to conform to his fantasy, to assume the form of a dead woman. Which is why the flashback after the first encounter between Stewart and Kim Novak *qua* the vulgar, redheaded Judy is so subversive: for a brief moment, we gain an insight into the endless suffering woman must bear as a price for embodying man's unconditional, fatal love.

2.   Richard Rorty, *Contingency, Irony and Solidarity,* New York, Cambridge University Press, 1989.

3.   Ibid., p. xv.

4.   Ibid., pp. 91, 93.

5.   Ibid., p. 179.

6.   Ibid.

7.   Ibid.

8.   Ibid., p. xv.

9.   Ibid.

10.   Freud, "The Ego and the Id," *SE,* vol. 19.

11.   The Lacanian formula "the only thing of which the subject can be guilty, ultimately, is ceding his desire," presents an exact inversion of the paradox of the superego, and is thus deeply Freudian.

12.   Colleen McCullough, *An Indecent Obsession,* London and Sydney, Macdonald and Co., 1981, p. 314.

13.   Immanuel Kant, "Anthropologie," in *Werke. Akademie-Textausgabe,* Berlin, 1907–1917, vol. 7, p. 230.

14.   Immanuel Kant, "Versuch . . .," in *Werke* vol. 2, p. 175.

15.   The fate of Emmanuel Mounier, the founder of personalism, is here very suggestive. In theory, he strove for the recognition of the dignity and uniqueness of the human person against the double threat of liberal individualism and totalitarian collectivism; he is remembered above all as a hero of the French resistance. A crucial detail of his biography is, however, as a rule passed over in silence: after the French defeat in 1940, Mounier for a whole year placed his hope in Petain's corporativism, apprehending it as a unique opportunity to reinstate the spirit of organic community. Only afterward, disillusioned by Vichy's "excesses," did he turn to the resistance. In short, Mounier strove for "fascism with a human face," he wanted fascism without its dirty obverse, and he renounced it only on experiencing the illusiveness of this hope.

16.   Cf. D. A. F. de Sade, *Philosophy in the Bedroom and Other Writings,* New York, Grove Press, 1966.

17.   Lacan, *Ecrits,* pp. 768–769.

Index of Works Cited

2 Popular Literature, Theater, and Opera

3 Other Writers and Artists Cited